KINGS AND CONSULS

Kings and Consuls

Eight Essays on Roman History,
Historiography and Political Thought

James H. Richardson

PETER LANG
Oxford • Bern • Berlin • Bruxelles • New York • Wien

Bibliographic information published by Die Deutsche Bibliothek
Die Deutsche Bibliothek lists this publication in the Deutsche Nationalbibliografie;
detailed bibliographic data are available on the Internet at http://dnb.ddb.de.

A catalogue record for this book is available at the British Library.

Library of Congress Cataloging-in-Publication Data

Names: Richardson, James H., 1976- author. | Richardson, James H., editor.
Title: Kings and consuls : eight essays on Roman history, historiography,
    and political thought / James H. Richardson.
Description: New York : Peter Lang, 2020. | Includes bibliographical
    references and index.
Identifiers: LCCN 2019059969 (print) | LCCN 2019059970 (ebook) |
    ISBN 9781789973860 (paperback) | ISBN 9781789974157 (ebook) |
    ISBN 9781789974164 (epub) | ISBN 9781789974171 (mobi)
Subjects: LCSH: Rome--Historiography. | Rome--Politics and
    government--Historiography.
Classification: LCC DE8 .R53 2020 (print) | LCC DE8 (ebook) | DDC
    937--dc23
LC record available at https://lccn.loc.gov/2019059969
LC ebook record available at https://lccn.loc.gov/2019059970

Cover image: *La table claudienne* (detail), Collection de Lugdunum, musée & théâtres
romains, num. inv.: br.002. Photo © Jean-Michel Degueule, Christian Thioc.

Cover design by Peter Lang Ltd.

ISBN 978-1-78997-386-0 (print) • ISBN 978-1-78997-415-7 (ePDF)
ISBN 978-1-78997-416-4 (ePub) • ISBN 978-1-78997-417-1 (mobi)

© Peter Lang AG 2020

Published by Peter Lang Ltd, International Academic Publishers,
52 St Giles, Oxford, OX1 3LU, United Kingdom
oxford@peterlang.com, www.peterlang.com

James H. Richardson has asserted his right under the Copyright, Designs and Patents
Act, 1988, to be identified as the author of this Work.

For Peter Wiseman

Contents

Acknowledgements

The dedication of this book to him hardly suffices to express my gratitude to Peter Wiseman, not only for his teaching and supervision, but also for years of advice and encouragement. The book owes its existence to Peter in more ways than one; indeed, it was even he who first suggested, after kindly reading a draft of the essay that forms Chapter 2, that I should try to publish a collection of my papers on early Rome. It is an additional pleasure and privilege to be able to offer it to him in the year, if not quite on the occasion, of his eightieth birthday.

Thanks are also due to Philip Dunshea, the commissioning editor at Peter Lang, for his help with organising the project and for his supportive approach from the very start, Lucy Melville, for seeing the book through the various stages of production and the press' anonymous referees for all their useful feedback. With such excellent advice from so many different sources, it goes without saying that all the problems and errors that remain are entirely my own. The research and writing of Chapters 1, 2 and 6 were greatly helped by a Marsden grant and I am extremely grateful to the Royal Society of New Zealand for its financial support. Finally, special thanks are also due to my wife Catherine and my son Aiden, for their support and for everything else.

It was Joachim Fugmann's incredibly useful and excellently produced commentary on the *De viris illustribus* that first prompted me to think of Peter Lang. It seemed altogether not without a certain appropriateness.

With one exception, all of the following essays have been published before: 'The People and the State in Early Rome', in Andrew Brown and John Griffiths, eds, *The Citizen: Past and Present* (Auckland: Massey University Press, 2017), 63–91; 'The Oath *per Iovem lapidem* and the Community in Archaic Rome', *Rheinisches Museum für Philologie* 153 (2010), 25–42 (Bad Orb: J. D. Sauerländers Verlag); 'Rome's Treaties with Carthage: Jigsaw or Variant Traditions?', in Carl Deroux, ed., *Studies in Latin Literature and Roman History* XIV, Collection Latomus 315 (Brussels: Éditions

Latomus, 2008), 84–94 (Leuven: Peeters); 'Ancient Historical Thought and the Development of the Consulship', *Latomus* 67 (2008), 328–41 (Leuven: Peeters); 'The Roman Nobility, the Early Consular *Fasti*, and the Consular Tribunate', in Jeremy Armstrong and James H. Richardson, eds, *Politics and Power in Early Rome (509–264 BC)*, *Antichthon* 51 (Cambridge: Cambridge University Press, 2017), 77–100; '"Firsts" and the Historians of Rome', *Historia: Zeitschrift für alte Geschichte* 63 (2014), 17–37 (Stuttgart: Franz Steiner Verlag); 'L. Iunius Brutus the Patrician and the Political Allegiance of Q. Aelius Tubero', *Classical Philology* 106 (2011), 155–61 (Chicago: University of Chicago Press).

I am grateful to the several publishers for their permission to reprint these works. I have made some modifications to each, to try to take into account more recent work, where it may be useful or may have affected the argument, to address various other matters and also to reduce some of the repetition of material between the different chapters. It should be noted, however, that a certain amount of repetition could not be avoided: although this is a book, designed to be read like most other books, from start to finish, I wanted to ensure that each individual essay nonetheless remained intelligible in and by itself. I have also added translations of the Greek and Latin.

Introduction

For early Rome, historiographic study must precede historical.[1]

It is now twenty-five years since the publication of T. J. Cornell's magisterial history of early Rome, *The Beginnings of Rome: Italy and Rome from the Bronze Age to the Punic Wars (c. 1000–264 BC)*. And it is some measure of Cornell's achievement that, even after a quarter of a century and even though recent archaeological discoveries have made sections of it obsolete, his book remains the standard work of its kind on the subject in the English language. At the time of its publication, reviewers were full of praise. The book was welcomed as 'a truly magnificent achievement', and rightly so.[2]

As any good book should, *The Beginnings of Rome* also prompted disagreement and debate. There was one issue in particular about which many expressed reservations, and that was Cornell's handling of the literary evidence, in the historicity of which he had placed considerable confidence. For a number of reviewers, that confidence was misplaced.[3]

The problem is simple: while the Romans generally came to date the foundation of Rome to sometime in the mid-eighth century BC, no one at Rome wrote history until the end of the third century, and it is not clear that Rome's first historians had access to anything much in the way of genuine or reliable evidence from more than a century or so before their own day. Recent archaeological discoveries, which have pushed Rome's origins further back in time, have only (or ought only to have) made the

---

1 Pinsent 1971, 272.
2 Wiseman 1996, 315.
3 See most notably Wiseman 1996; McDonnell 1997; Oakley 1997b. Since Cornell's book contains large sections of material reworked from his contributions to *The Cambridge Ancient History*, it is also worth noting the comments of Billows 1992, 193–4 in his review of that volume.

situation worse. Since historians of antiquity are so used to dealing with lengthy periods of time, on account of the paucity of the evidence, it is all too easy to overlook the sheer length of time involved and all that that means. How could Fabius Pictor, Rome's first historian, have possibly known anything much, or even anything at all, about what had happened several hundred years before his own day?

Further complicating matters is the fact that Fabius Pictor's work has not survived, while the literary evidence for early Rome that has comes from some century and a half later, and often even later still. Much had happened during that time, and not all of it was beneficial to the preservation or reconstruction of an accurate account of the events of Rome's past. A lot of it may have been detrimental. There are all manner of issues that need to be taken into account, from questions of evidence, research, methods and purpose, to conceptions of truth and plausibility, standards of honesty, the influence of later events on the traditions of the past, and even the simple understanding of historical change and development. It cannot just be taken for granted (although it often is) that people living more than 2,000 years ago consistently worked with methods and to standards that are recognised today and that the only difference is one of degree.

It is really very easy to see why Cornell's reviewers did not share his optimistic assessment of what the Romans had to say about Rome's distant past. And yet, despite the nature and scale of the problem, the seriousness of the criticism and, it must be said, the overwhelming persuasiveness of many of the objections to Cornell's position and approach, it is fair to say that Cornell's general assessment of the literary evidence has nonetheless been influential and can readily be detected in the work of a number of British scholars in particular. Even more significant, however, is a recent assessment of Cornell's book as 'more skeptical' in its handling of that evidence.[4] That claim was made in comparison with the work of A. Carandini and should be understood in that context, but it nonetheless stands in striking contrast to the views of a quarter of a century ago. So what has happened to move scholarship so far in the direction of the very position, and indeed even beyond it, that had earlier invited so much stern and valid criticism?

4   Armstrong 2016, 1.

The specific circumstance behind Carandini's optimism – that optimism that makes Cornell's position one of scepticism by comparison – is, of course, the discovery of traces of what may be a wall at the foot of part of the Palatine hill, a discovery that has prompted Carandini to claim that the foundation myth of Rome is actually historical.[5] And it may well seem to follow that, if the stories the Romans told about the very origins of Rome are somehow historical, then what they said about later times ought to be historical too.

The position of Carandini and his followers is not new. A comparable reaction can be found in scholarship – work that has long since been abandoned – from about a century ago, following the archaeological discoveries of G. Boni, in this case in the Roman Forum. At that time, as more recently, the archaeological evidence was used to justify the almost complete rehabilitation of the literary evidence; the existence of Rome's mythical founder was announced as a matter of fact; and the optimists, now fully vindicated (or so some of them claimed), could openly declare their faith to the world.[6]

It is difficult not to draw a very different conclusion. Instead of proving the existence of Romulus, which the archaeological evidence does not do and has never done, these different discoveries appear instead simply to have been used as justification for those who already wanted to believe that the literary evidence for early Rome was reliable to go ahead with their beliefs. The issue is not the archaeological evidence (which ought to be important in its own right) and the sorts of questions that such evidence can and cannot answer, but instead the preconceived views of a group of scholars and their appropriation of that evidence to validate those views.[7]

---

5   Carandini is immensely prolific; the specific work with which Armstrong compares Cornell's book is his *Rome: Day One* (Carandini 2011b); this work is described simply as 'optimistic' (Armstrong 2016, 1), which hardly seems sufficient to describe a work of what may be called selective faith. Cornell, it should be noted, does not follow Carandini; see Cornell 1995, 30; Cornell 2012; Cornell 2014b.

6   See pp. 47–8 below.

7   As Feeney 2007, 91–2 says: 'If the ancient tradition had fixed on 1000 as the "real" date [of Rome's foundation], then these scholars would all be focusing on the exiguous human remains at Rome from around 1000 as "corroboration."'

Even when the archaeological evidence is not misused in this way, there is still plenty of evidence for the influence of the will to believe in the reliability of the literary evidence.[8] Indeed, for some, it seems that it is simply inconceivable that ancient accounts of Rome's early history are altogether unreliable, so much so in fact that it has even been asserted that the burden of proof lies with those who doubt the historicity of those accounts.[9] The problem is, the proof exists, but those who believe in the reliability of the evidence simply dismiss it or otherwise seek to explain it away.

Since his work has been lost, no one today knows for sure where Fabius Pictor got his material or even what material he used. But for those who maintain that ancient accounts of Rome's early history are broadly reliable, it simply follows that Pictor must have had access to good evidence. It is possible, moreover, to identify some of his potential sources: he could, it seems, have consulted family records, state documents and archives made

8   The phrase 'will to believe' was used by Finley of those who insist that 'the tradition of the expedition against Troy must have a basis of historical fact'; Finley commented: 'In the absence of literary or archaeological documentation, there is no immediate control over this will to believe' (1964, 2). In 1979, Wiseman used the phrase with reference to the writings of Rome's republican historians: 'Nowadays we have learned to pay lip-service, at least, to the danger of accepting annalistic material as reliable, but the will to believe is still strong' (1979b, 52–3). In 2016, Wiseman devoted a short chapter to the topic (29–37); as he puts it there: 'If you *want* to believe in something strongly enough, you may find it easy to overlook the arguments against it' (34). Note Billows 1992, 194 on the coverage of early Rome in *The Cambridge Ancient History*: 'Too often ... [the] rules of logic are dispensed with by authors seeking to make a partisan case.'

9   Cornell 1995, 16: 'Given what we now know about the extent and uses of writing in archaic Rome, the burden of proof clearly lies on those who wish to deny the authenticity of a public document cited in our sources.' It does not follow, of course, that evidence for Roman literacy proves the authenticity of any early public document recorded in the sources (consider, for instance, Romulus' treaty with Veii, mentioned by Dion. Hal. *Ant. Rom.* 2.55.6). Cf. Momigliano 1969, 15: 'why should the Romans say that two yearly *praetores* or *consules* replaced the king, if that was not the truth? How could they forget the character of the momentous change from monarchy to Republic?' On Cornell's approach, see Wiseman 1996, 312–13, on Momigliano's, Wiseman 1995, 105.

by priestly colleges, the pontifical in particular.[10] The very nature of the material sounds reassuring: official, serious and safe (but no doubt for that reason, anachronistic, although the early existence of such material is regularly taken for granted). And since Pictor was an historian, it apparently follows that he must have been consistently engaged in an activity that – while admittedly different in many respects – was fundamentally the same as that of a modern historian, at least one concerned primarily with the military and political history of Rome. That assumption is implicit in the very question of his sources.

One serious difficulty with this view is the fact that the Romans themselves were aware that extremely few documents – some laws and a few treaties only – had survived from early times. They explained these circumstances with the story that Rome had been sacked by the Gauls in the early fourth century BC.[11] For many years, this was a problem with which modern historians also had to contend. After all, if ancient accounts of Rome's early history are reliable, then Rome must have been thoroughly burnt by the Gauls.[12] And if the city and the documents in it had been destroyed, how could anyone at Rome have known anything about Rome's early history?

The Roman account of the destruction of Rome was long seen as necessitating a deeply sceptical reaction to the literary evidence for early Rome, although those who wanted to have faith in the evidence certainly sought ways to get around what was for them an inconvenient problem.[13] It has, however, since been discovered that there is no archaeological evidence

---

10   Bispham and Cornell 2013, 175–8 for Pictor's possible sources; cf. also Cornell 1995, 9–16; Oakley 1997a, 22–72 (with a focus on later times); Forsythe 2005, 69–77; Armstrong 2016, 21–39; Rich 2018, *passim*, etc.

11   Livy 6.1.2, 6.1.10; cf. Plut. *Numa* 1.2; on the documentary evidence mentioned in the literary sources, see Ampolo 1983a; on the treaties, see Richardson 2017, 264–71.

12   Diod. 14.115.6, 14.116.8–9; Livy 5.41.10–43.1, 5.55.3–5; Plut. *Cam.* 22.6, 31–32.3, etc.

13   For example, Roberts 1918; Ogilvie 1965, 6 n. 1 ('I believe ...'); Heurgon 1973, 249: "'most of [the archives] perished", says Livy, and the Romans, one supposes, set about reconstituting them immediately after ... we should think not of masses of annals that could have been destroyed in the fire, but of a few inscriptions on stone or bronze, which might have survived ... In any case, if they were made up again, to reconstruct a hundred years is not beyond the powers of memory of a primitive people.'

for widespread destruction and so the story of the sack of Rome has been happily dismissed, along with all the implications of it for the historical record.[14] Documentary evidence could have survived after all and so Roman accounts of Rome's early history can, it seems, be taken as broadly reliable. That position is already a stretch, and not only because it involves a *non sequitur*. It is also based on the assumption (one made by the Romans themselves but clearly anachronistically) that documents had been made in archaic times in the first place. It is likely that the story of the loss of records was invented to explain the absence of records; after all, if such documents had actually existed, their absence would not have required an explanation. But that general absence is probably just what should be expected in an essentially oral society, as archaic Rome was. As for the production of anything along the lines of 'state' or 'public' records, since that requires not only the existence of a state, but also of a state able and concerned to produce such material, the very absence of documents is potentially significant evidence in its own right. It should not be argued away, and especially not on the basis of some belief (whether ancient or modern) that such material simply *must* have existed.

---

14   Scullard 1980, 408: 'It has sometimes been maintained that all the old temples perished in the fire. Archaeological research has shown that this is not true in the main ... And if the Gauls spared the temples they probably spared the archives and records which they contained.' Cornell 1995, 318: 'the belief that the scarcity of documentary sources for early Roman history was due to their destruction at the hands of the Gauls ... is a false solution to a non-existent problem. The important point to make about records in relation to the sack is not that so many ancient documents, buildings, monuments and relics were destroyed, but rather that so many of them survived. The best explanation of all the evidence is that the Gauls were interested in moveable booty ... They ransacked the place, and made off with whatever they could carry ... This conclusion is in line with common sense and is moreover consistent with the fact that no archaeological trace of the Gallic disaster has yet been positively identified.' And earlier, 24: 'we know that many important documents, not to speak of buildings and monuments, did, in fact, escape. In any case it is unlikely that the Roman authorities, who were careful to send the Vestal Virgins and their sacred cult objects to Caere, did not take similar precautions to protect their archives when they heard news of the impending Gallic attack.' See also Delfino 2009; Rich 2013a, 149; Rich 2018, 22–3.

There is a certain irony in the fact that the solution to what was un-doubtedly the single biggest problem for the study of early Rome was the discovery that the Gauls had not destroyed the city after all. The historicity of what the Romans had to say about early Rome had been saved, apparently, because the archaeological evidence had disproved the historicity of one of the things the Romans had to say about early Rome. With the unwanted story safely out of the way, all the rest of what the Romans said suddenly had the potential to be useful evidence for what had actually happened. The objection is obvious: if one story – and one story long considered to be sound – should have been invented, then why not others or even, for that matter, the rest? (Part of the answer to that question, no doubt, is that the rest is not quite so inconvenient.)

The Roman historian Livy certainly drew attention to problems in his sources. Some of these problems are very serious indeed. Livy complained about inconsistencies in the lists of magistrates;[15] he lamented that funeral speeches and the like contained mendacious material, material that had found its way into other accounts of the events of the past;[16] he complained

---

15 See Chapter 6 in particular.

16 Livy 8.40.3–5: *nec facile est aut rem rei aut auctorem auctori praeferre. vitiatam memoriam funebribus laudibus reor falsisque imaginum titulis, dum familiae ad se quaeque famam rerum gestarum honorumque fallente mendacio trahunt; inde certe et singulorum gesta et publica monumenta rerum confusa. nec quisquam aequalis temporibus illis scriptor exstat quo satis certo auctore stetur.* [It is not easy to prefer one account to another or one authority to another. I think the record has been cor-rupted by funeral speeches and false inscriptions for the masks of ancestors, as each family claims for itself with deceitful lies the fame of deeds and honours; assuredly as a result both the achievements of individuals and the public records of events have been thrown into disorder. Nor is there extant any writer contemporary with those times on whose authority it would be sufficient to depend.] On this problem, see also Cic. *Brut.* 62: *et hercules eae quidem exstant: ipsae enim familiae sua quasi ornamenta ac monumenta servabant et ad usum, si quis eiusdem generis occidisset, et ad memoriam laudum domesticarum et ad illustrandam nobilitatem suam. quamquam his laudationibus historia rerum nostrarum est facta mendosior. multa enim scripta sunt in eis quae facta non sunt: falsi triumphi, plures consulatus, genera etiam falsa et ad plebem transitiones, cum homines humiliores in alienum eiusdem nominis infunderentur genus; ut si ego me a M'. Tullio esse dicerem, qui patricius cum Ser. Sulpicio consul anno x post exactos reges fuit.* [[Funeral speeches] are certainly extant: for the families themselves used to keep them as their marks of honour and

about the distortions, exaggerations and lies of the historian Valerius Antias (whose work he nonetheless used);[17] and he also observed that the historian Licinius Macer was unreliable when he wrote about his own family.[18]

For those who believe that the literary evidence for early Rome is generally reliable, what Livy has to say is a problem that clearly needs to be got rid of. The names of magistrates that can be extracted from Livy's work and from Dionysius of Halicarnassus' are broadly consistent and so, it supposedly follows, must be historical;[19] funeral speeches and other such family records can only have been a source of minor corruption, apparently;[20] Valerius Antias was, it seems, actually a serious historian who carried out extensive research in the archives of the Senate and, if there were problems in his work, that was the fault of his sources (the Senate's archives excluded, of course);[21] as for Licinius Macer, his work was not really all that unreliable either.[22] Besides, no one at Rome could possibly have distorted or misrepresented the events of the past and hoped to get away with it. Everyone knew what had happened, so any lie would have been so quickly rooted out that no one would have even attempted to tell it in the first place.[23]

The fact that Livy had actually read the works of Antias and Macer, which no one today can do, is often ignored. So too is the fact that no

---

as memorials, and for use when any member of the family died, both as a record of the house's distinctions and to illustrate its nobility; and yet, by these eulogies, our history has been made quite faulty. For many things are written in them which did not happen: false triumphs, too many consulships, even false genealogies and transitions to the plebs, as men of humbler birth were mixed into another family of the same name, as if I should say that I was descended from M'. Tullius, who was a patrician consul with Ser. Sulpicius ten years after the expulsion of the kings.]

17 Livy 26.49.3, 30.19.11, 33.10.8, 36.38.5–7, 38.23.8, 39.41.6, 40.29.8, 42.11.1, etc.
18 Livy 7.9.5: *quaesita ea propriae familiae laus leviorem auctorem Licinium facit.* [The glory that he seeks for his own family makes Licinius an authority of lesser weight.]
19 See Chapter 6.
20 Cornell 1995, 10 on Cic. *Brut.* 62 and Livy 8.40.2 (n. 16 above); cf. Smith 2011a, 26 and Glinister 2017, 71 on Cic. *Brut.* 62.
21 See in particular Rich 2005 and Rich 2013b.
22 Smith 2011a, 31.
23 Cornell 1986, 80, 82; Oakley 1997a, 31–2, 39–40; Cornell 2005, 49, 52; Glinister 2017, 71–2.

Roman funeral speech survives; moreover, the evidence for them that does exist is frequently played down or just passed over.[24] Also played down is the fact that the extant evidence for the names of magistrates comes mostly from works from the first century BC, and that the nature and content (and even the existence) of lists of such names in the second, third, fourth and fifth centuries BC are unknown. As if that were not enough, Livy's assessment of Macer's work has been rejected on the basis of what Livy himself had to say about it, as if Livy were incapable of assessing the work properly and also so incompetent as to reveal that fact.[25] As for Antias, if he had indeed done all that research, why should he have also used sources that were patently unreliable? Why does Livy criticise specifically him and not those sources or his use of them? And does it ultimately make any difference, whether Antias or his sources were to blame for the problems that Livy encountered? But there is simply no evidence to support the claim that Antias conducted research in the Senate's archives anyway.[26]

As for the idea that distortion and fabrication were impossible, because everyone knew what had really happened, not only is that evidence of a certain determination to believe in the historicity of the literary evidence no matter what, but it is also evidence of wilful blindness to a substantial body of evidence to the contrary (ancient Rome would need to be somehow unique in human history).[27] Besides, arguments of this kind potentially result in a paradox: if Rome's historians could not distort, misrepresent

24 In addition to Livy 8.40.3–5 and Cic. *Brut.* 62, which are effectively just dismissed (see n. 20 above), see Livy 27.27.12–14 for variant accounts; Suet. *Iul.* 6.1, where the claims are demonstrably unhistorical; Plin. *HN* 7.139–40, in which the exaggerated nature of the claims is self-evident; note also the inconsistencies between the claims made in the *elogium* of Scipio Barbatus (*ILLRP* 309) and Livy's account of Scipio's consulship of 298 (10.12.3–8); the *elogia* of the Scipios may owe something to funeral speeches, cf. Zevi 1969–70, 66–7. On the evidence for the events of 298, see Oakley 2005b, 173–4: most solutions involve some combination of the different accounts, even though they are incompatible. On *tituli*, see Livy 4.16.3–4, 4.34.6–7.

25 See Smith 2011a, 28–31.

26 Richardson 2018.

27 Of course, it was not unique: see, for example, Cic. *Att.* 6.1.17–18 for Metellus Scipio's ignorance about the history of his own family. See Armstrong and Richardson 2017, 6–8.

or lie about what everyone knew to be true, then Livy's comments about the works of Antias and Macer would have to be untrue; but Livy was an historian too and his comments can hardly be dismissed as mistakes or accidents, or as unimportant. The position of the optimists often seems, in the end, ultimately to be based not only on a refusal to see the wood for the trees, but also on the belief that each individual tree should be chopped down, using one means or another as required in each instance, so that the wood does not even exist.

The combination of sometimes extraordinary confidence in the historicity of the literary evidence, a growing body of archaeological evidence for early Rome and the belief that that evidence can be interpreted with reference to the literary evidence (which it is supposed, in an entirely circular way, to verify) has had predictable enough consequences. Those who work on the literary evidence for early Rome may well now find themselves confronted with the expectation that they should advance a positive thesis about the history of early Rome, even when the case they are making involves a deeply sceptical assessment of that evidence. They may also find that they are now expected to incorporate the archaeological evidence into their discussion as a matter of course, even when the discussion is concerned with issues to which the archaeological evidence cannot actually contribute. (As it happens, the limits of the archaeological evidence can be easily discerned in certain recent work on early Rome, in which that evidence is quickly left behind in favour of the literary evidence, even in the work of those who declare themselves to be archaeologists.)[28]

When the arguments in defence of the reliability of the literary evidence for early Rome are as unpersuasive as they generally are, and when the underlying will to believe in the historicity of the evidence is so readily apparent, there is every reason to dismiss the optimistic assessment and simply accept what ancient authors have to say about the lack of material from early times and about the problems in the material that was available

---

28   Carandini 2011b, 4. Carandini's book, *Rome: Day One*, provides an overview of his findings and reconstruction of Rome's origins. It includes an appendix in which the relevant literary evidence, free from Carandini's interpretation of it, is set out at length (123–63); there is, however, no comparable appendix containing the raw archaeological data.

to them. The results of such an approach need not just be negative. What the Romans said about the origins and early history of Rome may reveal little about Rome's actual origins and early history, but it does have the potential to shed light on all manner of other issues; and while those issues may have little to do with archaic Rome, they may reveal something about later circumstances. It may well be that the study of Rome's earliest history is just as much, indeed probably even more so, the study of the ideas, views and thinking of later times.

The quote that appears at the start of this introduction (namely that, 'For early Rome, historiographic study must precede historical') was originally used as the epigraph for the essay that forms Chapter 5 of this book. Since the observation is pertinent to the work as a whole, it made sense to put it at the very beginning. Not only does it remain as valid as ever but, given certain recent trends and developments, it may be that it is in need of some emphasis. The extant literary evidence for early Rome comes mostly from the late first century BC, and what is found in the works of Livy, Dionysius and the rest is the outcome of centuries of story-telling and several generations of the writing not just of history but clearly also of pseudo-history. It is the outcome of research of various kinds involving material of differing nature and value, but also of learned conjecture, speculation and invention, whether simply of a plausible nature, for entertainment's sake or for more partisan purposes. These circumstances also explain why the archaeological evidence cannot simply be used to verify Roman accounts of the past. To pick only one simple and obvious problem: how is it possible to distinguish between a reliable account of some early monument and a plausible-sounding story invented outright in later times to explain that monument?

* *

One of the main themes of this book is the development of the Roman state and its system of government (which, if only for convenience, will sometimes be referred to simply as the constitution). It will be useful therefore to summarise the Roman account very briefly, as it is found in the extant sources.

The Romans came to believe that Rome had been founded, that is to say, that their city and state had been created at one moment in time and by one individual. That moment was calculated to be sometime in the mid-eighth century and the individual was usually said to have been Romulus, although there were other dates and other candidates.[29] After it had been founded, Rome was subsequently ruled by a series of kings, most of whom were effectively elected to office and each of whom was said to have contributed in some way to Rome's development. When the last of those kings, L. Tarquinius Superbus, proved to be an abusive tyrant, the Romans expelled him and decided to do away with their monarchy. The kings were immediately replaced with two annually elected magistrates called consuls. Unlike the kings, who had ruled for life, the consuls were in office for only a year and, unlike the kings who had ruled alone (a brief period of co-regency during Romulus' reign aside), the two consuls shared their power. The consulship, with its collegiality and limited tenure of office, became synonymous with the free Republic.

Much of this has long been accepted as broadly historical and much of it, at least at first sight, may seem plausible enough. More confidence has generally been placed in the evidence for later events than earlier, although there are some who would accept almost the entire account largely as it stands. On closer inspection, however, there is much that is problematic. The view that cities were founded was prevalent in antiquity, but it is hardly historical in Rome's case and there is an abundance of evidence to show this (see Chapter 1 in particular). The idea that each of Rome's kings contributed to Rome's development certainly has some semblance of historical reality, but it does not follow from that that the Roman account is therefore historical. One obvious and significant problem is that, while the regal period supposedly lasted for some 250 years, there were in total just seven kings, and that is simply absurd. Several of those kings are quite clearly unhistorical too. The whole account looks to be an artificial reconstruction, and that assessment is further supported by the quite distinctive nature of the depiction of some of the kings.[30] Rome's development was, moreover, so closely tied to those seven kings that it was possible for the Romans to conceive of them as a series of founders. And when that idea gets used in turn to argue that Rome was superior to other states, precisely

29   See Wiseman 1995, 160–8 for the evidence.
30   See pp. 121–4 on Romulus, Numa and Servius Tullius. Note Flor. 1.8.

because those states had had only the one founder, there is further reason to be suspicious.

The idea that Rome was the work of many founders and was for that reason superior was inevitably strengthened by the Romans' belief that they had – somewhat uniquely – elected their kings and so had been able to choose the best men for the job. It was an established view, on the other hand, that hereditary succession leads to bad rulers. It can hardly be a co-incidence that only one of Rome's kings was said to have been bad and that that king was also the only one said to have acquired his position on hereditary grounds. But, if the Romans always chose their kings, how else could such a man have ever come to power?

A bad king was needed, but only the one. That was enough to provide a plausible explanation for why the Romans had brought an end to the rule of kings and established the free Republic. It also allowed for Rome's earlier kings to be assessed positively; after all, since they were Rome's founders, it would not do to make them all into abusive tyrants. What sort of state would such men have established? The whole reconstruction is patently contrived, and the surprisingly widespread evidence for stories about Rome's kings that presuppose hereditary succession suggests that it was probably a later development; even the story of the bad king whose abuses led to the end of the monarchy may well be unhistorical.[31] Much of this reconstruction is nonetheless widely accepted today. These matters are considered in Chapter 2.

Although the Romans later believed that their kings had been immediately replaced with magistrates known as consuls, there is good evidence to show that that was not the case. The consulship may have actually been created as late as the fourth century BC (see Chapters 3, 5 and 6). That means that the anti-monarchic ideology that was associated with it must have developed at a later date and in a different context. The most obvious context in which the Romans might have found it useful to set their republican institutions in direct opposition specifically to the rule of kings is when they came into conflict with the kings of the Hellenistic world. The benefits of such a reinterpretation are obvious. When, for instance,

---

31 See p. 99, n. 50 for the evidence and arguments that Lars Porsenna, the king of Clusium, may have been responsible for ending Tarquinius Superbus' reign.

the Romans later did away with the ancient and illustrious Macedonian monarchy, they established annually elected magistrates in its place and thus were able to present their actions as a benefaction. The Macedonian people, they claimed, were now free (see Chapter 5). That, of course, involved a definition of freedom no Hellenistic king could possibly entertain.

* *

For the Romans, the events of the past were always relevant and they were so in ways that they are simply not today.[32] The final chapter explores how the descent – both asserted and denied – of M. Iunius Brutus from L. Iunius Brutus, the legendary founder of the Roman Republic, was an important and contentious issue in the first century BC. L. Brutus had led the conspiracy to oust Tarquinius Superbus, while M. Brutus was a prominent figure in the plot to assassinate Iulius Caesar. Marcus' descent from Lucius evidently mattered; it helped to justify his involvement in Caesar's murder, which is precisely why his opponents challenged it. The achievements of ancestors were important, whether they consisted of getting rid of a king or something a little more commonplace, such as reaching the consulship, the magistracy that was the 'hallmark' of Rome's office-holding nobility (a topic explored in Chapters 6 and 7). It is hardly surprising, therefore, that Livy should have complained precisely about problems in the lists of magistrates, the making of false claims in funeral speeches and Licinius Macer's unreliability when he wrote about his own family. Similar charges have since been levelled against other Roman historians (see Chapter 7).

The events of the past could be contentious in other ways too. The Romans were not the only ones to write about Rome's history. Others did so as well and not all were admirers. Some were opponents, and these circumstances no doubt also help to account for some of the different interpretations and reconstructions that can be found in the literary evidence. One notable detractor was Philinus of Agrigentum, whose account of the First Punic War was later used by the historian Polybius. Polybius knew that Philinus' work was unfavourable to Rome and unreliable for

---

32   See Richardson 2012, 17–55; the bibliography on the role of the past in Roman society is considerable; see for instance Gallia 2012; Galinksy 2014; Roller 2018, all with various references to further work.

that reason, just as he knew that his other main source for the war, Fabius Pictor's history, was favourable and so unreliable too. Polybius himself had much higher standards, but the simple fact that he felt it necessary to insist that the writing of history requires impartiality is good evidence of what generally went on.[33]

Polybius had no difficulties at all showing up Philinus' account of the start of the First Punic War.[34] He went to greater lengths, however, to disprove Philinus' claims about the terms of the treaty between Rome and Carthage that was in place at the time of its outbreak, terms that unsurprisingly and somewhat suspiciously put the Romans wholly and unambiguously in the wrong.[35] Polybius' efforts led to the discovery and publication of some extremely important evidence.

Rome and Carthage had long had dealings with one another and they had on several occasions made treaties with each other. Polybius got access to a number of these, which had evidently been inscribed on bronze, and he discussed the terms of them in his work. Given the considerable lengths of time involved (Polybius dated the earliest treaty he found to the first year of the republican period), as well as the partisan nature of some accounts, the fact that there are uncertainties, inconsistencies and even incompatible claims in the evidence for Rome's early dealings with Carthage is perfectly understandable. The record may well be incomplete too, although gaps often do tend, by their very nature, to be undetectable.

Given these circumstances, the confidence with which so many have written on this topic in modern times may well come as a surprise. No less extraordinary is the method that is widely employed when dealing with this material. Despite the many and often obvious problems, the evidence is treated not only as reliable but also as complete. No one source preserves intact the whole record of Rome's dealings with Carthage, but it is usually assumed that the several different sources have somehow managed to do this between them. All that needs to be done is for the different pieces of that record to be picked out of those different accounts and put back together. The fact that the pieces are often selected and reassembled to suit

---

33   Polyb. 1.14, 1.15.12, cf. also 3.8–3.9.5.
34   Polyb. 1.15.1–11.
35   Polyb. 3.21.9–26.7.

the desired reconstruction is neither here or there, apparently, nor is the fact that some of the pieces are incompatible with one another.

This method and the specific problem of Rome's treaties with Carthage are the focus of Chapter 4, but the importance of the issue extends far beyond this specific body of evidence. This is because the use of this method – and the accompanying willingness to ignore not only the existence of divergent accounts but also the very implications of their existence – is not confined to this one topic. The evidence for Rome's origins has likewise been handled in a highly selective manner in some recent work, although in this case the desired interpretation of the archaeological evidence has often provided the criterion for what is to be accepted and what ignored.[36]

It is worth repeating that the extant literary evidence for early Rome consists of a mix of material, some of which is older, but some newer, some of which is based on evidence, but a good part of which owes its existence to argumentation, reconstruction, interpretation and even invention. It needs to be handled accordingly.

* *

So where does this leave early Rome? Polybius' research into Rome's treaties with Carthage turned up some early material which he presented in his work (some of this was evidently newly discovered and the implications of that for the efforts or attitude of Rome's first historians should not be overlooked, nor should the absence of this material from subsequent works). Some of what Polybius found is especially significant because it seems to be inconsistent with the extant Roman accounts. That should probably not come as a surprise, although some have responded to this by dismissing what Polybius found in favour of what the Romans themselves had to say. But that is to champion later reconstruction over early evidence. This matter is discussed in Chapter 3.

In Livy's work a comparable piece of early evidence can be found. Livy records the content of an early inscription in which, it would appear, the chief magistrate of the state was called the *praetor maximus*. That name is

---

36   As Ridley 2017, 50 says, 'History is not reconstructed by simply choosing the source which suits you.'

inconsistent with later Roman accounts (including Livy's own), in which the chief magistracy of the state was the consulship, and it is also difficult to reconcile with the collegiality and power-sharing that were associated with the consulship. As with Polybius' evidence, some have responded by dismissing what Livy relates in favour of those Roman accounts, but that is again to champion later reconstruction over what appears to be a good piece of early evidence. These matters are addressed in Chapters 3, 5 and 6.

Evidence of this kind is significant, not only because it is contemporary with early times, but also because it raises doubts about what the Romans themselves said in much later times. Scattered throughout the literary evidence is a small body of material that is incompatible with the general account of events that is found in Livy, Dionysius and the rest. It does not automatically follow, of course, that this material is therefore reliable, but it seems less likely that it should have been invented. And what Polybius says about the content of Rome's first treaty with Carthage is certainly based on early evidence and what Livy says about the *praetor maximus* appears to be so too.

Another important early document is the so-called Lapis Satricanus, an inscription from the late sixth century BC that, in this case, actually happens to survive. This inscription provides evidence for a group of people who defined themselves with reference simply and only to one individual. Circumstances such as these are difficult to reconcile with ideas of fully developed states and citizenship (see Chapters 1 and 3). And if the literary evidence contains a few stray stories that appear to involve comparable groups, stories that some accounts struggle to accommodate or cannot adequately explain, it is not unreasonable to suppose that they may conceivably reveal something of earlier circumstances (whether only in the context of story-telling and the development of the Roman account, or of actual historical realities).

There is also early inscriptional evidence that confirms the existence of the position of *rex* [king] at Rome.[37] This evidence appears to associate the *rex* with religious matters but, beyond that, its value is actually quite limited: the powers of this *rex*, the way in which he acquired them and the manner in which he exercised them are all unknown. It cannot even

37 See Cristofani 1990, 58–9.

be assumed that they were his for life. On the other hand, the significance of the very act of setting up such an inscription should not be overlooked. That alone is important evidence.

There is one other type of evidence that has the potential to be contemporary with early times. Whatever the origins and original nature and purpose of such structures as the *curiae* and the tribes may have been, their names appear to have been kept in continuous use and thus preserved unchanged. The tribes that Romulus was said to have set up are problematic and they were clearly mysterious even in antiquity,[38] but the tribal system that Servius Tullius was said to have established is potentially much more helpful. Some of the Servian tribes – the earliest, it seems – were named after *gentes* ('clans' is the usual translation, although it does come with baggage). This would seem to suggest that some *gentes* or perhaps individual members of them were especially prominent and influential, and that possibility is not at all incompatible with the sorts of circumstances implied by the Lapis Satricanus and by some of what Polybius has to say about Rome's first treaty with Carthage.

When brought together, even if only loosely (but that is often all that is really possible), much of this evidence suggests that this was a world where the idea of the city-state was inchoate, and where powerful individuals and their followers and families could assert themselves, act independently and perhaps even take control of the pre-urban settlement and its inhabitants and, later, the city. The possibility that powerful individuals might have established themselves as 'kings' of some description (the meaning of the word need not have been stable or uncontested), on occasion no doubt by force of arms, whether actual or merely understood,[39] certainly seems more plausible than the Roman account of an elective monarchy, stable

---

38   Hence the various etymologies for, and uncertainties about, their names (Cic. *Rep.* 2.14; Varro *Ling.* 5.55; Livy 1.13.8; Plut. *Rom.* 20.1; Ps.-Asc. in Cic. *Verr.* 2.1.14; Paul. Fest. 106L, etc.), and the alternative view that they were equestrian centuries (see, in particular, Livy 1.13.8; *De vir. ill.* 2.11; Fugmann 1990, 135–8); on their names, see Rix 2006. But the Romulean tribes may not have actually ever even existed as such, see Bormann 1893 and the comprehensive discussion in Poucet 1967, 333–410.

39   Cf. Vaahtera 1993 for the clashing of weapons as a means to signal approval; Richardson 2019, 286–7.

and indeed static from the start; that idea is undoubtedly anachronistic, certainly for early times, and also unhistorical, envisaging as it does little or no change.

This is not, of course, to deny the possibility that some men may have ruled Rome by popular consent or that some may have come to power following the rule of another member of their own family. Given the nature of the evidence, it is impossible to know how Rome's kings had acquired their powers or even, for that matter, what powers they had. If it happened that, later on, towards the end of the sixth century, there was growing resistance to the idea that Rome should continue to be ruled by one man, a period of change, uncertainty and perhaps even experimentation when it came to the replacement of the king and the creation of the earliest magistracies would hardly be surprising, as different groups sought to secure influence for themselves and also to set limits on the powers and activities of others, and as the new city-state began to develop and assert itself. It goes without saying that this is all necessarily tentative and hypothetical, but the Romans' own account is no less a matter of later reconstruction.

As will become apparent, no attempt is made here to offer any sort of detailed or systematic account of the history of early Rome, even within the narrow scope of the concerns of this book. This is because the evidence simply does not allow for it. The extant literary evidence is demonstrably problematic and there is simply insufficient reliable material to permit anything more than a few conjectures about early circumstances (which is precisely why a series of essays offers a suitable way to approach things). And – to address in advance that other expectation – the issues with which this book is primarily concerned are ones to which the archaeological evidence for the early inhabitation of the site of Rome contributes little. The results of the archaeological work that has been carried out during the last thirty or so years may have made sections of Cornell's *The Beginnings of Rome* obsolete, but Cornell's assessment of the value of the archaeological evidence remains unaffected by that: 'archaeology,' he says, 'cannot tell us much about the details of social structure or institutions ... If we want to know about the earliest institutions of the Roman state, it is to the literary sources that we must turn.'[40]

40 Cornell 1995, 114. And hence Carandini (see n. 28). The basic point was made long ago, see Thuc. 1.10.2 (although his concern is power).

CHAPTER I

The People and the State in Early Rome

I

Countries and states – that is, sovereign states under a single government – are today by and large synonymous, and they are also both generally taken for granted. This is still the case, even though the country, which is a relatively recent invention, is arguably starting to look out of date in some respects (think, for instance, of the exploitation by multinational companies of workers in countries with a low, or no legal minimum wage; think too of the moving of profits offshore, and of tax havens and what their use means; or, for a positive example, think of the European Union). In antiquity, there were no countries. The main political structure in the Classical world, or at least the one that is the most prevalent in modern discussion and in the modern imagination more generally, was the individual city-state. The most famous of those are of course Athens, Sparta and Rome, although there were a great many others. Each of these cities was a state in its own right, with its own laws and customs, its own citizen populace, its own territory and so on.

When it comes to the question of how cities came into existence, the Romans had really quite specific ideas, and since, in antiquity, cities were usually city-states, these Roman ideas were as much concerned with the establishment of states as they were with the actual cities themselves. First of all, cities were usually founded at a precise moment in time and usually by one individual, or so the Romans believed (and they were not alone in this). In the case of Rome, that individual was Romulus, and the moment in time was 21 April 753 BC.[1]

In order to found his city (and founders were usually, although not always, men), the founder needed to perform a variety of rituals, the precise details of which differ somewhat from account to account. What appears to have been the most important of these rituals required the founder to plough a ditch around the site where the city was to be built, using a pair of oxen, one male and one female, and – at least, according to some – a plough fitted with a bronze ploughshare.[2] Since this ditch supposedly marked out the location of the walls of the city (and – again, according to some – it also marked out the city's sacred boundary, the *pomerium*), the founder had to lift the ploughshare out of the ground wherever he wanted to have a gate in the city wall, and carry it over to where the wall was to begin again. This idea led to the questionable derivation of the word for a gate, *porta*, from the verb to carry, *portare*.[3]

According to M. Terentius Varro, who was writing in the first century BC, this ploughing ritual was, it would seem, absolutely fundamental to a city being a city. Varro's argument, however, is scarcely persuasive. He

1   According to some; Timaeus put the foundation of Rome in 814 BC, while Fabius Pictor put it in 747 BC, Cincius Alimentus in 728 and Cato the Elder in 751 (see Dion. Hal. *Ant. Rom.* 1.74.1–2). Naevius and Ennius made Romulus the grandson of Aeneas (Serv. Dan. *Aen.* 1.273), while Sallust claimed that Rome was founded by Trojans under the leadership of Aeneas (*Cat.* 6.1); on that sort of chronology Rome would have been founded in the twelfth century BC (although that does of course depend on how the fall of Troy gets dated). See Wiseman 1995, 160–8 for sixty-one different versions of the foundation myth of Rome. All these dates, the more familiar one of 753 included, are unhistorical; they are not based on evidence, but instead on various calculations and synchronisms; see Feeney 2007, 86–100. Bickerman's classic paper (1952) is also relevant in this context.

2   See Cato *FRHist* 5 F66 (= Serv. *Aen.* 5.755; Isid. *Orig.* 15.2.3); Varro *Ling.* 5.143. For the performance of this ritual by Romulus, see Dion. Hal. *Ant. Rom.* 1.88.2; Plut. *Rom.* 11.2–3. Further evidence can be found in Carandini 2006, 183–219, and also 433–4 on the ritual itself.

3   Isid. *Orig.* 15.2.5: *ubi portam vult esse, aratrum sustollat et portet, et portam vocet.* [Where [the founder] wants there to be a gate, let him lift the plough and carry [*portet*] it, and call it a gate [*portam*].] Varro, however, thought that gates were named from the carrying of goods through them (*Ling.* 5.142). See further Maltby 1991, 486.

supposed that cities (*urbes*) are so-called after the circle (*orbis*) formed by
the furrow that the founder ploughed around the site of his city, and after
the *urvum*, the curved part (the plough-beam) of the plough that he used
to make this furrow.[4]

What this particular ritual presupposes, obviously enough, is a very
clear idea from the outset, not only of where the city itself should be built
and where its boundaries should be (and consequently how big it would
be), but also where the gates, and so also the roads that went through them,
should be located. All this requires a considerable amount of planning,
as well as some awareness of the wider geographical, political and even
economic landscape.[5] More than that, it also requires a certain manner of
thinking and a certain type of knowledge, that is, the sort of thinking and
knowledge which can readily be expected of an urban dweller, but which
are less easily expected of someone used only to life in some sort of pre-
urban settlement, and which are hardly to be expected at all of someone
who does not even lead a sedentary life.

After his furrow had been ploughed, the founder – since he was
founding a city-state – would usually draw up a law-code, create a senate,
perhaps establish a political assembly of some kind, create a citizen populace,
enrol an army and so on.[6] In the case of Rome, various developments of a
constitutional nature took place during the course of the regal period and
during republican times too, but the Roman state itself nonetheless clearly
started with Romulus.[7] Indeed, some ancient writers took for granted the

---

4   Varro *Ling.* 5.143. For further ideas along these and other lines, see the evidence
     collected in Maltby 1991, 655.
5   See the entirely anachronistic discussion in Cic. *Rep.* 2.5–11 of Romulus' choice of
     site. But Cicero's Romulus lived in a literate and enlightened age, see *Rep.* 2.18–19;
     cf. Wiseman 2008, 125–6.
6   See, for instance, Virgil's imaginative depiction of the founding of Carthage in
     book one of the *Aeneid*; at 1.425 there is an allusion to the ploughing ritual; the
     very next line reads: *iura magistratusque legunt sanctumque senatum.* [They choose
     laws and magistrates and a venerable senate.]
7   Note especially Dion. Hal. *Ant. Rom.* 2.3–29 (on which, see Wiseman 2009, 81–
     98); also Plut. *Rom.* 13; Livy 1.8.1 on Romulus' establishment of law, 1.8.4–5 on the
     big, and consequently empty, city that Romulus supposedly built. The literary evi-
     dence is collected in Carandini 2011a; see also Franciosi 2003, 3–57.

existence of citizenship, elections and even magistracies during Romulus' reign.[8] Once again, all this presupposes a significant amount of planning, as well as the existence of a range of sometimes fully developed social and political ideas, including of course the very idea of a state and, along with it, the idea of citizenship.

If these Roman ideas about the formation of city-states are assessed in the context of much later times and of the founding by the Romans of something like an autonomous colony, there are no significant difficulties with them. But if they are assessed in the context of the origins of the earliest city-states of Italy, of which Rome was one, they are quite obviously problematic. How could the very first founders have come to possess all the knowledge and expertise that these ideas presupposed they had? Recently, A. Carandini – an archaeologist who has managed to convince himself that the foundation myth of Rome is actually historical – has hit upon a possible solution.[9]

According to Varro, the ploughing ritual was – despite Varro's various Latin etymologies – actually Etruscan, and Plutarch, in his biography of Romulus, says that Romulus summoned people from Etruria to instruct him.[10] Carandini says: 'Romulus sent for priests from Etruria, from whom he learned how to found an *urbs* (which implies the prior foundation of *urbes* on the right bank of the Tiber).'[11] This, however, only really pushes the problem back in time: when and how did the Etruscans learn how to found an *urbs*? Moreover, since the ritual was believed – rightly or wrongly – to be Etruscan, it would be a very easy assumption to make that Romulus must have turned to the Etruscans for help (as the Romans in later times did on occasion for various issues). But it is in some ways an unnecessary assumption, since the city of Alba Longa, from whose kings Romulus was

8   According to Serv. *Aen.* 7.709, after Romulus and Titus Tatius made their treaty, the Sabines received Roman citizenship, although they were not given the right to vote and so could not elect magistrates; for the election of magistrates in Romulus' day, see also Iunius Gracchanus *ap.* Ulp. *Dig.* 1.13.1.*pr.*

9   An overview of Carandini's ideas about the origins of Rome can be found in his book, *Rome: Day One* (2011b). The significance of the title is obvious.

10 Varro *Ling.* 5.143; Plut. *Rom.* 11.1.

11 Carandini 2011b, 50.

said to have been descended, was also an *urbs*.[12] It would, therefore, be comparable (certainly as far as the value of the evidence goes) to suppose that Romulus could have learnt how to found an *urbs* from his own family.[13] Furthermore, the ruling house of Alba Longa was allegedly descended from the Trojan hero Aeneas and, according to Virgil, Aeneas certainly knew how to perform the ploughing ritual, as did – or so it is implied – even the settlers from Tyre who founded the north African city of Carthage.[14] They, presumably, had not called on the Etruscans for help. It would seem that the details of this supposedly Etruscan ritual were very widely known, or so the Romans could imagine; clearly they just took the performance of the ritual for granted, no matter how improbable the results.

When it comes to the supposed foundation of Rome, none of this evidence, the story of the Etruscan priests included, is of any historical value whatsoever, not least because the very idea of a foundation, prior to which Rome did not exist and after which Rome did, is unhistorical. And, it hardly needs to be said, Romulus is himself an entirely mythical figure. He simply did not exist. What this evidence does show, however, is just how ingrained the idea of the city-state was in the Roman mindset (as the country perhaps is in the contemporary mindset), and this has quite significant implications for the nature of the evidence (see below).

It may come as no surprise that it has long been argued that these Roman ideas about the way cities were founded actually developed at a much later date. It appears that they developed out of Roman colonising activities (and note that, in the fully developed version of the story, Rome was a colony too, of Alba Longa). While the Romans may have come to believe that they founded their colonies in the same way that Romulus had supposedly founded Rome, it is much more likely that they simply

12   For Alba Longa as an *urbs*, see, for example, Cic. *Rep.* 2.4; Livy 1.3.3, 1.29.4–6; Virg. *Aen.* 8.47–8.

13   Dionysius (*Ant. Rom.* 1.86.1, 1.87.1, 2.3.1, 2.4.1 and 2.30.2) in fact has Romulus seek and follow the advice of his grandfather Numitor, the king of Alba Longa, when founding Rome. See Livy 1.7.3 for Romulus performing rituals 'in the Alban manner' (*Albano ritu*).

14   See, for example, *Aen.* 5.755: *interea Aeneas urbem designat aratro* [meanwhile Aeneas marks out the city [*urbem*] with a plough]; for the Tyrians and Carthage, see n. 6 above.

assumed that the rituals they used to found their colonies had been performed when Rome was founded.[15] Although, it must be said, not everyone agrees with that.[16]

In contrast to the idea that Rome was founded at a specific moment – indeed on a specific day – sometime in the mid-eighth century, the archaeological evidence shows that the site of Rome had actually been inhabited from a considerably earlier date and, more importantly, that the settlement and later city had developed over a long period.[17] Even without such evidence, it is reasonable enough to expect that the city and state of Rome took some time to develop, although that expectation is obviously difficult to reconcile with the ancient idea of a precise and dateable act of foundation. Under these circumstances, the only way in which the cake can be had and eaten too is to reduce the act of founding a city to little more than a ritual and/or political undertaking, something that could even be carried out inside an existing settlement, thus potentially marking out some part of that settlement from the rest of the surrounding community.

So it is that Carandini, who very much wants to have his cake as well as eat it (and in more ways than one, since his approach involves defending certain, selected ancient accounts of the foundation of Rome, while also effectively rewriting those accounts to solve all the problems that that initial defence creates), claims that the founding of Rome essentially amounted only to 'the invention of a new form of organization and government.'[18] Thus – contrary to what the ancient sources imagine – what Romulus did, Carandini claims, 'involved not the realization of any plans for a city but a series of ceremonial acts and sacred prohibitions that instilled into

15   Some time ago, Castagnoli 1958, 9; more recently, Wiseman 2004, 141; Rüpke 2007, 181–2; Wiseman 2013, 248. For another example of the Roman tendency to imagine that rituals performed in much later times had been performed from a very early date, see Richardson 2017.

16   Carandini aside, see for instance Grandazzi 2010 on the ritual itself.

17   See, for example, Fulminante 2014, 66–104, although the influence of the work of Carandini and his followers is palpable; on Rome's earliest walls, see Bernard 2012; the reconstruction and identification of several of the buildings Fulminante discusses are optimistic to say the least; see, for instance, Moormann 2001; Wiseman 2008, 271–92. See n. 56 below as well.

18   Carandini 2011b, 22.

the soil and the people a will to power expressed from the start in forms that we might term "modern" – that is, juridical, political, governmental, constitutional – masked but not negated by sacred and holy institutions.'[19]

But this approach just does not work. The story has Romulus found his city on essentially uninhabited land.[20] The literary evidence for the supposed foundation of Rome on the Palatine hill in the mid-eighth century BC cannot, therefore, be made to fit with the archaeological evidence for the much earlier and more extensive inhabitation of the site of Rome. Carandini's response to this objection is, typically, to dismiss those details in the literary evidence that do not fit with his reconstruction; hence, in this instance, he claims that 'Rome had to have arisen from nothingness [in the Roman accounts] so that Romulus's achievement could appear to have happened without prior groundwork and constitute a miracle: the founding.'[21] That, however, directly contradicts the ancient story (which Carandini, in this particular case, wants to retain) that Romulus had to call on the Etruscans to show him what to do. Why was that detail also not completely excised? There is after all nothing miraculous in following someone else's instructions.[22]

As for the political and, it could almost be said, 'constitutional' side of things, and the supposed establishment of the state, the details are quite clearly anachronistic. The very idea of a state – that is, of an organised political community under a single government – also had to develop, and there is similarly evidence that suggests that this too was something that took time and, moreover, that this was something that was variously asserted and contested in a number of different ways (see below).

---

19   Carandini 2011b, 28.

20   See, for example, Livy 1.4.5–9 and 1.6.3, 1.7.3; Tib. 2.5.55–6: *carpite nunc, tauri, de septem montibus herbas/ dum licet: hic magnae iam locus urbis erit.* [Graze now, bulls, on the grass from the seven hills/ while it is permitted: this will be the site of a great city.]

21   Carandini 2011b, 27.

22   Carandini's views are, unsurprisingly, extremely controversial and have been widely criticised on a variety of grounds; see, for instance, Poucet 2000, 160–81; Wiseman 2001; Moormann 2001; Wiseman 2004–6; Feeney 2007, 88–92; Wiseman 2008, 271–92; Testa 2012; Ampolo 2013; Hall 2014, 119–43. Carandini's basic approach and general argument are nothing new, see pp. 47–50.

What all this means is that, unfortunately, what the Romans have to say about the origins and early development of their city-state is largely unusable, simply because it takes for granted the existence of the city-state from the moment of Rome's supposed foundation and, even more improbably, presupposes the existence of the very idea of the city-state even before the creation of the city or state itself (although these are not the only reasons why the use of the literary evidence is extremely difficult). Once Rome had been founded, as far as later Romans were concerned – at least, the ones who wrote and whose works have survived – Rome existed as a city-state, with a citizen body, various political structures and so on. There are further consequences of this approach too.

II

At the time when the first city-states of central Italy were starting to come into existence, other social groups and structures already existed in the region, and indeed continued to exist. The first city-states did not, after all, appear from nowhere and out of nothing, as the archaeological evidence shows. It is not unreasonable to suppose that some of these other groups and structures may have been directly threatened by the emergence of the city-state, and that some may have also even threatened the first, fledgling city-states.

In the Roman literary tradition, however, the city-state is not just taken for granted, it generally predominates (and this is something that has, in turn, cast a long shadow over modern scholarship, and continues to do so in some quarters even to this day). Not only does Rome simply come into existence when Romulus founds it but, as noted earlier, Romulus himself is connected with another, much older city-state, Alba Longa. Alba Longa was said to have been founded by Ascanius who, like his father Aeneas, had come from the city of Troy.[23] Furthermore, when it came to his education,

23   See Livy 1.3.3; Dion. Hal. *Ant. Rom.* 1.66.1–2. Romulus' grandfather was Numitor, the rightful heir to the throne of Alba Longa; Numitor's position as king of Alba

the young Romulus supposedly went to school in the nearby city of Gabii (note, as well, that this presupposes that there was no school where he was raised, presumably because the site of Rome was, according to the story, essentially all pasture).[24] It is no wonder, then, that Romulus can so easily conceive of founding a city, and subsequently do so; he supposedly lived in a world where city-states had long existed and were the norm. This is obviously because later Romans just took the idea of the city-state for granted.

The almost inevitable result of all this is that, should the literary evidence happen to contain any material that may potentially shed some light on those various social groups and structures that predated and possibly even rivalled the earliest city-states (and it is an extremely difficult proposition: no one wrote history at Rome until the late third century BC), that material will undoubtedly have been reshaped in various ways on account of later assumptions and to conform with later expectations.[25] There is a further difficulty: any attempt to identify such material and to take that reshaping into account will usually and almost unavoidably result in a circular argument. Fortunately, however, there is some helpful archaeological evidence, and this evidence has the distinct advantage that it is contemporary.

In the late 1970s archaeologists working at the site of the temple of Mater Matuta in Satricum, a city that lay to the south of Rome, found a slab of stone on which an inscription had been written. The stone had been reused in the construction of the temple and that reuse provides a *terminus ante quem* for the inscription of about 500 BC.[26]

The inscription records a dedication to the god Mamars by a group of individuals who identified themselves simply as the *suodales* of Poplios Valesios. The word *sodales*, 'companions', could be used in a number of contexts including, perhaps most significantly, a military. Whatever the

---

Longa was secured by Romulus and his brother, Remus (for a succinct account, see Livy 1.3.10–6.2). As noted above (see n. 14), Virgil has Aeneas found cities using the appropriate ritual.

24   Dion. Hal. *Ant. Rom.* 1.84.5; Plut. *Rom.* 6.1. For Gabii as an *urbs*, see Livy 1.53.4.

25   On the tendency for Roman writings about the past to be anachronistic, see, for example, Wiseman 1979b, 41–53; Cornell 1986, 83–4; Gabba 1991, 80–5, 159–66; Poucet 2000, 285–328; Cornell 2005, 59–60, 62; Raaflaub 2005, esp. 187–8; Drogula 2015, 2–4; see n. 15 above.

26   For the inscription, see Stibbe 1980.

precise context of the word's use in the inscription (which does, note, record a dedication to Mars), the inscription provides evidence for a group of individuals who defined themselves with reference simply, and indeed entirely, to another person.[27]

There is a small body of further evidence that seems to fit with this idea of an individual and his companions. The bulk of it is literary, and so from much later times, which means that its value and use are extremely difficult. Much of it consists of stories of prominent individuals who move from one city to another (usually their destination is Rome, but that is doubtless only because the literary evidence focuses on Rome), and who take with them large numbers of followers. If these followers thought of themselves in any way as belonging to, or even as citizens of, the city-state they were leaving behind, then presumably their ties to their leader were greater.

It is on account of this and other evidence for mobility that archaic Rome has been called an 'open city',[28] although it may be anachronistic to make anything much of this. When city-states were still comparatively new, and indeed still developing, and when urban lifestyles were new along with them, and when the concept of citizenship, of belonging to a city-state, was equally new, or only starting to emerge,[29] the idea that a city could be 'closed', in the sense of having a definite and fixed body of citizens or of simply refusing to admit immigrants, may conceivably have been more novel than the idea that one could be 'open'.

One such story of mobility which, it has been very persuasively argued by F. Zevi, appears to have been recorded in an early source involves a man called Lucumo. Lucumo was said to have been the son of a Corinthian merchant called Demaratus who had settled in the Etruscan

27   The inscription reads: '[...]IEI STETERAI POPLIOSIO VALESIOSIO SVODALES MAMARTEI' [The companions of Poplios Valesios set this up[?] to Mars]; on *sodales*, see Versnel 1980, 108–27; Versnel 1997, esp. 181–2.

28   See the classic study of Ampolo 1976–7; also, for example, Cornell 1995, 157–9; Cornell 2003, 86–7; Bradley 2015, 102–5. Rome's nobility actually long remained open to outsiders; much of the evidence was assembled long ago by Münzer 1920, 46–97; this openness may have been more extensive than the evidence suggests: most people are usually not visible; see pp. 135–45.

29   As Cornell 1995, 158 says, 'such concepts as nationality and citizenship are anachronistic in the context of the seventh and sixth centuries BC.'

city of Tarquinii. After his father died, Lucumo left Tarquinii and moved to Rome, taking with him all his family's wealth and all his followers.[30] Another equally famous but much more difficult story involves a man called Attus Clausus. He was also said to have migrated to Rome, in his case from Inregillus, a Sabine town, and he similarly took with him very large numbers of followers.[31]

The story of Lucumo has further significance because, after he moved to Rome and after the incumbent king of Rome, Ancus Marcius, had died, Lucumo managed to succeed him. He became Rome's fifth king, Lucius Tarquinius. ('Lucumo' was Romanised as 'Lucius', and Lucumo took the name 'Tarquinius' from the city of his birth.)[32] As far as the Romans certainly of later times were concerned, this was nothing extraordinary. Their monarchy, they believed, had never been hereditary, and most of their kings had supposedly come from elsewhere.[33] It may be that the model of powerful men (men like Poplios Valesios, Attus Clausus, as well as Demaratus and obviously Lucumo) and their followers provides an explanation for any number of Rome's kings.[34]

It is in this same context that the word *sodalis* reappears too, although it does so in a text from the first century AD, so extreme caution is needed.[35] The Emperor Claudius gave a speech, the text of which has been partially preserved in an inscription that was found in Lyon in 1528, in which he argued in favour of allowing Gauls from Gallia Comata into the Senate.

30 Livy 1.34; Dion. Hal. *Ant. Rom.* 3.46.3–48.2. See Zevi 2014, also for further references to the ancient evidence and, for the early source, see Alföldi 1965, 56–72 as well; Gallia's objections to this argument (2007) are not convincing.

31 Livy 2.16.4–5; Dion. Hal. *Ant. Rom.* 5.40.3–5; Suet. *Tib.* 1.1. For references to further evidence and an analysis of the various differences in the several accounts, see Wiseman 1979b, 59–64.

32 Livy 1.34.10, 1.35.1–6; Dion. Hal. *Ant. Rom.* 3.48.2, 3.49.1.

33 Succinctly stated by Claudius, *ILS* 212: *quondam reges hanc tenuere urbem, nec tamen domesticis successoribus eam tradere contigit. supervenere alieni et quidam externi.* [Kings once held this city, yet they were not able to pass it on to successors of their own line. Strangers intervened, and even some foreigners.] On these matters, see Chapter 2.

34 See, for example, Momigliano 1989a, 97–8; Cornell 1995, 141–50.

35 See Versnel 1980, 120–1 and Maras 2010 for optimistic assessments.

As part of his case, he pointed out that Rome had always been open to outsiders, and he illustrated this with several examples, one of which is particularly important. According to Claudius,

> If we follow our Roman sources, [Servius Tullius, Rome's sixth king] was the son of Ocresia, a prisoner of war; if we follow Etruscan sources, he was once the most faithful companion (*sodalis fidelissimus*) of Caelius Vivenna and took part in all his adventures. Subsequently, driven out by a change of fortune, he left Etruria with all the remnants of Caelius' army (*Caelianus exercitus*) and occupied the Caelian hill, naming it thus after his former leader. Servius changed his name (for in Etruscan his name was Mastarna), and was called by the name I have used, and he obtained the throne (*regnum*) to the greatest advantage of the state (*res publica*).[36]

In this story too there is a prominent individual, Caelius Vivenna (or Caeles Vibenna, as he is usually known), and his followers, at least one of whom, Mastarna, is called a *sodalis*. Like Lucumo, Mastarna allegedly became king at Rome after moving there from Etruria; in his case, he changed his name to Servius Tullius. Servius was Rome's sixth king, so that makes Mastarna Lucumo's successor. It has been argued that Caeles Vibenna may have ruled Rome too, for a time, although he is not included in the canonical list of kings. But that list unrealistically has a total of just seven kings, even though Rome's regal period supposedly lasted for two and a half centuries, so there are good grounds for supposing that Rome had other, otherwise unknown rulers.[37]

---

36   Claud. *ILS* 212: *Servius Tullius, si nostros sequimur, captiva natus Ocresia, si Tuscos, Caeli quondam Vivennae sodalis fidelissimus omnisque eius casus comes, post quam varia fortuna exactus cum omnibus reliquis Caeliani exercitus Etruria excessit, montem Caelium occupavit et a duce suo Caelio ita appellita[vit], mutatoque nomine (nam Tusce Mastarna ei nomen erat) ita appellatus est, ut dixi, et regnum summa cum rei p(ublicae) utilitate optinuit.* The translation is Cornell's (1995, 133–4).

37   For Caeles as a possible king, see Alföldi 1965, 212–31 (Claudius' story implies that Caeles had died, but there were other versions); a slightly stronger case can be made in favour of Caeles' brother, Aulus Vibenna; again, see Alföldi's discussion; Cornell 1995, 144–5. On the problems in the king-list and the chronology of the regal period, see De Cazanove 1988; De Cazanove 1992; Cornell 1995, 121–6; Forsythe 2005, 98–9; Feeney 2007, 88–91; various problems were already observed in antiquity, see Cic. *Rep.* 2.28–9 and Dion. Hal. *Ant. Rom.* 4.6–7. See further Chapter 2.

Claudius also speaks of Caeles' army, and it may be that the term *sodales* is applicable here too, to the soldiers in that army, or at least to some of them, those who were closest to their leader. The army, in any case, was *Caeles'* army (*Caelianus exercitus*, says Claudius), and what was left of it following a setback of some kind and the death of Caeles – both of which are usually inferred from Claudius' account – appears to have been passed on to Mastarna. This is quite clearly not the army of the city-state of Vulci, the 'hometown' of Caeles Vibenna; it is Caeles Vibenna's own personal army. These are his men, and subsequently they become Mastarna's.[38]

What Claudius has to say about Caeles Vibenna and his most faithful companion, by chance, gets some support from a fourth-century BC Etruscan tomb painting from Vulci, which depicts a naked and bound 'Caile Vipinas' being freed by 'Macstrna' (the figures are identified by inscriptions).[39] This certainly fits perfectly well with the Etruscan context that Claudius mentions and seems to confirm the friendship between the two men, although it does not necessarily verify anything else, or even those details. The painting is still more than 200 years later than the purported events.[40]

As the city of Rome developed, another type of group appears to have emerged, if it did not already exist. These were the *gentes*. A *gens* was essentially a group of people who shared a common *nomen*; there was a notional idea that each *gens* ultimately originated from one individual, but these individuals are usually mythical and the extent to which individuals from different branches of the same *gens* were actually biologically related to one another is unclear. It is, however, unlikely that they were.[41]

It used to be believed that the *gentes* existed before the city-state, but the more prevalent view today is that they probably developed at about

---

38   Cf., for example, Cornell 1995, 144; Cornell 2003, 88; Torelli 2011, 230.

39   For the frescoes, see for instance, Moretti Sgubini 2004, and especially the chapter in the same volume by Andreae (2004, 52–4); further bibliography can be found in Richardson 2015.

40   On the handling of the evidence for Caeles Vibenna, see Richardson 2015.

41   See Smith 2006b on the *gentes* in general, and 32–44 on mythical ancestors; see also Kvium 2008 for a different approach.

the same time.[42] That does not mean, however, that they were necessarily all developing in the same direction.[43] It may also be the case that clear distinctions should not be imposed, at least early on, between individuals and their *sodales* and the *gentes*.[44] *Gentes* too, or some of them at any rate, may perhaps have once also had individual leaders. Attus Clausus, the man who took all his followers to Rome, changed his name once he got there to Appius Claudius. The story explains the origins of the *gens Claudia* at Rome. Having said all that, the evidence does generally suggest that the *gentes* were acephalous, certainly in historical times.

The *gentes* were powerful groups who appear to have long been able to pursue their own ambitions, and even behave in ways that may have been contrary to the idea of the state. The best example is found in the story of the private war that was said to have been waged by the *gens Fabia* with the Etruscan city of Veii (or, it may be, just with a rival group based in that city). The evidence for this war is, however, deeply problematic, and it has long been recognised that the story of the Fabii's expedition has been modelled on the famous, and essentially contemporary, exploits of the 300 Spartans at Thermopylae; like the Spartans, the Fabii were 300 or so in number and, like the Spartans, they were all killed, and the parallels do not stop there.

Whether or not it is possible to strip away all the parallels between these two episodes, and whether or not anything of value would be left, if they were removed, is anyone's guess.[45] Yet it may be that the story is not wholly fabricated, simply because it fits so poorly with all those assumptions about the Roman state and its army (namely that both had been created by Romulus, and so existed from his day onwards). It is telling that it is also possible to detect various attempts to harmonise the story of the Fabii's campaign with those assumptions. In Diodorus' account, for instance, the Romans fought a great battle with the people of Veii in which they were

---

42   Momigliano 1989a, 99; Cornell 1995, 84–5; Smith 2006b; and see below for the approach of Terrenato.

43   Cf., for instance, Torelli 2011, 226–7, and below for the hypotheses of Terrenato.

44   See Momigliano 1989a, 98–9; Versnel 1997, 182; and the hypotheses of Kvium 2008. See the next note as well.

45   For the various issues, see, for example, Richard 1990a (note 255–6 on the Fabii and their *sodales*); Richardson 2012, 81–3, 106–7, 119–20, 139–42, 150–1.

defeated; among the dead were the 300 Fabii.[46] The private war of the Fabii
is thus effectively made, in Diodorus' version, into an affair of the state.

The power and influence of the *gentes* can be seen as well in the Roman
tribal system. Rome's territory came to be divided up into regions called
tribus [tribes]. The earliest of these were named after *gentes*. One was called
the *tribus Fabia*, the Fabian tribe, and it has been suggested that this tribe
should be located in the direction of Veii, on the principle that the 300
Fabii were fighting to defend their own land. It is reasonable to infer that
these early tribes were named after those who dominated the land in question, and that was clearly not the state.[47] Later on, however, when Roman
territory expanded and new tribes were created, they were instead named
after geographical features.

The first of these new tribes seems to have been the *tribus Clustumina*,
following the defeat of Crustumeria; it was perhaps created in 495 BC, if
the literary evidence can be trusted.[48] Whether or not it can, it is significant that no further tribes were said to have been added for over a century,
which is a considerable period of time. Four were created in 387 BC, then
two each in 358, 332, 318, 299 and 241, and these tribes were almost all given
geographical names.[49] Clearly, by this time, the state had become more
powerful and so tribes ceased to be named after *gentes*.

46   Diod. 11.53.6. Cf. Richard 1990a, 248–51.
47   On the location of the *tribus Fabia*, see Taylor 2013, 40–1 and Linderski's defence
      of her argument (p. 363 of the same volume). On the tribes named after *gentes*, see
      Cornell 1995, 173–9; Wiseman 2004, 56; Taylor 2013, 4–6, 35–7.
48   See Livy 2.19.2 for the capture of Crustumeria; at 2.21.7, Livy says only that twenty-
      one tribes were created (*tribus una et viginti factae*), which is an ambiguous phrase.
      Among Livy's twenty-one tribes was presumably the *tribus Clustumina*.
49   Livy 6.5.8, 7.15.11, 8.17.11, 9.20.6, 10.9.14, *Per.* 19; Taylor 2013, 47–68. The *tribus
      Poblilia* appears to have been named after the Publilii; this may be the result of pol-
      itical circumstances, see Taylor 2013, 50–2.

III

From this necessarily brief and patchy overview, it is possible to see that, alongside the developing city-state of Rome, there appears to have existed various other social groups, and it seems that these groups could, for some time, act entirely independently of the state, if they so chose, even when they were based at Rome. The most obvious conclusions to draw from this are that the Roman state was at first under-developed and comparatively weak, and also that not everyone subscribed to the idea of it.

The difficulty then is working out why, how and when the state and the idea of being a part of it and belonging to it – so, essentially, citizenship – became firmly established and more influential than, say, adherence to a man like Poplios Valesios or Attus Clausus, and also why, how and when those men themselves came to commit to the idea of the state, and to the idea that they too were citizens of it.

These questions are, not surprisingly, unanswerable in any precise way, not just because the city and state of Rome were not founded at some particular moment in time, but also because the evidence is simply insufficient to answer questions of this kind in anything other than the most general of terms. The only contemporary evidence is the archaeological evidence, and archaeological evidence can only very rarely be used to answer questions about political ideas and practices. This is part of the reason why Carandini has ended up having to draw increasingly on the literary evidence for Romulus' foundation of Rome, although he thinks that that evidence is reliable, or at least that some of it is. Not only do Carandini's selective handling of the literary evidence and his need to reconcile it with the archaeological evidence (which points in a different direction) undermine his approach, but the basic assumption that the literary evidence for Romulus and the foundation of Rome sheds light on the origins of Rome is simply untenable.

Contemporary textual evidence is what is really needed, but barely a handful of inscriptions from archaic Rome have been discovered and only two of those are relevant to questions pertaining to the state, and even then only vaguely so. What makes those two inscriptions relevant is simply that some form of the word *rex* appears on them. Moreover, one of the inscriptions was carved on a stone stele that was set up in the Forum, and the very act of setting up such a monument is in itself highly significant, while the other inscription is on a fragment of a bucchero cup that was found at the site of the Regia (the regal connotations are clear from the building's name).[50] Nonetheless, while this evidence confirms that Rome had in fact once been ruled by kings,[51] and while it also helps to reveal something of the wider context, its value is somewhat more limited than it may seem at first sight.

The ideas associated with the word *rex* evidently changed over time,[52] and this makes it very difficult to use any of the evidence for the king's position in the state (viz. the writings of Rome's historians, antiquarians and so on), simply because that evidence dates to the second and first centuries BC and, in many cases, even later still. That evidence was also written in the belief that the Roman state, of which the king was said to have been a central part, had existed from the time of the city's foundation and that Rome's first king was Romulus. The inscriptional evidence certainly proves that Rome had once been ruled or in some way led by individuals whose title was *rex*, but it does not prove that these kings had the powers, status or position in the state that later writers claimed they had, nor that the state itself existed to the extent or in the way that those writers assumed it did.

A further piece of evidence, which can to a certain extent be treated as contemporary, lends some support to this conclusion. Sometime supposedly in the late sixth century BC the Romans made a treaty with the city of Carthage. The treaty itself does not survive but, fortunately enough,

50 See Cristofani 1990, 22–3, 58–9 for the evidence. On the symbolic value that an inscription could have, see the discussion in Williamson 1987.

51 It is telling that even this could have once been doubted, as it famously was by Pais, who argued in the first volume of his *Storia di Roma* (1898) that Rome's kings were in origin gods; unfortunately for Pais the inscription from the Forum was discovered in 1899, so just after his book had appeared. That Pais could have even argued what he did at all is nonetheless a reflection of the immense difficulties that exist in the literary evidence. It is worth noting as well that ancient authors who mention the stele from the Forum had absolutely no idea what it was and offered all manner of explanations for it. On these matters, see pp. 47–50.

52 See Chapter 2.

Polybius saw the text of it on a bronze tablet and – with the help of some learned Romans who were able, for the most part, to decipher the archaic Latin in which it was written – included a translation of it in his work.[53] The treaty shows that, by this time, Roman influence spread over parts of Latium, the region to the south of Rome. More significantly, the oath that was sworn when this treaty was made was sworn by only one individual and the divine punishment envisaged in that oath, should the treaty be broken, was to be meted out only to that same individual. Polybius' account of the oath has been rejected by modern scholars, precisely because it does not involve the state, but that is to beg the question. The account Polybius provides fits perfectly with the evidence discussed so far which suggests that individuals could dominate Rome and that the state was weak by comparison.[54]

The difficulties involved in attempting to trace the emergence of the Roman city-state have also been made worse by problems of methodology. One common approach for identifying the moment when Rome qualifies as a city-state has been to begin with questions of definition and with establishing a set of criteria that will allow for that moment to be identified.[55] As these criteria are themselves a matter of debate, the date inevitably changes with the criteria. Under these circumstances, the value of any attempt to identify some point in time when Rome can be called a city-state is naturally limited. The same applies, *mutatis mutandis*, to trying to identify the moment when some sense of allegiance to the state came to the fore, and when the idea of citizenship developed.

Despite all these difficulties (and equally, because of them), a good number of hypotheses about the formation of the Roman city and state have been entertained.[56] Outside influences, such as trade, warfare and

---

53   Polyb. 3.22, 3.25.6–9.
54   For an attempt to put aside assumptions about the state and to take Polybius' evidence seriously, see Chapter 3. In the same context of treaty-making, assumptions about the existence and nature of the Roman state have also led to various anachronistic retrojections being accepted as historical, see Richardson 2017.
55   See the discussion in Ampolo 1983b and Cornell 1995, 97–103.
56   See the various discussions (some of which are now out of date in some respects) on the formation of the Roman city and state (the two need not go together and may, in fact, have not) in, for example, Ampolo 1980; Drews 1981; Ampolo 1983b;

the influence of the cities of the Greek world (which of course included southern Italy) on the development of the Italic city-states in general have been frequently discussed. The role of internal factors has also been included in the debate although the evidence for them is often especially difficult. Trade with outside peoples usually leaves traces in the archaeological record, the context of which often also reveals something of the distribution of wealth and of social stratification, while something like the construction of defensive works or the destruction of a settlement is also often visible archaeologically. Evidence for developments driven by internal social, political or economic factors, on the other hand, can be much more difficult to detect,[57] where such evidence even happens to exist, and more often than not, it is unlikely to do so. Again, contemporary textual evidence is what is needed, but there is none from those early times, while the much later literary evidence takes the existence of the city and state from the very outset for granted. Arguments about internal developments and processes are usually therefore of a considerably more theoretical and conjectural nature.

N. Terrenato, for instance, has recently argued that it was actually the *gentes* who were responsible for the creation of the Roman state, a proposition that inevitably requires him to address the very big question of why they, of all groups, should have been concerned to do such a thing. To answer this, Terrenato considers the various roles that a city-state could have played in diplomacy, politics, trade and religion, as well as in warfare and domestic conflict. In his view, the state was simply 'one of many political tools that clans [*gentes*] had at their disposal', although, for this argument to work, Terrenato inevitably has to depict Rome as long an extremely weak state. Indeed, he views it as 'a weak and fragile entity' that suffered from 'congenital frailty' and 'inherent instability'; it was in fact nothing more than a puppet of the *gentes*. But this is a picture that may start to seem at odds with Rome's growth and military success.

Cornell 1988; Cornell 1995, 81–118; Forsythe 2005, 82–93; Hall 2014, 138–41; Fulminante 2014, especially Chapter 1 for a discussion of various approaches to urbanisation and state formation (but cf. n. 17 above).

57   Does some indication of increasing specialisation in the production of pottery, for instance, reflect internal developments or external influences?

Terrenato's model is, moreover, entirely top-down, so much so in fact that the state can be described as the *gentes*' 'toy' which 'they felt fully entitled to tear ... apart whenever they grew tired of it.'[58] It may reasonably be asked, however, why the Roman people should have gone along with this, and why they should have tolerated the idea that the nascent city-state where they lived and with which they may have identified, and of which they were or were becoming citizens, was little or nothing more than a plaything of the powerful, and potentially a transitory plaything at that, one that could be cast aside at any moment.

The views of the Roman people are, of course, unknown, since there is hardly any evidence for them and certainly none that is anywhere near contemporary. Even apart from the question of what they may have been prepared to put up with, it would nonetheless be rash simply to deny them any role in the formation of the Roman state, and to suppose that the state's formation was due entirely, or even largely, to the activities of the powerful few, and even more so when the powerful few were the ones who stood to lose the most (even if there were also some potential gains to be made).

As it happens, it may just about be possible to detect something of the role that the people may have played in the formation of the Roman state. The argument does require that all ideas of a foundation moment are dismissed entirely,[59] and that much greater prominence is given to the evidence that suggests that the formation of the Roman state was the result of a very lengthy process, one that saw advances as well as steps backwards (or even sideways) and one that was affected in various ways by conflicting needs and ideas. If the case that has been made so far has been at all persuasive, such an approach should not seem problematic in the least.

---

58   Terrenato 2011 (see 236, 237 and 243 for the several quotes).

59   The influence of such ideas is still detectable in recent work; even apart from Carandini's own work (where the influence is obviously predictable), note for instance Terrenato 2011, 235, who talks of 'the time when the decision to create a city-state was taken'; 241, 'cities were the result of conscious decisions made by individuals.' But it is most unlikely that, at least as far as the earliest city-states are concerned, individuals did indeed make conscious decisions at some particular moment in time to create a city-state: this is the ancient model, which is entirely unsatisfactory.

IV

The main theme, according to the Romans' own accounts, of Rome's social and political history during the fifth and fourth centuries BC is the so-called 'conflict (or struggle) of the orders'. The Roman citizen body was, or so the Romans believed, neatly divided into two orders, the patricians and the plebeians; the division is, however, over-schematic and quite probably unhistorical, at least for early times.[60] From the beginning of the republican period (that is, after the kings had been expelled and replaced with elected annual magistrates), the patrician families allegedly dominated the state, as only patricians could hold the magistracies and priesthoods of the state. The phrase 'the conflict of the orders' refers to the struggles of the plebs to gain protection from abuse at the hands of the rich and powerful, to gain representation in the state and subsequently to gain access to the state's magistracies and priesthoods.

According to the ancient accounts, the plebs – who made up at least some part of the Roman army and the bulk of the labour force more generally – organised several secessions, in which they simply withdrew from the city, in order to force concessions from the patricians. The result of the first of these secessions (in the mid-490s BC) was the creation of a new magistracy, the plebeian tribunate, whose role seems to have been to protect the plebeians and represent their interests.[61] This magistracy was one to which people were elected, and so its creation required the organising of a suitable electoral assembly, one for plebeians only. The plebs supposedly also began to keep official records, although that claim may be anachronistic, for the fifth century at least, but probably for much of the fourth too. It was the plebeian movement as well that was said to have been responsible

---

60   The division was, predictably enough, said to have gone back to Romulus' time: Cic. *Rep.* 2.14 and 2.23; Livy 1.8.7; Dion. Hal. *Ant. Rom.* 2.8; Plut. *Rom.* 13.1–3. The reality may very well have been much more complex; see, for instance, Cornell 1983; Cornell 1995, 242–58.

61   Livy 2.32.2–33.3; Dion. Hal. *Ant. Rom.* 6.45–89. On the tribunate, see, for example, Smith 2012, with references to earlier work; in this context, note Drogula 2017.

for getting Rome's first ever law-code drafted and set up in public. That was in the mid-fifth century BC.[62]

As far as later writers were concerned, the activities of the plebs looked like they amounted to a state and, since these writers took the existence of the Roman state for granted (they believed, after all, that it had been created centuries earlier by Romulus), they conceived of the plebeian movement as leading to the formation of a state within the state. This idea has been carried over into modern scholarship, most notably by Th. Mommsen in the nineteenth century, although it has more recently been defended by T. J. Cornell.[63]

Cornell's defence of the idea focuses on the question of whether or not the plebeian movement can be viewed as something that can reasonably be called a state. He takes the existence of the wider Roman state for granted.[64] On the one hand, he is absolutely right to do so – it would be extremely difficult, if not even perverse, to argue that the Roman state simply did not exist at all by the early fifth century BC – but, on the other,

62   Assembly: the evidence is difficult; Livy says that a law was passed in 471 BC to allow plebeian tribunes to be elected in the tribal assembly (2.56.2–58.2; also Dion. Hal. *Ant. Rom.* 9.41–9), but Livy does not say how they had been chosen previously; some sources say that they had been elected in the curiate assembly (Asc. 76C; Dion. Hal. *Ant. Rom.* 6.89.1, 9.41.2); for different assessments, see, for example, Ogilvie 1965, 380–1; Cornell 1995, 260–1; Forsythe 2005, 177–9. For the keeping of records, see Livy 3.55.13; Pompon. *Dig.* 1.2.2.21; Zonar. 7.15. For the plebeians' efforts to get a law-code drafted, see Livy 3.9.2–32.7 *passim*; there are various difficulties in the evidence, see Ogilvie 1965, 411–13, 449–54; Cornell 1995, 272–6; Forsythe 2005, 202.

63   Livy 2.44.9: *duas civitates ex una factas, suos cuique parti magistratus, suas leges esse* [two states had been created out of one; each faction had its own magistrates, it own laws], also, for example, 2.24.1, 3.19.9; see Dion. Hal. *Ant. Rom.* 6.88.1 for the concern that two states might be formed in one (μή ποτε δύο πόλεις ποιήσωμεν ἐν μιᾷ); Mommsen 1887b, 145; Cornell 1995, 258–65; see also Momigliano 2005, 178–80. For arguments against this idea, see Forsythe 2005, 176.

64   Note Cornell 1995, 265: 'The later vestiges of the [plebeian] movement ... were gradually recognised and integrated with the institutions of the state. ... What is remarkable is not only the way in which plebeian institutions matched those of the state, but the fact that their organisation was in many ways more advanced and sophisticated. In the period down to 367 BC the plebeian institutions were either integrated into the constitution, or were themselves imitated by the "patrician state".'

it may be premature to think that it existed in an uncontested or straight-forward manner, or that it was an idea to which everyone fully subscribed.

The private war of the *gens Fabia* was supposedly fought in the early 470s BC, some thirty years after the expulsion of the kings (that was in 510/509 on traditional chronology, with the first elected magistrates sup-posedly holding office in 509). Cornell has argued that the campaign of the Fabii 'represents one of the last vestiges of an archaic form of social organisation which was probably already in an advanced state of obsoles-cence.'[65] That may very well be so, although the phrase 'advanced state of obsolescence' is perhaps something of an overstatement.[66] When it comes to the question of private wars of this kind, the argument is based on very little evidence indeed; but the lack of evidence pertains to earlier times just as much as it does to later, thanks no doubt in part to Roman assumptions about the establishment by Romulus of the Roman army. All this inevitably makes the demise of such practices extremely difficult to date; the absence of evidence is clearly not necessarily evidence of absence. There is, however, some evidence for behaviour that is not entirely unrelated.

When it comes to those powerful individuals and their followers, they did not just disappear along with the Roman monarchy. Attus Clausus was said to have migrated to Rome in the early years of the republican period.[67] There are also various stories of individuals who allegedly sought to estab-lish themselves as kings of Rome, even in republican times. The evidence is, as always, extremely difficult, and it is clear that many of these stories have been heavily modified (if not, in some instances, perhaps even invented outright) at a later date and in light of later events. As with the expedition of the 300 Fabii, it is impossible to know what, if anything, lies behind the evidence as it currently stands, or whether or not it is possible to try to put aside that subsequent manipulation and shaping. Nonetheless, the evidence does have a certain cumulative force and, more significantly, not

---

65   Cornell 1995, 311; see also Richard 1990a.
66   Compare Cornell's comments in 1988, 94: 'Si può, però, facilmente sospettare che guerre gentilizie di questo genere fossero un fenomeno comune e forse caratteristico dell'epoca.'
67   See n. 31 above. There was another version, which put his migration in Romulus' time; but on this, see Wiseman 1979b, 59–61.

all of what it suggests fits quite so neatly with the expectations that the literary evidence may otherwise engender.[68]

The most famous of the would-be kings were Sp. Cassius, Sp. Maelius and M. Manlius Capitolinus, each of whom was in the end killed for his activities and alleged aspirations, but there were others.[69] Also relevant in this context is the story of Ap. Herdonius. Herdonius was a Sabine, like Attus Clausus; like Clausus, he too was said to have gone to Rome although, in his case, he was said to have seized the Capitoline hill in a bid to take over the city (this was in 460 BC).[70] He supposedly had with him 2,500 followers (or perhaps more), according to Livy, and it may be tempting to think of Caeles Vibenna, his faithful *sodalis* Mastarna, and his army, or of Poplios Valesios and his *sodales*. By 460, however, Rome had been a Republic for half a century and the rule of kings was a thing of the past. Herdonius, the aspiring monarch, was out of date; he was automatically bad, and his followers are all cast by Livy as exiles and slaves.[71]

68   As Badian 1990a, 215 notes, 'the inscription [from Satricum] calls into question the whole interpretation of the Roman social and political structure that we get in Livy: the *suodales* cannot be plausibly matched, or fitted into the background we are given. They point to a social organization plausible in itself, but irreconcilable with the late Republican version of the "Struggle of the Orders" that we have come to take for granted.' This is perhaps something of a slight exaggeration, since there is other evidence that seems to fit with the circumstances implied by the inscription, but it certainly is true that such evidence only rarely accords, and never easily, with what is implied and assumed by Livy.

69   See, for example, Smith 2006a; and also Forsythe 2005, 193–5, 239–41, 259–62 for a sceptical assessment of the evidence.

70   Livy 3.15.5–18.10; Dion. Hal. *Ant. Rom.* 10.14–16.

71   Livy 3.15.5: *exsules servique, ad duo milia* [Ogilvie, *OCT: quattuor milia*] *hominum et quingenti* [exiles and slaves to the number of 2,500 [Ogilvie: 4,500] men]; Dion. Hal. *Ant. Rom.* 10.14.1, in contrast, has Herdonius gather together his clients and the most courageous of his attendants (συνήθροιζε τοὺς πελάτας καὶ τῶν θεραπόντων οὓς εἶχε τοὺς εὐτολμοτάτους; on θεράποντες, see Versnel 1980, 117); Herdonius' plan, however, Dionysius says (10.14.3), nonetheless involved calling on exiles, slaves, those in debt and the like. Cf. Torelli 2011, 232. Livy's choice of words is, however, likely to be due to first-century influences, see Ogilvie 1965, 423–5, also Forsythe 2005, 205.

It is also possible to think of someone like Cn. Marcius Coriolanus. Cornell has argued that Coriolanus' career should perhaps be understood in the same general context of powerful, independent individuals who do their own thing, look out only for their own interests and do not think of themselves as under the authority of any government, or indeed of anyone. Consequently, when Coriolanus' activities in Rome did not work out, he simply left and went to join the Volsci.[72] This too was supposedly in the early fifth century.

The literary evidence for all these individuals and events is extremely problematic. The point does need to be stressed. Nonetheless this evidence does fit very well with the circumstances implied by the inscription from Satricum, and also with the evidence (likewise problematic) for powerful individuals from the regal period and for *gentes* that appear to have once been more powerful than the state. The evidence certainly suggests some element of continuity with those times.

While the difficulties involved in basing an argument on textual evidence written centuries after the events in question need always to be kept in mind, it is worth giving careful consideration to the plebeian movement in the context of state formation. To what extent did the activities of that movement – restricting the actions of the powerful, creating magistracies and an assembly, keeping records, campaigning to get a law-code drafted and published,[73] and so on – play a role in the formation of the Roman state? Developments of this kind are just the sort of thing that ought to be expected when a state comes into existence. And, although it is the view of later writers who were drawing on an anachronistic literary tradition, the idea that the plebeian movement itself amounted to a state (albeit within a state) is nevertheless suggestive.

The nature of the evidence, unfortunately, may not allow for the argument to go much further than this, that is, beyond simply suggesting that 'the conflict of the orders' was not just about securing and advancing plebeian rights, but that it may well have also played a role in the formation of the Roman state, in its early stages at least. This possibility is certainly

---

72 Cornell 2003, 84–91.
73 Note Maras 2010, 189, 195 for the evidence that the Twelve Tables contained legislation aimed at restricting the actions of *sodalitates* with respect to public law.

significant, not only in itself and for what it may reveal about the origins of at least one state, and, on its own terms at least, one extremely successful state. It is also significant for contemporary discussion, about states in the twenty-first century, about the roles that they should play and about their duties and responsibilities, as well as the duties and responsibilities of their citizens. For, in the case of Rome, it may be possible to see something of how the state was created – to some extent – by the people, and for the people, for their protection, to rein in those wealthy and powerful individuals who were concerned only with their own agenda and interests, to get them to adhere to the idea of the state and to behave responsibly towards it and their fellow citizens, as well as to try to address at least some of the inequalities in Roman society.

CHAPTER 2

The King and the Constitution: Elections and Hereditary Succession in Regal Rome

I

At the end of the nineteenth century, scepticism in the historicity of the literary evidence for early Rome could hardly have been greater. This was a time when it could be claimed in all seriousness that Rome's kings had never existed and that the kings the ancient authors wrote about were nothing other than river, solar or other such deities.[1] In an environment such as this, the discovery made by G. Boni of an archaic inscription on which the word *rex* appeared was inevitably revolutionary.[2] Scepticism in the historical value of the literary sources was now untenable, optimism justified and the optimists vindicated, or so it could be claimed. As so often happens, in all the exuberance, there was also a considerable amount of excess. The inscription and the complex in which it was located accorded with ancient accounts of what was said by some to be the tomb of Romulus,[3] and so the discovery was even hailed as proof that

---

1   Pais 1898, for example, and bluntly, 378: 'i sette re di Roma non sono altro che divinità'; and later too, Pais 1906, for example, 150: 'Romulus, Tullius, Numa and Ancus Marcius were all solar deities'; but equally, 200: 'Numa and Tullius, kings of Rome, were merely river and solar divinities.'

2   For the inscription, see Cristofani 1990, 58–9. For Boni's excavations, see Sisani 2004, 62–3.

3   Ps.-Acr. on Hor. *Ep.* 16.13–14; Porph. on Hor. *Ep.* 16.13–14; Fest. 184L; for a monument to Romulus, cf. Dion. Hal. *Ant. Rom.* 2.54.2; Plut. *Rom.* 24.3; see Coarelli 1999.

Romulus himself had existed. Indicative of the enthusiastic mood are the somewhat self-satisfied comments of R. Lanciani:[4]

> Since the discovery of the Heroon Romuli in the Comitium and of the archaic stele, – whatever the meaning of its legend may be, – the history of ancient Rome cannot longer be written in the distrustful spirit of the hypercritical school. The future rests with our conservative party, of which I was a convinced member even at a time when it required a certain amount of courage to be recognized as such and to meet the accusation of credulity, when a lecturer could not name the founder of the City as a man who had actually existed, without blushing before his audience.

The problem is, the ancient sources also said that the complex was the tomb of Faustulus and the tomb Hostus Hostilius too.[5] Of course Boni's discovery no more proved the existence of Romulus than do more recent discoveries, for which all the same problems with the literary evidence exist, including that most fundamental difficulty of its relationship (or better, lack thereof) with the archaeological evidence.

Ironically enough, even though the inscription does confirm the existence in the sixth century of a *rex* – whatever a *rex* may have actually been at that date – the fact that ancient writers could describe the inscription and its immediate physical context quite accurately while clearly having only a vague notion of what the complex was is good reason for scepticism.[6] What is also remarkable is that no one knew either what the inscription itself was actually about, even though they could still see it, for a time, and certainly in better condition than it is in today (not least because a substantial part of it has been lost). Some said it was an account of Romulus' deeds, others, Hostus Hostilius', and he was not even a king.[7] Clearly no one could even

---

4   Lanciani 1901, 30; see also Gallup 1905 (and Platner 1906 for a reply). Cf. Wiseman 1992, 126–8; Grandazzi 1997, 19, 23–5; Sisani 2004, 63. For Pais' response, see Pais 1906, 15–42.

5   Fest. 184L; Dion. Hal. *Ant. Rom.* 1.87.2, 3.1.2.

6   As already Pais 1906, 41: 'we have here a new example of the arbitrary manner in which the ancient annalists described and determined the age of the earliest monuments', which remains true, regardless of Pais' fourth-century dating of the monument.

7   Dion. Hal. *Ant. Rom.* 2.54.2, 3.1.2.

begin to read it, or was concerned to try.[8] And that state of affairs doubtless applies to any other documents that may have survived from that same era and even more so in the case of anything older.[9]

So what, then, did later Romans *really* know about the regal period and their kings? And, if they did happen to know anything veracious, *how* did they, if documents from such early times were unintelligible in later and when no one wrote history at Rome until the end of the third century BC, that is, until some 300 years after the regal period had ended? Moreover, given the sorts of documents the sources claim had survived from that era – a few laws and treaties but not much else[10] – how were Rome's historians able to produce any sort of narrative of events, which is what ancient historiography was primarily concerned to produce, from such material, even if it *was* intelligible?

As for the appearance of the word *rex* on the inscription, all that that proves is that the title was in use at the time when the inscription was set up. It does not prove anything much more than that, although a religious role of some kind for the *rex* in question (who may conceivably have been a *rex sacrorum* in any case) can perhaps be inferred from the extant parts of the inscription without too much risk. It certainly does not follow that the literary evidence for Rome's kings is in any way veracious, and, strictly speaking, does not even disprove the argument that the kings the ancient authors wrote about were in fact just euhemerised gods.[11] The extraordinary

8 As is usually acknowledged; Ampolo 1983, 23–5; Holloway 1994, 82; Briquel 2016, 41–2. Cornell 1991, 28–9 finds the misinterpretation 'disturbing' but, as Wiseman observes (2008, 10), this 'is just what we should expect.'

9 Note the problems Polybius had reading Rome's first treaty with Carthage (Polyb. 3.22.3); the several treaties with Carthage appear to have been newly discovered evidence (cf. Walbank 1957, 336–7), but subsequent historians do not seem to have been interested.

10 See Ampolo 1983, 15–16 for the evidence. The story that early documents were destroyed in the Gallic sack is clearly aetiological, to explain the lack of documents; note that Livy 6.1.10 has material – precisely laws and treaties – recovered after the Gauls' departure; see pp. 149–50. On the evidence for Rome's early treaties, cf. Richardson 2017, esp. 266–70.

11 Scullard (1980, 50) – still reacting against Pais' views decades later – offered a better objection: 'The attempt to dismiss [the kings] as gods is discredited, since no cult of kings existed and there is no sure indication of their divine origin either in their names or legends.'

confidence of scholars like Lanciani was as premature as it was unwarranted. But, however unjustified it may have been, that confidence is nonetheless important evidence. It is evidence of the sheer will of some to believe in the historicity of the Romans' accounts of even the earliest history of Rome despite all the evidence and arguments that show that such an approach is neither justified nor sustainable.[12]

Although there has of late been something of a resurgence of similar uncritical exuberance, as a result of more recent archaeological discoveries,[13] it is fair to say that the overwhelming majority of scholars today would not want to claim that Romulus was an historical figure. Most would be unlikely to suppose either that there is anything truly historical in the evidence for Numa Pompilius, Tullus Hostilius or Ancus Marcius, the three kings who were said to have come after him. The Tarquins and Servius Tullius may be another matter but, even in their case, comparatively little of what the Romans said about them would seriously be taken as reliable evidence for what those men actually did, even if there is reason to suspect that they probably did exist.[14] And yet, despite these circumstances, it nonetheless remains the case that various parts of the evidence, even for the very early kings, are regularly accepted as genuinely historical, to some extent at least. It is what may be called the 'constitutional' aspects of the monarchy that are usually deemed the most trustworthy.[15] In particular – and perhaps most importantly of all for understanding the regal period as a whole – it

12   On the 'will to believe', see pp. 3–11 and n. 8.
13   The allusion is, of course, to the work of Carandini and his followers (on which, see Chapter 1), whose fundamental approach seems little different from that discernible in the passage quoted from Lanciani above: the literary evidence is handled selectively; the passages chosen are made to fit with the archaeological evidence; the archaeological evidence is then supposed to verify the literary evidence. The fate of Carandini's reconstruction is bound to be comparable too; certainly no one today would want to adopt Lanciani's position.
14   Typical views in, for example, Momigliano 1989a, 90–3; Cornell 1995, 119–21; Forsythe 2005, 96–7; Bianchi 2010, 4–5. On the Tarquins, note Zevi 2014.
15   Note the comments of Cornell 1995, 119 and Glinister 2006, 17. Glinister argues that there was no reason for anyone to distort details of the regal system, because it was 'an incidental part' (!) of the account; as will be seen, there were very good reasons why the system might have been modified (see section IV below).

is the idea that Rome's kings did not inherit the throne but were elected or somehow chosen by the Senate and people that is most often accepted as historical.[16] It is in fact fair to say that this view represents the orthodoxy in scholarship on the period.

The idea that Rome's monarchy was not hereditary is almost universally accepted as a simple matter of fact. T. J. Cornell, for instance, says that 'No king of Rome inherited the throne from his father.' Tarquinius Superbus, the son of Tarquinius Priscus, was 'a usurper who seized the throne illegally' and so is the 'exception that proves the rule'. B. Linke is equally emphatic. 'A form of hereditary kingship', he says, 'did not exist'.[17] It has even been claimed that hereditary succession was not even a feature of the Roman mentality.[18] Some have, however, been a little more cautious, but only comparatively so.[19]

As for the way in which Rome's kings supposedly did come to power, modern reconstructions are many and varied, but they almost all have in common the fundamental belief that the kings were selected somehow and their position subsequently ratified. The only exceptions are those kings – usually the last two – who are supposed to have seized power by force or acquired it by some other illegal means, although even these men, some maintain, will still have got their position approved in some way.[20] Several

16   The words 'king' and 'throne' come with anachronistic baggage; they are used here for convenience, although anachronism may not be out of keeping.

17   Cornell 1995, 141; Linke 2010, 185–6, referring to Rome's early kings; later kings were Etruscan mercenary leaders (188). Cf. also Mommsen 1887a, 8; Stuart Jones 1928, 407; Heurgon 1973, 113, 140–1; Kunkel 1974, 347–8; De Sanctis 1980, 350; Scullard 1980, 69; Bernardi 1988, 189; Wieacker 1988, 208; Momigliano 1989a, 97, 102, 105; Blaive 1998, 72–4; Briquel 2000a, 79–80; Briquel 2000b, 43; Glinister 2006, 30 n. 21; Bringmann 2007, 5; Valditara 2008, 13; Capogrossi Colognesi 2014, 17.

18   Bianchi 2010, 8 n. 17: 'il principio ereditario rimase sempre estraneo alla mentalità romana'; Bianchi refers to Bernardi 1953, 283–5 (see 285 for precisely the same view).

19   For example, Forsythe 2005, 98; Fronda 2015, 51; Armstrong 2016, 60–1.

20   For example, Valditara 2008, 33–5: the position of Rome's Etruscan tyrants was sanctioned by the army's acclamation. Different solution in Glinister 2006, 23: 'in practice the *interregnum* is an option and not a prerequisite.' Green 2007, 191–200 tries, albeit unconvincingly, to explain early Latin monarchy in general with reference to the *rex Nemorensis*, who acquired his position by murdering the incumbent *rex*.

accounts of the process by which the kings were supposedly appointed can be found in the ancient evidence, and they are variously handled. Some scholars follow the sources closely, others only generally, sometimes drawing on them selectively, picking out and emphasising (and sometimes modifying too) specific details and basing their reconstructions on those details alone.[21] There is considerable variation, but there is nonetheless an underlying consensus: Rome's kings did not inherit their position; they were elected, selected or approved in some way, or otherwise held power illegally.

All this is, however, vastly more uncertain than is usually acknowledged. This is not just because there is good reason to suspect – as is in fact widely accepted – that ancient accounts of the way in which Rome's kings were appointed are based on the anachronistic retrojection of later ideas and practices. It is also because – and this is something that does not receive the attention it deserves – the literary evidence is filled with stories that presuppose that the sons of kings could inherit the throne, or at least make a credible claim to it on hereditary grounds. The several extant accounts of the regal period regularly juxtapose stories based on ideas of hereditary succession with stories of the Senate and people choosing the next king. Modern scholarship has accepted the latter to varying degrees, but has failed to offer an adequate explanation for the existence of the former (which it has in fact generally ignored), even though both sets of stories can usually be found side by side in the very same accounts.

21   Niebuhr 1851, 339–43; Mommsen 1887a, 6–10; Stuart Jones 1928, 412–14; Gjerstad 1973, 206–10; Heurgon 1973, 114, 124, 126–7; Kunkel 1974, 350–63; De Sanctis 1980, 350, 357–9; Scullard 1980, 68–9; Bernardi 1988, 195; De Martino 1988, 352, 355; Wieacker 1988, 200, 210–11; Momigliano 1989a, 96–7, 105–6; Cornell 1995, 142–3; Linke 1995, 50–1, 61–2, 101–3; Blaive 1998; Briquel 2000a, 79–81; Briquel 2000b, 43; Forsythe 2005, 110; Glinister 2006, 18–23; Bringmann 2007, 5–8; Valditara 2008, 12–13; Linke 2010; Capogrossi Colognesi 2014, 17–19, 22–3; Fronda 2015, 51; Mouritsen 2015, 148; Armstrong 2016, 59, 61–3, 72, 85, 94, 127, 134, 166, 173–4; Mouritsen 2017, 19, 22–3, 26, etc. Mommsen, De Sanctis, Kunkel, Forsythe and – but often to a lesser degree – others view much of the process as anachronistic retrojection; on the question of anachronism, see also Magdelain 1968, 30–3. See Bianchi 2018, 628–35 for a discussion of several recent attempts to assess the position of the *rex* with reference to the priest known as the *rex sacrorum*; such approaches are similarly based on a selective and often quite arbitrary handling of the evidence and, as Bianchi shows, are unpersuasive.

In the following section (II), the question of hereditary succession will be discussed and the numerous stories that presuppose it will be considered. In the section after that (III), the process by which Rome's kings were said to have been appointed will be assessed. In the final section (IV), an entirely new explanation for the nature and shape of the account of the regal period in the extant sources will be offered.

II

Rome was a colony of Alba Longa, or so the Romans believed, and the kings of Alba Longa (from whom Romulus, Rome's founder and first king was descended) were said to have inherited their throne.[22] No one today supposes that there is anything historical in any of this and it is accepted that the Alban kings were simply used as a chronological device to bridge the gap between the fall of Troy and the foundation of Rome.[23] That does not mean, however, that the evidence for them is of no value. On the contrary, it is very important. Whoever invented the Alban dynasty clearly found it natural to think in terms of hereditary succession, even for Rome's mother-city.[24]

The Roman king-list, on the other hand, has usually been taken as evidence that things were different at Rome and that Rome's monarchy was not hereditary in nature. Apart from Tarquinius Superbus, none of the kings is a direct, patrilineal descendant of any other. While it is often

22   Hereditary succession can be inferred from some passages, such as Fabius Pictor *FRHist* 1 F4b (= Plut. *Rom.* 3.2): τῶν ἀπ' Αἰνείου γεγονότων ἐν Ἄλβῃ βασιλέων [the succession of the kings of Alba, descended from Aeneas]; Cato *FRHist* 5 F8 (= Serv. *Aen.* 6.760): *Albani omnes reges Silvii dicti sunt ab huius nomine* [all the Alban kings were called Silvii from his name]. Other sources are often explicit: Diod 7.5.6–12; Livy 1.3.6–11; Dion. Hal. *Ant. Rom.* 1.70–1; Ov. *Fast.* 4.39–53; Zonar. 7.1.

23   For example, Ogilvie 1965, 43–4; Cornell 1995, 125; Feeney 2007, 95–6.

24   Although, as Kunkel 1974, 347–8 observes, this does allow for Romulus' ancestry to be traced back to Aeneas. The story of the twins' exposure also requires hereditary succession.

argued that their names (Romulus' aside) may well be genuine, that does not really amount to anything much, especially when the chronology of the entire regal period is so extremely problematic.

There are simply too few kings – supposedly only seven in some two and a half centuries – and the inevitable result is that their reigns are all improbably long. There were, in contrast, nearly four times as many emperors during the first two and half centuries of the principate.[25] And there are other problems. Numa was supposed to have been a student of Pythagoras, but that is a chronological impossibility.[26] Equally impossible is the chronology of the last three kings. The ancient solution in this case was to insert an extra generation of Tarquins, so that Superbus was made into the grandson of Priscus,[27] but that is too easy. Although the idea has, somewhat surprisingly, found a few modern adherents,[28] it is only a means to fix a chronological problem; it is not based on any evidence and is historically worthless, beyond its value as evidence for the way ancient historians sought to address the problems they encountered in the material they inherited.

The idea that there were just seven kings has been called a 'patent fiction' and with good reason.[29] With good reason, too, the king-list itself has been labelled 'a pseudo-historical construct'.[30] Scholars even of a conservative nature have regularly been prepared to shoehorn other figures into the list. The best example is undoubtedly the Vibenna brothers, one or both of whom are often supposed to have ruled Rome.[31] So, while some

25   Or, as Finley 1985, 9–10 puts it, the first seven emperors reigned for only a century; Cornell 2014b, 251: 'there is no historical parallel for a monarchical regime in which seven successive rulers lasted for two and a half centuries.' See p. 32 n. 37 for further references.

26   Cic. *Rep.* 2.28–9; Livy 1.18.2–3; Dion. Hal. *Ant. Rom.* 2.59, etc.

27   See below.

28   Gantz 1975; Facchetti 2000, 36; Laurendi 2010, 134, 142. It is sometimes argued that the 'missing' Tarquin is Cneve Tarchunies Rumach from the François Tomb, which is just absurd, and it is not certain that Priscus was supposed to have had sons in the alternative version anyway (see below).

29   Smith 2011b, 35.

30   Wiseman 2013, 241 n. 52, with reference to Wiseman 2008, 314–16; Cornell 2014b, 252.

31   For example, Momigliano 1989a, 94–7; Cornell 1995, 144–5.

of the names of the seven kings may be genuine, it is most unlikely that the sequence of them is complete and reliable. The king-list does not, on its own, provide compelling evidence against hereditary succession, not when there are so many problems with it, when it is itself almost certainly a later construct, and above all when hereditary succession is taken for granted in so very many of the stories the Romans told about their kings.

It will be useful to look at these various stories more closely, not only because they are usually just ignored in this context, but also because there are different versions of some of them. In one or two instances, it is possible to make inferences about the relative chronology of the different accounts. For all that there is evidence of disagreement among the sources, and variation in some of the details, the basic point nonetheless remains unaffected: the Romans told numerous stories about their kings that anticipated hereditary succession. These stories are most unlikely to reflect anything at all of the historical realities of regal Rome, about which Rome's historians knew probably nothing, but they certainly do reflect what later Romans said about their kings. And what they said is often entirely incompatible with modern views of the Roman monarchy.

When Romulus' reign came to an end (however that was supposed to have happened), he departed leaving no designed heir. In almost every account, Romulus did not have children,[32] which means that no argument either way can be made about hereditary succession. The only author, it seems, who claimed Romulus had children is the little known and poorly attested Zenodotus of Troezen, who wrote probably in the mid- to late second century BC, or possibly the early first.[33] According to him, Romulus married the Sabine Hersilia, with whom he had two offspring, but Plutarch, who relates Zenodotus' story, notes that others said Hersilia had married Hostus Hostilius.[34] As for the children, one was a daughter named Prima, the other a son called Aollius, but later Avillius, says Plutarch. Neither appears anywhere else, and T. P. Wiseman has plausibly suggested that

---

32   Dion. Hal. *Ant. Rom.* 2.56.7, 3.1.4 is explicit.

33   Wiseman 1987, 288–92; Ampolo and Manfredini 1988, 308.

34   *FGrHist* 821 F2 (= Plut. *Rom.* 14.7); on Hersilia, the identity of her husband and the evidence for her, see Ogilvie 1965, 73–4; Wiseman 1987, 288–9.

Avillius was invented to create a suitably prestigious ancestor for the Avillii.[35] Whatever the motive for the invention of the story, Prima's and Aollius' credentials are such that they are of no significance when it comes to the question of hereditary succession.

Several sources evidently claimed that Numa Pompilius, Romulus' successor, had children, but the nature of much of the evidence is clear from the children's names. Some said that Numa had four sons, Pompon, Pinus, Calpus and Mamercus, from whom were descended the Pomponii, the Pinarii, the Calpurnii and the Mamercii.[36] It is reasonable to assume that the story of these children is a secondary development; it is usually discussed in the context of legendary genealogies and also, in the case of Calpus, with reference to the work of the late second-century historian L. Calpurnius Piso.[37] Like the story of Avillius, the story of these children clearly exists only for the sake of creating eponymous ancestors and it does not go beyond that immediate concern. Moreover, not everyone agreed, and some, according to Plutarch, said that Numa had only one child, a daughter called Pompilia.[38] This was evidently the earlier version of the story. It is hardly significant that there is no suggestion that Numa's daughter was ever a candidate to succeed her father.

Pompilia was said to have been married to Marcius,[39] the son of the man who had persuaded Numa to accept the Romans' invitation to become

35   Wiseman 1987, 290–1.
36   Plut. *Numa* 21.1. On Mamercus, see Wiseman 1987, 209.
37   Wiseman 1979b, 11; Rawson 1991, 258 n. 69; Forsythe 1994, 201–7; Gabba 2000, 43.
38   See Plut. *Numa* 21.1 for the claim that Pompilia was his only child, and 21.2 for those who rejected the story of Pompon, Pinus, Calpus and Mamercus; Dion. Hal. *Ant. Rom.* 2.76.5 says most historians claim he had four sons and one daughter, but Cn. Gellius (*FRHist* 14 F22) says he had just the one daughter. Wiseman 1979b, 11 suggests Gellius' claim was 'a deliberate contradiction' of Piso's story; Rawson 1991, 178; Forsythe 1994, 202–3; Gabba 2000, 43. Note Zonar. 7.6: Numa left no successor.
39   Plut. *Numa* 21.3 suggests agreement, but others do not say to whom she was married (e.g. Livy 1.32.1; Dion. Hal. *Ant. Rom.* 3.35.3), while Cic. *Rep.* 2.33 has Laelius and Scipio agree that nothing is known about Ancus' father; Zetzel 1995, 188 suggests: 'Julius Caesar ... boasted descent from Ancus through the noble plebeian family of the Marcii Reges; Laelius' comment may indicate aristocratic condescension.'

their king. After Numa's death, Plutarch says, the elder Marcius, Pompilia's father-in-law, had competed with Tullus Hostilius for the throne. He was unsuccessful and subsequently starved himself to death. His son stayed on in Rome, however, and he and Pompilia had a child of their own, Ancus Marcius. When Numa died, Ancus was just 5 years old, says Plutarch. Plutarch is not explicit, but he hardly needed to be: Ancus cannot have been a contender to succeed his grandfather and become king, if he was only a small child.[40] He did, however, become king in the end.

Tullus Hostilius died in suspicious circumstances. His house burnt down while he, his wife and his children were all inside. According to one version of the story, Tullus had been struck by lightning following a botched attempt to perform certain rites that Numa had carried out. According to Dionysius of Halicarnassus, some said the lightning was sent as punishment for the neglect of certain rites and the importation of others.[41] Why Tullus' entire family should have been killed as well is not explained, but it may be that these versions are later. The majority, says Dionysius, gave a different account (one that, significantly, *does* explain why Tullus' family was also killed). According to the majority, Ancus Marcius and some supporters murdered the king and his children and then set fire to their house. It seems that Ancus was not happy; he was Numa's grandson, he was of royal descent and yet he was not king. To make matters worse, Tullus had children, and Ancus was worried the throne would go to one of them after Tullus had died.[42]

The underlying assumption in all this is quite obviously that the monarchy was hereditary. Ancus Marcius thought that he should be king, because he was Numa's grandson. He was also concerned that one of Tullus' children would inherit the throne from his father. Neither circumstance ought to have applied, however, if Rome's monarchy was never hereditary. Dionysius, as it happens, preferred the story of divine punishment. He

---

40 Plut. *Numa* 21.3–4; also 5.2 and 6.1–3 for the elder Marcius and his role in getting Numa to go to Rome.

41 Calpurnius Piso *FRHist* 9 F15a–b (= Plin. *HN* 2.140, 28.14); Livy 1.31.8; *De vir. ill.* 4.4. Dion. Hal. *Ant. Rom.* 3.35.1–2; cf. also Cic. *Rep. ap.* August. *De civ. D.* 3.15; App. *Reg.* 2; Val. Max. 9.12.1; Plut. *Numa* 22.7; Eutr. 1.4.2.

42 Dion. Hal. *Ant. Rom.* 3.35.2–4; Zonar. 7.6.

points out that Ancus could not have known that the Romans would choose him to be the next king.[43] The observation is a valid one. If the Senate and people chose the king, why should Ancus have felt entitled to reign? What did he hope to gain by murdering the incumbent king? And why should he have been worried that the throne would go to one of Tullus' children? What this story clearly must presuppose is a stage in the development of the tradition when hereditary succession was believed to have existed at Rome and when the Senate and people did not have a say in who would be their next king. Otherwise, the story makes no sense at all.

It was during Ancus Marcius' reign that Lucumo moved to Rome from Tarquinii. Once he got there, Lucumo changed his name to Lucius Tarquinius (Priscus). Tarquinius was said to have been an ambitious man who aspired to become king. He worked to ingratiate himself with the Roman people and their king, and soon became Ancus Marcius' friend.[44] As a result, in his will, Ancus named Tarquinius the guardian of his children.[45] He had two sons, one or both of whom had nearly reached adulthood.[46]

After Ancus had died and when his successor was about to be chosen, Tarquinius sent Ancus' sons away on a hunting expedition, to get them out of the city. It seems they were a threat to his chances of becoming king; that is, they were rivals to the throne, and that can only have been because they were the king's sons.[47] But why should Ancus' children have been rivals, if there was no hereditary basis to the Roman monarchy? And why should they in particular have been rivals, if it was entirely a decision of the Senate and people who would be the next king? Why did Tarquinius not send

43   Dion. Hal. *Ant. Rom.* 3.35.5.
44   Polyb. 6.11a7; Cic. *Rep.* 2.35; Livy 1.34; Dion. Hal. *Ant. Rom.* 3.47–8, 4.6.2; Strabo 5.2.2; Claud. *ILS* 212; Cass. Dio fr. 9; *De vir. ill.* 6.1–5; Zonar. 7.8.
45   So Livy 1.34.12, 1.40.2 and *De vir. ill.* 6.5; Cass. Dio fr. 9.1 and Zonar. 7.8 have him put in charge of the children's supervision earlier.
46   Livy 1.35.1; Dion. Hal. *Ant. Rom.* 3.45.2; Zonar. 7.8.
47   Livy 1.35.1–2. Zonar. 7.8 has the Senate and people set to elect Ancus' sons; Tarquinius intervenes, sends the sons away and gets himself elected on the understanding that, when Ancus' sons had reached adulthood, the throne would be restored to them. The story clearly presupposes hereditary succession. Note also *De vir. ill.* 6.5.

all the men who were potential candidates for rule away on that hunting expedition? It is obvious that this story presupposes hereditary succession.

So too does Livy's account of a much later episode in which Tarquinius' reign is mentioned. In his fourth book, Livy gives a lengthy speech to the tribune C. Canuleius, in which Canuleius observes that Tarquinius was made king while the sons of Ancus were still alive.[48] The continued existence of Ancus' sons would only be of significance, however, if they had some claim to the throne, that is, if they were the heirs to it. Canuleius' observation clearly also presupposes the existence of some form of hereditary claim to rule.

At the same time, however, the several versions of the story of his accession have Tarquinius appointed by the Senate and people of Rome; some even have him campaign for office.[49] In these accounts, therefore, two different sets of circumstances appear to be juxtaposed, with little attempt being made to reconcile them. The story of Ancus' children presupposes that the monarchy was hereditary, while the story of Tarquinius' canvassing and appointment is based on the idea that the kings were freely chosen for the position.

Like their father, the sons of Ancus Marcius were greatly aggrieved at missing out on what they believed was theirs by hereditary right.[50] They also knew that a child who had been raised in the Tarquin household like a son and who was now a son-in-law was being marked out as successor (in particular, because certain omens had marked him out).[51] They decided to

---

48   Livy 4.3.11.

49   Enn. *Ann.* 138Sk (cf. Skutsch 1985, 295); Cic. *Rep.* 2.35; Livy 1.35.1–6; Dion. Hal. *Ant. Rom.* 3.46.1; Zonar. 7.8. On Livy's account, cf. Penella 2004.

50   Livy 1.40.2; Dion. Hal. *Ant. Rom.* 3.72; Zonar. 7.8. Note also that Dionysius has Tanaquil suppose that, were Ancus' sons to gain the throne, they would murder Tarquinius' descendents (i.e. get rid of those who had a hereditary claim to the throne), see *Ant. Rom.* 4.4.3–4; see also 4.11.3–4 and 4.33.2 where Dionysius has Servius repeat the idea.

51   Cic. *Rep.* 2.37 for Servius Tullius (*itaque Tarquinius, qui admodum parvos tum haberet liberos, sic Servium diligebat, ut is eius vulgo haberetur filius* [and so Tarquinius, whose children were at that time very small, became so fond of Servius that the latter was commonly regarded as his son]); Livy 1.39.1–4 for the omen, Tanaquil's assessment of it, the raising of Servius Tullius (*inde puerum liberum loco coeptum haberi* [after that, the boy began to be looked on as a son]) and his marriage

act. They arranged for two farmers to quarrel in the vestibule of the palace, in the hope they would be brought before the king. The plan worked, and the farmers, having got access to Tarquinius, promptly killed him.[52] The story has invited ridicule. Why kill the king and not the designated heir? Livy offers an answer: were they to kill the heir, the king would simply choose someone else and, besides, Ancus' sons would have also had an angry king to contend with.[53] They could hardly have anticipated subsequent events: the pretence of Tanaquil, Tarquinius' widow, that her husband was still alive and on the mend, and the scheme whereby Servius Tullius secured his position by acting as regent while Tarquinius supposedly recovered from his wounds.[54] Thus Servius Tullius, the one whom the gods had favoured and the son-in-law of the king, became king.

Tarquinius had sons, however, and Servius Tullius knew the risk. To counter the threat they posed, as the legitimate heirs to the throne, Servius arranged for them (there were two) to marry his daughters (fortuitously enough, he had two).[55] The marriages were mismatched and ill-fated, however, and before long, the ambitious and unscrupulous son, Tarquinius Superbus, and the ambitious and unscrupulous daughter, the younger Tullia, had dispatched their spouses and married each other. With Tullia driving him, Superbus began to scheme to secure the throne that he – and Tullia too – believed was his by hereditary right. And when Superbus

---

to Tarquinius' daughter, also 1.41.3; 1.40.2–3 for the views of Ancus' sons; Dion. Hal. *Ant. Rom.* 3.72.7, 4.3.4, 4.4.2, 4.4.4, 4.4.8, 4.9.1; Val. Max. 1.6.1; Plut. *Mor.* 323C–D (some of which comes from Valerius Antias, *FRHist* 25 F20); Flor. 1.6.1; Serv. *Aen.* 2.683; *De vir. ill.* 7.1–4; Zonar. 7.8–9.

52   Cic. *Rep.* 2.38 (but with no details); Livy 1.40.4–7; Dion. Hal. *Ant. Rom.* 3.73.2–4, 4.4.1; Zonar. 7.8.

53   Livy 1.40.4. See Cornell 1995, 131, 141 ('this mysterious tale is rather nonsensical, since the assassination produced the very result the Marcii had set out to prevent'); Ridley 2014, 95 suggests some Greek parallels.

54   Cic. *Rep.* 2.38; Livy 1.41; Dion. Hal. *Ant. Rom.* 4.4.2–5.3; Plut. *Mor.* 273C, 323D; Flor. 1.6.2; *De vir. ill.* 7.4; Zonar. 7.9.

55   Livy 1.42.1; Dion. Hal. *Ant. Rom.* 4.28.1 (although Dionysius' account differs in several important details; see below); *De vir. ill.* 7.15; Zonar. 7.9.

usurped the throne, he justified his actions on hereditary grounds: he was the son of King Tarquinius Priscus.[56]

Dionysius' version of the story is different. According to him, Tarquinius Superbus was not Priscus' son, but instead his grandson, and was only a small boy at the time of Priscus' death. He therefore posed no immediate threat and, in fact, he and his brother were put into the care of Servius Tullius and his wife. Servius, it seems, was to function as something of a regent or guardian (ἐπίτροπος [guardian] is the term Dionysius uses most frequently) until Priscus' grandchildren were old enough to inherit the throne, although, as it happened, the people subsequently ratified Servius' position as king.[57] It is difficult to know how much of this is Dionysius' own invention and how much of it he got from Calpurnius Piso's account (since it was Piso who first argued that Superbus must have been Priscus' grandson and it was Piso whom Dionysius followed for this).[58]

As for Priscus' children, Dionysius says that he had two daughters, but no sons.[59] When setting out his case for the existence of three generations of Tarquins instead of the usual two, Dionysius observes that, had Priscus left adult sons, Tanaquil would not have helped to secure the throne for Servius Tullius, nor would those sons have allowed Servius to become king.[60] That observation quite obviously presupposes hereditary

---

56 Diod. 10.1; Livy 1.46.1–48.7; for the hereditary claims, see 1.47.2–4, 1.48.2; Dion. Hal. *Ant. Rom.* 4.27.7–39; for hereditary claims, see 4.29.2–3, 4.31–2, 4.37.3 (again, Dionysius' account differs from the others; see below); Ov. *Fast.* 6.587–610; *De vir. ill.* 7.15–19; Zonar. 7.9.

57 For Servius as a regent, see Dion. Hal. *Ant. Rom.* 4.4.6–5.2, 4.8.1, 4.9.1–5, 4.11.4, 4.31–3, 4.40.3; cf. Flor. 1.7.2: *hic* [Superbus] *regnum avitum, quod a Servio tenebatur, rapere maluit quam expectare* [Superbus preferred to seize rather than wait for the kingdom of his grandfather, which was being held by Servius]; Zonar. 7.9: καὶ πρῶτον μὲν τοὺς τοῦ Ταρκυνίου παῖδας προυβάλλετο ὡς αὐτὸς τὴν ἡγεμονίαν ἐπιτροπεύων [at first he put forward Tarquinius' sons as his excuse, claiming that he was the guardian of their royal office]. For the appointment of Servius as king, see Dion. Hal. *Ant. Rom.* 4.12, 4.34–5 (a speech in which Servius champions the right of the people to choose the king and denies that the monarchy is hereditary; see also 4.37.3–4), 4.40.3; Zonar. 7.9.

58 Dion. Hal. *Ant. Rom.* 4.6–7; *FRHist* 9 F18.

59 Dion. Hal. *Ant. Rom.* 3.65.6, 3.72.7, 4.1.1, 4.3.4, 4.7.4, 4.9.1.

60 Dion. Hal. *Ant. Rom.* 4.6.6.

succession. The story that Priscus only had daughters offers an easy solution: there were no adult male heirs; Tanaquil helped Servius to become king, but entrusted him with the care of Priscus' grandchildren (a story that also presupposes hereditary succession). This solution, however, creates a problem of its own. If Priscus only had daughters, Tarquinius Superbus would not have been a Tarquin; he would have taken his father's name, not his maternal grandfather's.

Dionysius seems to have become aware of this problem. In contradiction to his comments elsewhere, he later claims that Priscus did have a son after all. To get around some, at least, of the difficulties this son's existence ought to have created, Dionysius introduces him only to say he had recently died, leaving two infants.[61] Nonetheless, his existence inevitably still raises awkward questions about Servius Tullius' early prominence in Priscus' household, not to mention Dionysius' previous silence about him, but that is presumably why he is mentioned briefly and only ever in passing.

It seems that Dionysius was simply working out different solutions to the various problems as he went along, and that that is the explanation for the contradictory claims and other difficulties in his account.[62] What is most noteworthy is that all of this could have been avoided completely with the simple argument that Rome's monarchy was not hereditary, but that argument does not appear to have occurred to Dionysius at this point. It would, however, be somewhat unfair to criticise him for this. After all, he must have known what was said to have happened in the alternative version, in which Superbus was Priscus' son, he himself told how Ancus' sons were responsible for Priscus' murder and, although he rejected it, he also knew the story in which Tullus Hostilius had been murdered by Ancus Marcius. This was a tradition filled with stories that took hereditary succession for granted. Dionysius can hardly be blamed for doing the same.

Given the existence of these stories, which all presuppose that Rome's monarchy was hereditary, is it really possible simply to say that Tarquinius

---

61   Dion. Hal. *Ant. Rom.* 4.4.2; he is alluded to elsewhere: 4.33.2 (Tanaquil was the mother of Superbus' father); 4.79.4 (Tarquinia, Servius Tullius' wife, was the sister of Superbus' father).

62   A change in source is unlikely; Dionysius says (*Ant. Rom.* 4.7) that Piso alone made Superbus Priscus' grandson.

Superbus is the exception that proves the rule? The actions of Ancus Marcius – following the story that Dionysius said the majority told – are really no different at all, nor are those of Ancus' sons;[63] the main difference in these stories is that Ancus was also said to have been made king by the Senate and people (see section III below), while his sons were outwitted by Tanaquil and Servius Tullius. The other difference is that the account of Superbus' deeds got written up at length, while the stories of Ancus and his sons get little attention and, when it comes to Hostilius' death, there were other versions too. As for straightforward views such as Linke's, namely that 'a form of hereditary kingship did not exist', they are surely impossible to maintain without the adoption of a highly selective approach to the evidence. But how could the various stories discussed here have ever come into existence, if the Romans had always believed (or knew, as modern scholarship supposes) that their monarchy had never been hereditary? These stories are obviously not historical, but why should anyone have invented them, if they were simply incompatible with accepted ideas?

III

The current orthodoxy is not based just on the idea that Rome's monarchy was not hereditary. It is also based on the idea that there existed, as F. Glinister, for instance, has put it, 'a formal electoral process by which a man became king'.[64]

Modern discussion of this electoral process has usually focused on the process itself and not specifically on the evidence for it. This has allowed for the inconsistencies and other problems in the evidence to be played down or even just ignored, for different accounts to be conflated or handled selectively, and it has also allowed for some misleading conclusions, especially when it comes to Tarquinius Priscus. It is necessary to take a

---

63   For further parallels, see Ogilvie 1965, 191; Vasaly 2015, 50.
64   Glinister 2006, 18.

different approach, to focus on the evidence itself, set it out in full and also handle each account separately, so that the differences between the several accounts are made clear.

Numa Pompilius was the first man said to have been made king by this electoral process. The story of his appointment is unique in some respects, which is perhaps unsurprising, but the fundamental elements of the process itself were nonetheless supposed to have been established at this time.[65] They were, moreover, supposed to have been established in their final form. It is true that the handling of the appointment of subsequent kings does vary slightly on occasion, but there is never any sense that this is due to any change in the system itself. There is also variation in the details between the several different accounts but, since each appears to be internally consistent, this does not look to be evidence of change either. The same methods, it appears to have been assumed, were used to appoint Tullus Hostilius, Ancus Marcius and Tarquinius Priscus. Servius Tullius and Tarquinius Superbus did not acquire power in this way, as has been seen, but there are stories of criticism aimed at both of them for precisely this.[66] On traditional chronology, therefore, the system for appointing a new king was supposedly in place (even if it was not always used) for more than two centuries, during which time it does not appear to have ever really changed.

While they do not agree on all the details, Cicero, Livy, Dionysius and Plutarch all claim that the senators initially tried to rule Rome themselves following Romulus' death; these circumstances continued until the people would no longer tolerate them.[67] In his account, in book two of the *De re publica*, Cicero has the senators establish the first *interregnum* at this point.[68] Following the senators' recommendation, the people invited Numa to come to Rome and become the king. Although he had already

---

65   Although the inauguration ritual could be traced back to Romulus: Livy 1.18.6; Dion. Hal. *Ant. Rom.* 2.6.1.

66   Servius: Livy 1.46.1, 1.47.10; Dion. Hal. *Ant. Rom.* 4.8.2, 4.10.5, 4.31.2, 4.34.5, 4.40.1–3; Superbus: Livy 1.49.3; Dion. Hal. *Ant. Rom.* 4.78.1, 4.80.1–3 (Brutus' speech; note that hereditary succession is nevertheless taken for granted at 4.79.4 and 4.81.3–4).

67   Cic. *Rep.* 2.23; Livy 1.17.1–8; Dion. Hal. *Ant. Rom.* 2.57.1–3; Plut. *Numa* 2.6–3.1.

68   Cic. *Rep.* 2.23.

been chosen in the *comitia curiata*, when he got to Rome, Numa arranged for a curiate law to be passed, to ratify his command (*imperium*).[69]

After Numa died, the *comitia curiata* met once again, under the presidency of an *interrex*, says Cicero, and chose Tullus Hostilius to replace him. Tullus likewise got his *imperium* ratified by a curiate law.[70] After Tullus' death, Ancus Marcius was chosen by the people; he too had a curiate law passed ratifying his *imperium*.[71] Following the death of Ancus, the people voted for Tarquinius Priscus, who also got his *imperium* ratified by a curiate law.[72] Next, came Servius Tullius and, after him, Tarquinius Superbus, who both came to power by other means.

Livy's account is somewhat different. He has the senators decide that the people should choose a new king; that choice, however, would not be valid until it had been ratified by the Senate.[73] When it comes to Numa's appointment, Livy claims that the people, called to assemble by the *interrex*, handed the decision back to the senators, who chose Numa Pompilius. Once he had come to Rome, Numa instructed that the auspices be taken, as they had been by Romulus. The necessary omens were received and thus Numa became king.[74] This last detail, the taking of the auspices, Cicero did not include; for his part, Livy says nothing about Numa, or any other king, getting his *imperium* ratified by a *lex curiata*.

Livy also appears to have known another version of Numa's appointment. In the speech he gives to Canuleius, he has the tribune say that Numa ruled by order of the people and with the Senate's approval.[75] This follows the sequence by which Livy has the other kings appointed.

Following the death of Numa, Livy says, the state reverted to an *interregnum*. Tullus Hostilius was then made king by the people. The senators ratified the decision.[76] There was another *interregnum* after Tullus' death;

---

69   Cic. *Rep.* 2.25.
70   Cic. *Rep.* 2.31.
71   Cic. *Rep.* 2.33.
72   Cic. *Rep.* 2.35.
73   Livy 1.17.9–10.
74   Livy 1.17.10–1.18.
75   Livy 4.3.10.
76   Livy 1.22.1.

the state returned to the senators, who appointed an *interrex*. The people elected Ancus Marcius and the senators ratified this.[77] Following Ancus' death, the people made Tarquinius Priscus king, after he had campaigned for the job and argued his case before the people.[78] Livy does not add that the decision was ratified by the Senate, but that is probably only an oversight on his part; he is clearly just more interested in Priscus' political manoeuvres.

Like Livy, Dionysius has the senators choose Numa Pompilius to be Romulus' successor; the people were ordered to assemble and the decision was announced by the *interrex*. Once Numa had arrived at Rome, the tribes voted for him by *curiae* and the patricians ratified the assembly's decision. The augurs took the auspices, which were favourable, and so Numa became king.[79]

After Numa's death, the Senate, having gained control of the state, appointed *interreges* and Tullus Hostilius was chosen to be king. He was appointed by a vote of the people, in accordance with the laws, and the decision of the people was confirmed by the auspices.[80] After Tullus' death, *interreges* were appointed once again. They chose Ancus Marcius as the new king; their choice was ratified by the people and then by auspicious signs. Ancus performed all the things required by custom (what they were, Dionysius does not say) and then took up his position.[81] *Interreges* were again appointed after the death of Ancus; they assembled the people and chose Tarquinius Priscus. Omens ratified the people's decision.[82]

Numa's accession is covered by Plutarch, in his biography of the king. Unable to agree on a replacement for Romulus, Plutarch says, the senators established the interregnal system. Later, after they had been accused of changing the form of government, they resolved that Numa should be king. The people were informed of this, and Numa, although he initially rejected the invitation, was soon persuaded to come to Rome. Once there, the

---

77 Livy 1.32.1.
78 Livy 1.35.1–6.
79 Dion. Hal. *Ant. Rom.* 2.58.2–3, 2.60.3.
80 Dion. Hal. *Ant. Rom.* 3.1.1–3.
81 Dion. Hal. *Ant. Rom.* 3.36.1.
82 Dion. Hal. *Ant. Rom.* 3.46.1. Note also *Ant. Rom.* 4.40.2, 4.80.2; 4.12 is unhelpful, as the circumstances (Servius' election) are clearly unusual.

interrex in office, Spurius Vettius, called the people together and everyone voted for Numa. Before taking up the insignia of his position, Numa first made sure that the gods approved. The auspices were favourable.[83]

There are some obvious discrepancies in these accounts. Cicero alone claims that the kings got their *imperium* confirmed by a *lex curiata*;[84] Dionysius, and Livy and Plutarch (in the case of Numa) have the kings get divine confirmation of their appointment, but Cicero does not; Livy has the people's decision subsequently ratified by the Senate, but the sequence is different in Dionysius' account. Despite these differences, each individual account is nonetheless by and large internally consistent; at least, the inconsistencies that are found in them do not appear to be of any real significance. Cicero, for instance, mentions the *interrex* only in his account of Tullus Hostilius' appointment but, elsewhere, he speaks of *interregna* (they made the regal period longer),[85] and it would in any case be extremely difficult to argue that Cicero had meant to imply by his silence that *interreges* had not been appointed on the other occasions. And Livy does not explicitly say that the senators ratified the people's choice of Tarquinius Priscus, but his silence is probably of no significance either. Indeed, given the importance of the Senate's ratification, had it supposedly been refused, that is something Livy is likely to have stated directly and not merely hinted at.[86] The only innovation, beyond the initial creation of the whole system, appears to come in the story that Tarquinius Priscus campaigned for office,[87] but that does not affect the nature and workings of the system itself.

The variation between the different accounts suggests that they are unlikely to be based on reliable documentary evidence, but such a case hardly needs to be argued. What record of such procedures would have been kept from such early times, or even made in the first place? The details

83 Plut. *Numa* 2.4–7.3; for his appointment and inauguration, see 7.1–3.
84 It has been maintained that Tac. *Ann.* 11.22 makes the same claim (e.g. Magdelain 1968, 30), but there is reason to doubt this, see Vervaet 2014, 308.
85 Cic. *Rep.* 2.52. Cf. Walbank 1957, 666–8.
86 *Pace* Gjerstad 1973, 211, Capogrossi Colognesi 2014, 38 and others who want to emphasise the break following the arrival of the 'Etruscan' kings; see Cornell 1995, 127. In contrast, Armstrong 2016, 80 n. 22, 85 claims that the *curiae* granted *imperium* to Superbus, but this equally contradicts ancient accounts.
87 Livy 1.35.2.

of political procedures are rarely recorded even in considerably later times. Any attempt to explain away the variation or, worse, to combine details taken from different accounts, in order to produce some other version still of the interregnal procedures would be misguided.[88] Why should the ancient sources not themselves have described the correct procedures (if there ever even were such), but instead – as these sorts of approaches ultimately assume – have related only some details accurately, with other authors, by chance, preserving other details, all of which need only to be brought together for the 'correct' set of procedures to be recovered? It is telling (and unfortunate) that it should also need to be said that the requirements of the argument should not be allowed to dictate how the evidence is handled.

Most of the individual stages of this supposed 'formal electoral process' have come under suspicion at one time or another, and much of the system has been dismissed as the result of anachronistic retrojection of later practices.[89] The way in which the regal *interregna* were doubtless approached in antiquity was from the vantage point of the republican period. For many Romans, including Rome's first historians, their experience of an *interregnum* was contemporary, since *interreges* were appointed from time to time in the republican period to oversee the election of consuls when there was no consul available and no dictator.[90] This is, however, something of a problem. Roman thinking about the past, as has long been recognised, was generally anachronistic, with the result that contemporary circumstances were frequently assumed to have existed in much earlier times.[91] It is really no surprise that the regal *interrex* was said to have done much the same thing (*mutatis mutandis*) as the republican.

It has even been argued that the *interrex* was entirely a creation of the republican period,[92] but that is a more difficult proposition. The obvious

88   The method is, however, quite common; see the various works in nn. 17–21 above; cf. also Chapter 4.
89   See n. 21. Cf. Dion. Hal. *Ant. Rom.* 2.6.1 (continuity from Romulus' day in the inauguration rituals); Livy 1.17.6 (*nunc quoque* [now too]), 1.17.9 (*hodie quoque* [today too]).
90   See Jahn 1970, 28–9, 109–90 *passim*.
91   See p. 29 n. 25.
92   Friezer 1959, 308–9; Ogilvie 1965, 87–8; Forsythe 2005, 110, 170.

problem is how to explain the name, if the *interrex* was not an invention of the regal period. It is not easy to see what circumstances could have prompted the creation in republican times of a position with such a name. It is much easier to suppose that the *interrex* was indeed a relic of the regal period, but that does not necessarily amount to all that much, especially when even the precise meaning and significance of the word *rex* in archaic times are uncertain.

The word *interrex* (μεσοβασιλεύς in the Greek sources) implies a position of some kind held between *reges*. That is all that the word on its own means. The regal *interrex* could therefore, at least in theory, have functioned as something like, for instance, a guardian or regent, someone who could protect the throne and perform the king's duties until a new king could be found or perhaps if the heir to the throne were too young.[93] The evidence is certainly not historical, but it is still worth noting that, during the first *interregnum*, the Senate was said to have attempted to retain its control over the state using the *interreges*.[94] And, although it is part of his extended Tarquin dynasty, Dionysius claimed that Servius Tullius was charged with the care of the young Tarquinius Superbus until he came of age. Something similar is implied by the story that, in his will, Ancus Marcius appointed Tarquinius Priscus as the guardian of his children. The possibility of some kind of guardianship was at least clearly not unimaginable. Be all that as it may, the regal *interrex* is most unlikely to have done what the sources imagine he did and it is perfectly possible that he had actually done something really quite different. And, if he had, the idea that the kings had been elected loses its strongest support.

On the other hand, even if the regal *interrex* did happen to do something along the lines of what the sources imagine, it would be very unlikely that that had been the case throughout the entire regal period. Such a role

93   The question of inheritance aside, these ideas are not new; Ogilvie 1976, 57, for instance, calls the *interreges* 'a caretaker government', Momigliano 1989a, 103, the *interrex* 'the interim head of state'. Magdelain (1968, 32 and 1990, 279–303) assigns the *interrex* an annual role, connected with the Terminalia and the Regifugium; his argument is ingenious, but inevitably tenuous. Dovere 2009 argues unpersuasively that the *interregnum* was in effect the normal state of affairs.

94   See n. 67 above.

may have been in existence for only a part of that time, and that is a consideration that applies regardless of the nature of the role the regal *interrex* had actually performed. This means that any sweeping generalisations about the elective and non-hereditary nature of Rome's kings are dangerous and more likely than not to be incorrect, for some periods at least, if not for all. Given what the interregnal system presupposes, in terms of the development of the monarchy and the apparatus of the state (an independent Senate, an interim office, voting and an assembly in which to do it), a later date for its inception would be more plausible than an earlier one, although that is certainly out of keeping with ancient accounts.

The Romans maintained that it was Romulus who set up the Senate and organised the people into three tribes and thirty *curiae*. Even apart from the fact that Romulus never existed, there are difficulties. It is most improbable that these several political structures simply appeared fully formed, as they essentially do in the literary evidence, and the three Romulean tribes may be as unhistorical as Romulus himself.[95] The idea that the Senate was created at the very beginning of Rome's history doubtless reflects only the centrality of the Senate in the minds of the Romans (and Rome's first historians were senators after all), and the alleged nature of the regal Senate – it appears for the most part as an independent deliberative body – is almost certainly anachronistic. An important passage in Festus presents something entirely different: the Senate was chosen by the king, not the king by the Senate.[96] What makes this evidence especially valuable is not just that it is unlikely to be some pseudo-historical invention. Festus' comment is based on the circumstances presupposed by a piece of legislation that was passed in the later fourth century BC. What he says, therefore, could be perfectly reliable. There are, furthermore, good historical reasons why something along these lines might have been the case.

---

95   Senate: Cic. *Rep.* 2.14; Livy 1.8.7; Dion. Hal. *Ant. Rom.* 2.12; Plut. *Rom.* 13.1–2;
       three tribes (equestrian centuries, according to some): Cic. *Rep.* 2.14; Livy 1.13.8;
       Dion. Hal. *Ant. Rom.* 2.7.2–4; Plut. *Rom.* 20.1–2; thirty *curiae*: Cic. *Rep.* 2.14; Livy
       1.13.6–7; Dion. Hal. *Ant. Rom.* 2.7.2–4, 2.47.3–4; Plut. *Rom.* 14.6, 20.2, etc. Further
       references in Fugmann 1990, 131–40. On the Romulean tribes, see p. 18 n. 38.
96   Fest. 290L; see Cornell 2014a.

It has long been argued that Rome's kings (some of them, at least) were *condottieri*, warlords, men with their own private armies, who may have seized control of Rome with the use of force.[97] Such men, it is not unreasonable to imagine, may well have wished to fill whatever sort of Senate or proto-Senate happened to exist at the time (if one even did) with their own supporters, to reward the loyalty of their followers and to have trusted advisors to hand, and also to get rid of any possible opposition. In the case of the last two kings, Servius Tullius and Tarquinius Superbus, it is usually argued that they are best understood as tyrants, and it is not improbable that such men are also likely to have removed opposition – that is, after all, what the famous stories of the tall poppies and the feigned stupidity of Brutus imply – and any vacancies would naturally have been filled with allies, if they were filled at all.[98] So the evidence of Festus is not implausible. It hardly needs to be said that these arguments (about *condottieri* and tyrants) do not accord all that well with the idea that there existed some kind of formal process for selecting the king that operated on any sort of regular or consistent basis.[99]

As for the *curiae*, they are one of the great enigmas of Roman history and it is clear that the Romans of historical times were not all that well informed about their origins and original nature. Hence the story that Romulus had created all thirty *curiae*, and hence too the story that he had named them after thirty of the Sabine women, a silly idea that was already dismissed by some in antiquity.[100] Of the thirty *curiae*, the names of only a few are still known, but these names are nonetheless extremely important. Most of the evidence for the *curiae* comes from considerably later times and so quite probably reflects only later circumstances and ideas. The names of the *curiae*, however, are conceivably contemporary with their creation.

97   For example, Momigliano 1989a, 97; Cornell 1995, 143–5; Bianchi 2010, 7–8; more generally, Adam 2001; Torelli 2011; Ampolo 1976–7 is also relevant.

98   Livy 1.35.6, 1.49.2–6, 1.54.6–9, 1.56.7–12; Dion Hal. *Ant. Rom.* 3.67.1, 4.42, 4.56–7, 4.67.4–70, 4.77–83, etc. Much of this is of course part of the tyrant stereotype.

99   The idea that Rome's kings were *condottieri* is sometimes associated just with the later kings (e.g. Cornell 1995, 144), but why should earlier times, in which the state was even less developed, have been different?

100   See Cic. *Rep.* 2.14; Livy 1.13.6–7; Dion. Hal. *Ant. Rom.* 2.47.3–4; Plut. *Rom.* 14.6, 20.2; Paul. Fest. 42L; *De vir. ill.* 2.12; Serv. *Aen.* 8.638.

It is significant that some of the *curiae* appear to have been named after geographical areas, but others after *gentes*, or after individuals (that is what Varro evidently believed).[101] The names of two, however, are mysterious,[102] and it is conceivable that they were named on different grounds again. What all this suggests is that the *curiae* may not have been created all at once, but may have been set up over time and under differing circumstances.[103] This is certainly what happened with the so-called Servian tribes, which were similarly named on different principles, as they were set up under different circumstances; some were named after *gentes*, but others after regions and places, a few inside the city but most beyond it.[104] This does not mean that the *curiae* cannot have been involved in the appointment of a new king, but their development may well have had an influence on the nature of any involvement. None of this comes through in the sources, however. In the sources, the system for appointing the king is presented in static (and consequently unhistorical) terms. Indeed, just like the Senate and the *curiae*, the system for appointing a new king essentially appears fully formed.

There is, therefore, evidence that allows for the reconstruction of something really quite different from the circumstances described by the Romans. Any such reconstruction could of course only ever be conjectural and could not ever be proved (which is the usual, and all too easy, objection to such reconstructions), but accepting the Romans' own account is actually no different: such an approach equally involves conjecture and the results equally cannot be proved.

---

101   Areas: Foriensis, Veliensis; *gentes*: Acculeia, Faucia, Titia, Velitia. Varro *ap*. Dion. Hal. *Ant. Rom.* 2.47.4: some *curiae* were named after leading men, others after *pagi*; Plut. *Rom.* 20.2: many were named after places. For the names of the *curiae*, see Smith 2006b, 202–5.

102   Viz. Rapta, Tifata (although Paul. Fest. 503L: *Tifata iliceta* suggests a place).

103   Other evidence points in the same direction: see Fest. 180–2L on the *curiae veteres*; Smith 2006b, 356. See Richardson 2019, 295–6.

104   Tribes named after *gentes*: for example, Aemilia, Cornelia; after places inside the city: Collina, Esquilina; and outside it: Aniensis, Oufentina; while the first of the Servian tribes were said to have been set up by Servius Tullius, the last two were not established until 241 BC (Livy *Per.* 19).

Given the many difficulties and probable anachronisms in the evidence for the election of the kings, as well as the existence of all those stories that presuppose hereditary succession, the general and ready acceptance in modern scholarship of the idea that Rome's kings were indeed elected, if properly appointed, and that Rome's monarchy was never hereditary is really quite difficult to understand.

IV

Ancient narratives of Rome's regal period contain two elements that, at first sight, seem to be incompatible. Parts – sometimes very significant parts – of those narratives take for granted the idea that the kingship was hereditary and that the sons of the king had a credible claim to the throne. At the same time, however, whenever the king died, the state more often than not (on four out of six possible occasions) reverted to an *interregnum* allowing the Senate and people to choose a new king.

As it happens, a number of stories can be found in the evidence that justify these circumstances, although this role is not made explicit. The most significant feature of these stories is that they ultimately serve to explain why the throne was *not* inherited: Romulus had no children, while Numa had no sons; Ancus Marcius was only a child when Numa died; Tullus Hostilius was not murdered, but was struck by lightning, and his children were also killed in the ensuing fire; Tarquinius Priscus sent Ancus' sons away, to ensure that he and not one of them would become king, while Tanaquil similarly outmanoeuvred them, to make sure that Servius Tullius became king after Priscus; and finally, like Numa, Servius Tullius had no sons. Not one of these stories would have been needed, however, and the stories that presuppose that a son of the king would inherit the throne from his father ought never to have arisen in the first place, had it truly been the case that Rome's monarchy was simply not hereditary or was not ever believed to have been so. As for the electoral side of things, it is perfectly possible to use these same stories to construct a narrative of the regal period in which successors are chosen by the Senate and people simply because the king left no male heir and not because the king was normally elected. Tarquinius Priscus and his son aside, the only exception to this is Ancus Marcius, but his sons came up against the ambitious Priscus – the first man to campaign for the position – and later Priscus' widow and son-in-law.

Cornell, who accepts that Rome's kings were elected and that there was no hereditary principle at Rome, and who also tends to be in general optimistic about the historicity of the literary evidence, has attempted to reconcile the various stories in a different way. 'The most probable inter-pretation', he says, 'would seem to be that the Roman monarchy was an elective system, but one in which connections, sometimes blood relation-ships, existed between some of the kings and their successors. We are given to understand, for instance, that kings were able to designate their chosen successors by giving them positions of responsibility; thus Tarquinius Priscus was the "right-hand man" of his predecessor Ancus Marcius, and was succeeded in his turn by his own favourite, Servius Tullius.' He goes on: 'A further sign of this connection between kings and their succes-sors is that they were frequently related by marriage. Servius Tullius was the son-in-law of Tarquinius Priscus, and Tarquinius Superbus was the son-in-law of Servius Tullius ... In general the process means no more than that the most evident way a king can show favour to a would-be successor is to offer him his daughter's hand.'[105]

The usual problem with this sort of approach (which is certainly not unique to Cornell) is that, while it seeks to accommodate the evidence, it distorts elements of it in order to do so. For instance, while Priscus in-gratiated himself with Ancus Marcius, he still sent the king's sons out of the city, to ensure that it was he and not they who succeeded their father; although Servius Tullius was Priscus' son-in-law, he only acquired the kingship through deception and, according to Dionysius, he was only to function as a regent until the king's sons came of age; and, when Servius Tullius married his daughter to Tarquinius Superbus, he did so to secure his own position, not to elevate Superbus or mark him out as his successor.

105   Cornell 1995, 141–2.

A better way to account for the evidence is simply to recognise that what is found in Livy, Dionysius and the other sources is a conglomeration of different stories, some of which are older, some of which are newer, some of which are mutually incompatible and most, if not all, of which are unlikely to be historical. The account of the regal period that is found in the sources is not based on documentary evidence or some accurate, or even partial, record of actual events (see section I above). It is, instead, the product of several centuries of story-telling and should be treated accordingly.

The Romans were probably already telling stories about their kings during the regal period, and they need not have been reliable even then. During the centuries that followed their expulsion, stories about the kings will have been told, retold and no doubt modified in the retelling. New stories will certainly have been devised too, while others may well have fallen out of fashion. At some stage, the idea that there were only seven kings and the identity of those seven became established. Various developments, from the accounts of attempted coups (historical or otherwise) of would-be kings to Roman expansion into southern Italy and King Pyrrhus' invasion, are very likely to have influenced what the Romans thought and said about their kings. So too the advent of historiography;[106] certainly Greek historiography affected what stories the Romans told. The clearest example is the story of Sextus Tarquinius, Tarquinius Superbus and the tall poppies, which was copied directly from the story of Periander, Thrasybulus and the tall ears of wheat.[107] Stories such as this have played an important role in encouraging and supporting the idea that the Tarquins were tyrants. Then there are the kings who were contemporary with Rome's republican historians, the Hellenistic kings, most notably. Although they inhabited a world very different from that of Rome's kings, they, too, undoubtedly influenced what the Romans thought about their kings and the stories they told about them. And later events will have also affected Roman thinking.

---

106   Wiseman 2008, 315 connects the tradition that there were seven kings with literary historiography; Purcell 2003, 34; Feeney 2007, 90–1; Smith 2011b, 36.

107   Livy 1.54.5–8; Dion. Hal. *Ant. Rom.* 4.56; Hdt 5.92; Scapini 2011, 107–11, with further references and bibliography.

The careers of men like Tiberius Gracchus, Sulla and Caesar are obviously significant in this context.[108]

Whatever bearing these and other such factors might have had on the formation and shaping of the stories the Romans told about their kings, at some stage, there was clearly room for stories of hereditary claims to the throne and presumably also once the inheritance of it; hence the frequent appearance of stories that presuppose hereditary succession. At some other, probably later, stage, the idea that the kings had been elected (or ought to have been) ensured that they were almost all said to have been so, with, of course, the notable exception of the last who was said, in contrast, to have based his claim to rule entirely on hereditary grounds and never to have got his position ratified. It may not be possible to recover anything much of the precise chronology of these particular developments, but a few suggestions can at least be made for why the monarchy came to be conceived of in the way that it did.

Whatever the historical realities of regal Rome may have been, Roman historiography was a product of the republican period, when the Senate and people called the shots. The idea that Rome's kings had been elected allowed for the Senate and people to play an important role in Rome's history from almost the outset. There is indeed something of a republican feel to the several *interregna* of the regal period: the Senate and people choose their king, who is in many respects just like the consuls, although he holds office alone and for life.[109] What could be involved, therefore, is straightforward anachronistic thinking. The Senate and what was believed to have been the oldest assembly of the people supposedly existed from the earliest possible moment (Romulus' day), so it would not be much of a stretch to suppose that some of their most important functions had done

108   All this has long been recognised (the bibliography is consequently considerable); cf., for example (in most instances, *passim*), Ogilvie 1965; Giua 1967; Bellen 1991; Erskine 1991; Gabba 1991; Wiseman 1995; Gabba 2000; Wiseman 2004; Wiseman 2008; Scapini 2011; Ungern-Sternberg 2011; Humm 2014; Mineo 2014; Ridley 2014, with further references in the addendum.

109   On kings and consuls, cf. Sall. *Cat.* 6.7; Cic. *Rep.* 2.56, *Leg.* 3.8; Livy 2.1.7–8, 4.3.9, 8.32.3; Dion. Hal. *Ant. Rom.* 4.73.4, 4.74.2–3, 4.84.5, 5.1.2; Val. Max. 4.1.1; Flor. 1.9.2; Eutr. 1.9.

so too. The idea that an *interrex* had been involved from the outset is perfectly understandable, from a republican point of view: once the king had died, an *interrex* naturally would have been needed, as there would have been no one else to summon and preside over the assembly. But there must have been more involved. Why, after all, was it maintained that Tarquinius Superbus had claimed the throne on hereditary grounds?

In the *De re publica*, in his discussion of the circumstances leading up to Numa's appointment, Cicero supposes that the Romans realised something that Lycurgus, the founder of Sparta's constitution, had not. In a hereditary monarchy (as Sparta's was), the king's son comes to power regardless of whether or not he is fit to rule; the Romans, however, Cicero claims, saw that royal virtue and wisdom were more important than royal ancestry.[110] These are views that require some process of selection, one in which ancestry plays no role but in which the character of the king is the primary concern. If the king is chosen, the people can pick the best man available.[111]

Similar ideas can be found in Polybius' discussion in book six of his history. Polybius supposes that, in the past, those who were chosen to be king held their position into old age, as they brought security and abundance for their people and lived just as they did. But when the office was inherited, the kings felt secure and that, coupled with the availability of resources, led to luxury, display and lawless behaviour; the result was that the kingship changed into tyranny.[112] And Polybius argues for comparable developments in other forms of government too. Good governments rule with the consent of the people, but when power is inherited, it is invariably abused.[113] Hereditary succession, in short, leads to bad rulers, and that, in turn, leads to a change in the system of government.

---

110 Cic. *Rep.* 2.24; cf. 1.50.

111 Cf. Dion. Hal. *Ant. Rom.* 4.34.4, 4.40.2 (ἐκεῖνοι [the *interreges*] δὲ τὸν ἄριστον ἄνδρα, εἴτ᾽ ἐκ τῶν ἐπιχωρίων, εἴτ᾽ ἐκ τῶν ξένων, βασιλέα καθίστασαν [the *interreges* appointed the best man king, whether he was a native or a foreigner]; see Fromentin 2004 on Dionysius' handling of this theme; the idea that several of Rome's kings came from elsewhere is worth reconsidering in this context); App. *BCiv.* 1.98.

112 Polyb. 6.7.4–8; cf. Giua 1967, 326–7; Hahm 2000, 469.

113 Polyb. 6.8.2–6, 6.9.2–9.

Given the Romans' famous animosity towards kings and that they kicked theirs out at an early stage in their history, why should the qualities and character of Rome's kings have mattered? What difference did it make if they had been bad? The Romans had got rid of them after all (which presupposes that at least one of them had been no good). And what difference did it make if they had acquired power on account of their ancestry or because the Romans had chosen them for the position? As it happens, there is a very specific reason why these things did matter.

According to Cicero, the elder Cato maintained that Rome's constitution was superior to those of other states. This was because the constitutions of those states had been established by just one man, who had alone set up the laws and institutions. In contrast, Rome's constitution was due to the genius not of one man, but of many; it had been established over several generations and not in the lifetime of one single man. After all, no individual on his own and no one group of people alive at any particular moment in time can anticipate the future; experience and time are needed.[114]

Although Cicero presents this as something Cato 'used to say' (*dicere solebat*), it seems clear that he had found it in Cato's historical work, the *Origines*, as he hints in the next paragraph: like Cato, he too in his discussion will go back to the '*origines*' of the Roman people, he says, gladly borrowing from Cato the very word.[115] If that is correct, the structure of the *Origines* is potentially significant.

According to Cornelius Nepos' overview of the work, Cato covered the regal period in book one and the origins of the states of Italy in books two and three. It was on account of these books, Nepos supposes, that the whole work was called the *Origines*. The remaining four books covered Rome's history, from the First Punic War to the praetorship of Servius Galba (264–151 BC).[116] Given that structure and focus, it is difficult to see where else, other than in book one, that Cato could have demonstrated his thesis (assuming he had) about the formation of the Roman state. It may have also been in book one that he made his claim about the superiority

---

114   Cic. *Rep.* 2.2, cf. also 2.37.
115   Cic. *Rep.* 2.3. The argument in Cornell 1978, 135 and Cornell 2001, 43 is entirely convincing; Cornell's later caution (2013b, 151) seems excessive.
116   Nep. *Cato* 3.3–4.

of Rome's constitution; but even if, as has been suggested, the claim was made in a later book, the content of the first could hardly not have been of immediate relevance.[117]

Nepos' description of the first book was not entirely accurate. Cato appears to have included later events and gone at least as far as 458 BC; he may have even gone as far as the Valerio-Horatian laws of 449, by which date, according to some, the main stage in the development of the republican state concluded.[118] He also covered significantly earlier times.[119] Despite this greater coverage, a substantial part of the book was likely still dedicated to regal Rome, and that is probably the reason why Nepos described the book's contents in the way that he did. If Cato had sought to show that the Roman state had been the work of many men and had been established over several generations, it may be that he had assigned a good part of the state's creation to the regal period.[120]

Cato was a contemporary of Polybius, and Polybius, in his famous discussion of the Roman state, appears to have made a similar claim about its development. He says that Lycurgus created the Spartan state with foresight and reasoning, and was not taught by adversity; the Romans, in contrast, achieved the same end not through reasoning, but through many struggles and experiences, and by always choosing the best in light of their experiences.[121]

Polybius' discussion has unfortunately not survived intact, but it appears that it was at this point that he inserted his now lost account of Rome's early history. This account went back to the very beginnings and it certainly went down as far as the Tarquins, but there is good reason to

117 Novara 1982, 108–11 opts for book four (and argues for no good reason that Cato did not demonstrate his thesis). *Pace* Astin 1978, 225–7, who depicts Cato as a man essentially ignorant of political theory and incapable of organising his material.

118 *FRHist* 5 F25 refers to events of 458; for the idea that Cato may have gone as far as the Valerio-Horatian laws, see Cornell 2001, 46 and n. 23 for references to further work; Cornell 2013a, 207 and Cornell 2013b, 76–7 (again, with excessive caution). On the significance of the Valerio-Horatian laws, see Cornell 1995, 272; Cornell 2001, 46–7; Vasaly 2015, 12–14.

119 *FRHist* 5 F3–12.

120 Cic. *Rep.* 2.37 points in this direction.

121 Polyb. 6.10.12–14.

conclude that Polybius must have gone as far as the mid-fifth century, the drafting of Rome's first law-code, the Twelve Tables, and the subsequent passing of the Valerio-Horatian laws.[122] The point of his account was to show how Rome's constitution, which he maintained was a mix of monarchy, aristocracy and democracy, had developed, but it presumably also served to prove the point that the Romans learnt from experience during the course of their state's development.[123]

It is no surprise that Polybius does not appear to have argued, as Cato did, that Rome's state was superior to others precisely because it was not the work of one man but of many,[124] but Polybius does nonetheless appear to have had the Roman state created over a lengthy period of time and so inevitably by many men. In that respect at least, his account is comparable. And his account of the development of the Roman state must also have assigned a good portion of that development to the regal period, and so likely to Rome's kings.

It is difficult to know if Cato's ideas about the development of Rome were inspired by Polybius' discussion, or Polybius' ideas by Cato's discussion, or whether both shared a common source of inspiration. These ideas may very well have come from the work of a previous historian, but they may equally just reflect views that were in circulation at Rome in the second century, if not already in earlier times.[125]

---

122 Polyb. 6.11.1; Walbank 1957, 674. See further n. 118.
123 For example, Walbank 1957, 663–4; Gabba 2000, 266; Hahm 2000, 473; Moore 2017, 134.
124 *Pace* Novara 1982, 116–19, who has Polybius follow Cato, but see Polyb. 6.10.12–14: despite the different origins, the outcome was the same for Sparta and Rome; and later, when comparing states (6.43–56), Polybius uses different criteria. Cf. also Taifacos 1979, 12–13; Moore 2017, 134, 146.
125 See variously Garbarino 1973, 343–8; Musti 1974, 125–35; Nicolet 1974, 246–55; Eckstein 1997, 192–7; Lintott 1997, 73, 79–80; Cornell 2013b, 157–8; Moore 2017, 144–5; and n. 124 above for Novara's views; for ideas already in circulation, see also Classen 1965, 386–9; Ungern-Sternberg 2011, 125–37; cf. as well works in n. 108 above. Cornell 1978, 137 maintains that the tradition 'reflects, however vaguely, an authentic historical process' (apparently there existed 'a framework of authentic tradition'). It is highly unlikely that Romans in the second century possessed such knowledge (see section I above), and the contrast between Stadtgründung (cf. Chapter 1) and Stadtwerdung is hardly the result of awareness of Rome's historical

About a century later, Cicero wrote his famous treatise, the *De re publica*, in which he drew on the works of, among others, Cato and Polybius.[126] In the second book, Cicero has Scipio Aemilianus, the protagonist of the dialogue, give an account of Rome's history, from the foundation of the city to the passing of the Valerio-Horatian laws, in order to show the development and character of the Roman state.[127] In what remains of Scipio's discussion of the regal period, the focus is firmly placed on the kings and their individual contributions to the creation of the city and state. And from what survives of his account of republican times, it is clear that the development of Rome and the role of individual statesmen in that development continued to be important concerns. Furthermore, at the start of the book, Cicero has Scipio relate Cato's views about the superiority of the Roman state as the product of time and many men, and periodically throughout the discussion, Cicero has his interlocutors make observations about Rome's ongoing development. Two of these are especially significant. Romulus, Scipio maintains, left not a baby but a grown-up nearing manhood (a necessary claim, no doubt, if Numa was to be appointed by the Senate and people). And C. Laelius, another participant in the dialogue, notes later on how Cato's views are confirmed: the Roman state was not the work of one man or one moment in time; each king added good and useful things.[128] As Cato and Polybius had before him, Cicero too had Rome develop over a lengthy period of time and at the hands of many men, and Cicero must likewise have had the greater part of that development take place during the regal period.[129]

Livy covers the origins of Rome, the regal period and the expulsion of the Tarquins in the first book of his history. He begins his second with the announcement that henceforth he will be dealing with the achievements of the free Republic. Livy then goes on to claim that, with the exception

---

development; the contrast is deliberate and it is ideological and political; cf. Novara 1982, 113–16; and note Cornell 1995, 59–60.

126 Mentioned by name in several places: Cic. *Rep.* 1.1, 1.27, 2.1–3, 2.37 (Cato) and 1.34, 2.27, 4.3 (Polybius).

127 Cic. *Rep.* 1.70, 2.3, 2.63; Zetzel 1995, 222. See further n. 118.

128 Cic. *Rep.* 2.21, 2.37; note also 2.3, 2.22, 2.30, 2.33.

129 Cf. Cic. *Rep.* 2.22; Lintott 1997, 82–3.

of Tarquinius Superbus, Rome's kings could all be viewed as founders, at least of parts of the city. And, perhaps somewhat unexpectedly, he adds that, had Brutus deposed any of the earlier kings, he would have done the Romans a very great disservice.[130]

Although different in various respects, these several arguments all have in common a basic view of the origins of the Roman state: it was not created at one moment in time by one individual founder, but was the result of a long period of development and was consequently the work of many men. And although Cato, Polybius and Cicero evidently included the first decades of the republican period in their accounts, a significant part of them must nonetheless have been taken up with the regal period. That almost inevitably means that Rome's kings were believed to have played an important role in the formation of the Roman state.[131] That is certainly the case in Cicero's work, which is the only one of the three to survive to any significant extent. As for Livy's handling of things, he was explicit: each of the kings, apart from the last, was a founder.

With these views in mind, it is worth reconsidering the alleged nature of the Roman monarchy. If Rome's kings had played an essential role in the formation of Rome, then their characters and qualities become extremely important. For obvious reasons, it would not do to have Rome established by bad kings, that is, by people who abuse their power and act only for selfish ends. What sort of state would such men have created?[132] What sort of example would they have set? And what would imitation of their behaviour lead to?[133] It is in this context that those arguments about elections and hereditary succession become so significant. In a hereditary monarchy, the king's son inherits power regardless of his character, and he

---

130   Livy 2.1.1–3. Cf. Luce 1977, 234–41; Cornell 2001, 53–4; Vasaly 2015, 36–56.
131   See also Sall. *Cat.* 6.7: the rule of kings at first preserved liberty and increased the state; later, after it had changed into tyranny, the Romans began to elect two rulers who held power only for a year; and Flor. 1.8 for a summary of the qualities and benefactions of each king. Note as well the general absence of Rome's nobility from the regal period, on which see pp. 135–40.
132   On the importance of leaders and the constitution, cf. Hdt. 3.80–2, 5.66.1, 5.78; Thuc. 2.36.4; Polyb. 6.2.9–10, 6.47.1–4; Dion. Hal. *Ant. Rom.* 2.3.5–6, etc. Note Luce 1977, 289–90 on Livy's account of the formation of the Roman character.
133   Cf. Cic. *Rep.* 2.69; *Leg.* 3.30–2; *Off.* 1.140.

may be more prone to abuse his power, because he thinks it is safely his by right of inheritance. Hereditary succession is capricious and all too easily leads to bad rulers. If, in contrast, the king is chosen, then it is possible to pick the best man, a man of regal qualities but not necessarily of regal ancestry – which is what Cicero has the Romans realise at the very outset[134] – and a series of such men would be eminently more suitable (and credible) for the establishment of Rome and its superior constitution.

As for Tarquinius Superbus, the only king to inherit his position, Cicero's handling of his reign is entirely unsurprising. One bad king ruined the entire institution.[135] Thus the monarchy was abolished and the Republic established. In the end, even the one bad king contributed something necessary to the development of Rome's constitution: he provided an explanation for why the rule of kings was brought to an end.[136] For why else should the monarchy not have continued, if Rome had only been ruled by the best men? At this point, hereditary succession had an important role to play. The Romans, presumably, would not have chosen a man like Superbus to be their king. Hereditary succession and Superbus' unsuitability for office went hand-in-hand.[137]

The idea that Rome's kings had each played an important role in the formation of the Roman city and state works extremely well to explain the nature of the evidence and, in particular, why stories of hereditary succession appear to have been passed over in favour of the view that Rome's kings were elected. There is, however, one king who does not quite so readily fit. Servius Tullius, who was said to have set up fundamentally important parts of the constitution – the tribes, census and centuries – ought on this reconstruction especially to have been elected to office. On one hand, religious omens marked him out and for that reason he came to prominence

---

134 Indeed, he goes one step further; Cic. *Rep.* 2.18–19: Romulus lived in a literate and cultured age; cf. Zetzel 1995, 176. See also n. 111 above.

135 Cic. *Rep.* 1.62, 1.64, 2.47, 2.51, 2.52; Livy 2.1.2; Val. Max. 4.4.1; cf. Glinister 2006, 24–5. Hence, presumably, the handling of Ancus Marcius' appointment; cf. Giua 1967, 328; Penella 2004, 631–2.

136 So Flor. 1.8.7.

137 Note that Dion. Hal. *Ant. Rom.* 4.11.4 has Servius Tullius claim that Ancus Marcius' sons would have behaved like tyrants, had they got control of Rome.

in the Tarquin household but, on the other, it was initially only thanks to
the schemes of Tanaquil that he became king, thwarting the ambitions of
Ancus Marcius' sons in the process. Servius Tullius is a difficult case. He
clearly attracted considerable attention in antiquity and his reign could be
presented in a variety of ways.[138] His strengths are certainly recognised in
the evidence and, while it is not entirely an adequate solution, it is worth
noting that there is no account in which he claimed the throne on hereditary grounds (which he could only have done as Priscus' son-in-law, but
the claim would have been weaker than Superbus' anyway).[139] His origins
were said to have been servile, quite probably on account of his name, and
that may also be factor. Would it be plausible to suppose that the Romans
had chosen a man of such status to be their king? The story was evidently
a source of some embarrassment.[140]

It is also useful to keep in mind the nature of the tradition, the development of which did not cease and was never straightforward. Romulus
provides an excellent example. He could be the heroic founder of Rome,
later worshipped as the god Quirinus, or he could be the murderer of his
own brother and the man who instigated the rape of the Sabine women.
He could be a good king, or a tyrant, got rid of by the senators.[141] As with
any myth, the story could be changed to suit the needs of those telling it,
or those hearing it. Under these circumstances, it is inevitably very difficult
to try to identify individual influences and ideas that may have helped to
shape the tradition at large, not least because other and subsequent concerns also affected the nature and content of the stories that were being told.

---

138   See Ridley 2014 for a systematic discussion of the evidence; on Livy's handling of
       things, see Poletti 2013. It is, however, difficult to follow Giua 1967, 328 who claims
       'Il regno di Servio Tullio doveva rappresentare concretamente i pregi di un sistema
       monarchio in cui la scelta del sovrano è determinata soltanto dalla valutazione
       delle sue individuali capacità.'
139   The difficulties also get passed over: for example, Livy 1.48.8; Dion. Hal. *Ant. Rom.*
       4.80.1–2, although Dionysius is here contradicting his own account.
140   See Cornell 1995, 132–3.
141   Cf. various references in n. 108 above. Dionysius, unsurprisingly, presents Romulus
       as a Greek-style law-giver (cf. Cornell 1978, 136), but it is noteworthy that his
       account of Romulus' constitution (*Ant. Rom.* 2.7–29) came from Varro (see
       Wiseman 2009, 81–98). For later times, note Gassman 2017.

The particular issues that this discussion has tried to address are the related ideas that Rome's kings, from Numa onwards, were chosen by the Senate and people of Rome, if they were properly appointed, and that Tarquinius Superbus, the last and worst of the kings, was the only one to hold the throne on hereditary grounds. It is suggested that, instead of being broadly historical, as has long been and is still widely maintained, this depiction of the regal period is the result of specific views and arguments. It contains a mix of anachronism, Greek political thought (or perhaps only some rudimentary observations about the perils of hereditary succession and the benefits of elections) and ideas about the formation – and success and superiority – of Rome. As for the historical realities of Rome's monarchy, little can be said; it is difficult to conclude from the evidence that it was never hereditary, but equally, that Rome's kings were never appointed, or that they ever were.

One final point can be made. The idea that Rome's kings had played an important role in the development of Rome also provides a solution to a further problem. If the Romans loathed kings so very much, as they are supposed to have done, why did they treat their own so favourably? The answer to that question should now be obvious: they were the founders of Rome, the men who first established not only the Roman city and state, but also the very character of the Roman people. The potential consequences were considerable; after all, Horace could even explain Rome's civil wars with reference to Romulus' murder of Remus.[142] Better, therefore, that Rome should have been founded only by the best men.

---

142 Hor. *Epod.* 7.

CHAPTER 3

The Oath *per Iovem lapidem* and the Community in Archaic Rome

I

One of the few documents from early Rome the authenticity of which no one now seriously doubts is the first treaty with Carthage. Polybius says that the treaty, and two others that were subsequently struck with the Carthaginians, were recorded on bronze tablets and were preserved in the treasury of the aediles. There are some difficulties, but there is no reason to doubt what Polybius claims.[1]

Polybius offers a precise date for the treaty. He says that it was struck when L. Iunius Brutus and M. Horatius were consuls, a date that he then converts into something more accessible to his Greek audience: the treaty was struck twenty-eight years before Xerxes crossed to Greece.[2] Although some have accepted it, Polybius' precise date is worthless. Brutus is simply unhistorical.[3] Nor was he, according to the later tradition of events, ever a colleague of Horatius. In the later version, Horatius was only a suffect consul who came to office after Brutus' death.[4] Polybius is here simply following a variant tradition concerning the identity of the consuls of the first

---

1 Polyb. 3.26.1; on the 'treasury of the aediles', see Walbank 1957, 353–4; Serrati 2006, 122–3.
2 Polyb. 3.22.1–2; Walbank 1957, 339–40.
3 See, for example, Welwei 2000; Wiseman 2014.
4 References in Broughton 1951, 1–3. Cf. Wiseman 2008, 306–19; and see pp. 116–17 below.

year of the republican period.[5] This entails no serious difficulty, however, for the names of the two consuls do not appear to have come, and obviously cannot have come, from the text of the treaty.[6] Polybius may record a second variant tradition here as well, if it is not just a simple slip. He says that Brutus and Horatius dedicated the temple of Jupiter Capitolinus. Later tradition gave that honour to Horatius alone, although there was clearly some uncertainty about when he did this, and in what capacity.[7]

Polybius next provides his readers with translations of all three of the treaties with Carthage, or more accurately, with translations of parts of all three, and he also provides commentaries on the first two.[8] He carefully notes however, before relating the terms of the first treaty, that, while his translation is as accurate as he can make it, the Latin language has changed so much since the treaty was drafted that not all of the text can now be easily understood, even by the most intelligent Romans. This comment has often, and no doubt rightly, been taken as confirmation of the document's authenticity, and of its early date, but it has also allowed for some rather loaded speculation about the identity of the learned Romans to whom Polybius refers.[9] The comment naturally also has wider implications for the Romans' ability to read and understand early texts,[10] although, since

5   The tradition concerning Tarquinius Collatinus (Brutus' colleague in the more prevalent version; see Broughton 1951, 2 for references) may have developed in the fourth century, see Wiseman 2014, 137–9. If it did, then Polybius must be presenting a variant tradition instead of only an early one.

6   Cf., for example, Walbank 1957, 399; De Sanctis 1960, 239–40; Oakley 1998, 256; Serrati 2006, 116: '[Polybius] gives the date [of the treaty] as the consulship of Brutus and Horatius, 509. This is possibly an error that, if not featured on the treaty, would probably derive from either Fabius Pictor or Cato.' But the error could scarcely have appeared on the treaty, unless it had been added at a much later date, when no one knew (despite what they may have believed) who had really been in office at the time when the treaty was made.

7   Polyb. 3.22.1. See Broughton 1951, 3–4 and n. 3, 6 and n. 1; Walbank 1957, 340.

8   Polyb. 3.22.4–25.5.

9   Polyb. 3.22.3. Note, in particular, Cary 1919, 69–70, who suggests that Polybius may have got his information about the treaties from Cato, 'the last person in the world to give an impartial account of the relations between Rome and Carthage'; cf. also n. 6 above.

10   Cf. Ampolo 1983a, 19–26; Wiseman 2008, 8–15.

Polybius' account of the clauses of the treaty seems coherent, plausible and, most importantly, appropriate to the general era to which the treaty is now usually assigned,[11] it is perhaps reasonable to suppose that the treaty was simply difficult to read, and especially so in some places, but that it was not wholly incomprehensible.[12] Had it been unintelligible, Polybius can be trusted to have said so.

After he has set out his translations of the treaties, Polybius turns to the oaths that were sworn for each.[13] Although he deals with all the oaths together in a single paragraph that he appends to his discussion of the treaties, there is no reason to suppose that the information he supplies about the oaths does not come from the treaties themselves. Firstly, in his seventh book Polybius provides what appears to be the full text of the treaty that Hannibal made with Philip V. The treaty evidently included details of the oaths that were sworn on that occasion.[14] And secondly, what Polybius records, for the first treaty with Carthage anyway, is perfectly plausible but perhaps also a little unexpected;[15] had Polybius only been relating what his

11   Cf. Heurgon 1973, 253–6; Cornell 1995, 211–12; Oakley 1998, 256; Serrati 2006, 116. The chronology of the early treaties between Rome and Carthage is notoriously difficult; the first treaty has, in the past, been given a significantly different date; see, for example, Mommsen 1859, 320–5; De Sanctis 1960, 239–40; Alföldi, 1965, 350–5; see Chapter 4 on the methods used to date the treaties. The first treaty with Carthage was most probably struck sometime in the late sixth century or possibly in the early fifth.

12   Serrati 2006, 115–16.

13   Polyb. 3.25.6–9. The reading of Calore 2000, 86 seems forced; if Polybius was referring here only to the oaths that were sworn when the second and third treaties with Carthage were struck, he would have needed to make this clear. And why should he have remained silent about the oath that was sworn when the first treaty was made? Cf. n. 20 below.

14   Polyb. 7.9.2–3, on which see Walbank 1967, 42–51; of the works cited by Walbank, see in particular Bickerman 1944.

15   See, for instance, Vaahtera 2000, 257: 'an oath taken on behalf of the state in such form as described by Polybius appears quite implausible, since the formula explicitly imposes the obligation, and the possible future punishment, only on the person who pronounces the oath, not on the state'; after discussing Livy's account of the oath that was sworn on the striking of a treaty (on which, see below), Vaahtera concludes: 'it is clear that Polybius is in error. He has confused two distinct rituals: the oath *per Iovem lapidem*, and the Fetial oath completed by slaying a pig

learned Romans imagined the oath to have involved, it is fair to say that he would probably have recorded something quite different.

For the first treaty, Polybius says, the Romans swore, according to an old custom, by Jupiter lapis; for the second and third treaties, they swore by Mars and Quirinus. Polybius then offers an explanation of the oath by Jupiter lapis: the person who swears to the treaty takes a stone in his hand, swears in the name of his state, and declares that, should he not abide by his oath, he alone should be cast out, as the stone is cast; having said this, he throws away the stone.[16] This explanation can hardly have come from the text of the treaty. Polybius may here have been drawing on the knowledge of his learned Romans. This means that the precise wording of the oath may be nothing more than what Polybius' informants supposed it to have been, or it may simply be the wording that was employed in Polybius' day.[17] But other evidence for the oath sworn by Jupiter lapis, although it comes from later sources, certainly confirms one thing: the oath sworn *per Iovem lapidem* appears to have been binding only on the person who swore it.[18]

Discussion of Polybius' account of the oaths has tended to focus on the problems in it. There are various difficulties with the phrase 'Δία λίθον',[19]

---

with a *lapis silex*'; Rich 2011, 194; see also Ogilvie 1965, 110: '[Polybius] had only a confused understanding of the detailed institution because he was misled into identifying the fetial sacrifice of the pig by a flint (*silex*) with an entirely separate oath *Iovem lapidem*.' On the contrary, Polybius provides good, early evidence. If that evidence does not fit with modern expectations or preconceptions, then those expectations and preconceptions should be thoroughly questioned before the evidence is dismissed.

16   Polyb. 3.25.7–9. The concept of the scapegoat may come to mind, but it is wholly inapplicable: if the person who swore the oath was, potentially, to function as a scapegoat, this would mean that possible violation of the treaty had been envisaged and that measures designed to mitigate the consequences of that violation had been built into the oath itself; but clearly this would destroy the value of the oath.

17   Polyb. 3.25.7–8 mentions the state, the fatherland and the laws in his account of the oath, but compare that with the version in Paul. Fest. 102L, in which no such terminology is used (only property, the *urbs* and the *arx* are mentioned).

18   Cic. *Fam.* 7.12.2; Plut. *Sulla* 10.4; Apul. *de deo Soc.* 5; Gell. *NA* 1.21.4; Paul. Fest. 102L.

19   Cf. Strachan-Davidson 1888, 73–80; Reid 1912, 50–2; Wissowa 1924, 779–82; Walbank 1957, 351–3; Dubuisson 1985, 189–94; Vaahtera 2000, 256–7.

although the explanation of the rite that Polybius provides may help to dispel some of these, at least as far as present purposes require. Even though the explanation undoubtedly comes from elsewhere, it is nonetheless quite obviously an explanation of the type of oath that was recorded on the treaty. There are also difficulties with the idea of oaths sworn by Mars and Quirinus (in turn, for each of the two subsequent treaties perhaps, or maybe as a pair for both).[20] Something certainly does seem to be amiss with the later oaths, but that is unimportant as far as the oath for the first treaty is concerned. Polybius clearly implies that he had received help (in person, or from what he had read in some unknown work) to make sense of the first treaty. There is no reason whatsoever to suppose that that help was restricted only to translating the terms of the treaty; indeed, the explanation that Polybius provides of the form of the oath may well be evidence that he had received assistance in reading the whole of the treaty. If Polybius' account of the terms of the first treaty is reliable, and it is generally supposed that it is,[21] then his account of the oath should be treated as reliable too. Of course, it may be worth considering the opposite, namely that the difficulties discernible in Polybius' description of the oaths may suggest that there could be difficulties in his account of the terms. But the main difficulty is connected with the oaths for the second and third treaties, and the solution to that difficulty is actually very simple;[22] the oath sworn when the first treaty was struck, although unexpected, is certainly coherent;

20   Cf. Walbank 1957, 353; Vaahtera 2000, 256.
21   See the references in n. 11 above, where this is implicit.
22   Presumably the triad of Jupiter, Mars and Quirinus is meant, and mention of Jupiter has simply been omitted; cf. Wissowa 1924, 780–1; Walbank 1957, 353; Vaahtera 2000, 256; Richardson 2017, 270–1. Calore 2000, 85–7 offers a different solution, but one that is based on a difficult reading of Polybius' text (see n. 13 above); nor does Calore provide any real evidence to support his theory that quite different types of oath were sworn, when a treaty was first struck (the oath that Livy describes, for which see below), when that same treaty was later confirmed or renewed (the stone-throwing oath), and when new clauses were subsequently added to it (an oath sworn by Mars and Quirinus).

and, most importantly, there is good, independent evidence for precisely this form of oath.[23]

Before any consideration is given to what the employment of the oath *per Iovem lapidem* may imply, it will be useful to note first and briefly Livy's famous and much discussed account of the ritual that was, according to him, performed when a treaty was made. Livy provides his description of the ritual in his first book, in his narrative of the reign of King Tullus Hostilius. The ritual, he claims, was conducted as follows. One of the fetial priests began by asking the king if he, that is the king, ordered that the treaty be made; the king ordered that it be so. Next, the fetial asked the king for the *sagmina*, herbs taken from the *arx* of the Capitol; the king presumably provided them.[24] The fetial then asked the king for permission to speak for the Roman people of the Quirites. Once permission had been granted, another of the fetials was appointed as the *pater patratus*, so that he might complete the oath, the central element of which was a request made of Jupiter. The request was that, should the Roman people be the first to breach the terms of the treaty, then may Jupiter strike the Roman people as the fetial strikes a piglet. After he had made this request, the fetial then struck a piglet with a *silex* [a stone].[25]

It has been argued that all this is in fact an antiquarian reconstruction, an argument that may find support in Polybius' account of the oath that was sworn when the first treaty with Carthage was made.[26] Yet there is

23   Cf. n. 18. Cornell 1995, 211 and Oakley 1998, 253, 255 appear to accept that Polybius' account of the oath is genuine: both treat the oath (and rightly so) as evidence of the first treaty's early date.

24   Livy 1.24.4–5, cf. 30.43.9. On the *sagmina*, see also Plin. *HN* 22.5; Fest. 424–6L; Paul. Fest. 425L; Serv. *Aen.* 12.120; Marcian *Dig.* 1.8.8.1.

25   Livy 1.24.5–9, see also 9.5.3. On the piglet, see n. 27 below as well.

26   Ogilvie 1965, 110–12; cf. Richardson 2017. *Pace* Calore 2000 who accepts as good both Livy's evidence (43–5) and Polybius', and who further supposes that Livy and Polybius both refer to the oath *per Iovem lapidem* (cf. e.g. 39, 53, 55, 57, 60 n. 70, 87). Such an approach requires an explanation for the differences between Livy's oath and Polybius', but it is not enough simply to distinguish between a public oath (Livy's) and a private one (Polybius'), or between an oath sworn when a treaty was made, and one sworn when a treaty was later confirmed, or when a *sponsio* was made (e.g. 83–7, 105, 107; see n. 22 above). Not only does Polybius say that the oath *per Iovem lapidem* was used for a treaty, he also says that it was used for the *first* treaty between Rome and Carthage (so the context can hardly be deemed anything

good evidence, literary and numismatic, that shows that a piglet was indeed killed when a treaty was made.[27] The date at which the practice of killing a piglet was introduced is not known. The earliest evidence for it, which is numismatic, comes from the late third century B C. But the absence of the piglet may in fact make much better sense in an archaic context.[28]

If the piglet was to represent the Roman people, as Livy claims it was, and if the fetial priest was to speak for the Roman people, again as Livy claims, then that presupposes the existence of a number of important concepts. Most obviously, the concept of the Roman people must have existed, as it certainly appears to have done by the time Rome's first treaty with Carthage was struck, as the terms of the treaty show. But the existence of this concept cannot always be taken for granted, especially in a community that had its origins in several, in a community that was remarkably open to others, seemingly irrespective of their origins, language or ethnicity, and in a community where ideas of citizenship appear to have taken some time to develop and take root.[29] Along with the concept of the Roman people, there also had to exist a sense of a state, and indeed of a state that could be considered the Roman people's (so a *res publica* rather than a *res privata*).

---

other than public). The only parallel between Livy's rite and Polybius' is the use of a stone, but the use to which that stone is put in each is very different, as is its symbolic value. If the *silex*, as Calore 2000, 57 argues, 'non era un oggetto qualsiasi ma uno strumento consacrato ad una divinità precapitolina, quale Giove Feretrio, e gelosamente custodito dall'antico Collegio sacerdotale dei feziali nel tempio del dio', then it is extremely difficult to imagine (and this is a point that has been made before) that anyone would throw it away; nor is it probable that such an object could represent symbolically a person who had broken the terms of an agreement, and yet that is the precise symbolic value of the stone in the ritual that Polybius describes.

27　Varro *Rust.* 2.4.9; Cic. *Inv. rhet.* 2.91; Virg. *Aen.* 8.641; Suet. *Claud.* 25; Fest. 266L; Paul. Fest. 267L; Serv. *Aen.* 1.62, 8.641. For the numismatic evidence, see Crawford 1974, 144–5, nos. 28/1–2, 29/1–2 and 266–7, no. 234/1; Richardson 2008b; Richardson 2017.

28　Compare Hom. *Il.* 3.298–301, an oath that is unquestionably early (note esp. 3.300: ὧδέ σφ' ἐγκέφαλος χαμάδις ῥέοι ὡς ὅδε οἶνος [let their brains be poured out on the ground just as this wine is]).

29　Cf. Ampolo 1976–7; Ampolo 1988; Momigliano 1989a, 66–8, 75–6, 81, 91, 99–100; Cornell 1995, 92–103, 157–9; see pp. 95–6 below and also Chapter 1.

Furthermore, the ability to conceive of these ideas in a sufficiently abstract way to allow for them to be imparted into the piglet is also a prerequisite of the ritual that Livy describes.[30] None of these things, in contrast, had to exist for the oath that Polybius records.[31] The oath *per Iovem lapidem* was binding only on the person who swore it, and it is for this very reason that this form of oath may have been far more suitable for an archaic context, as it presupposes little more than the existence of a single leader or chief of some description.[32]

Although the first treaty with Carthage was struck at a time in Rome's history when concepts such as the state and citizenship undoubtedly did exist (even if they may not have done so in a fully developed form, and even if they may not have been ideas to which everyone yet or fully subscribed),[33] there nonetheless remain several possible contexts in which the oath *per Iovem lapidem* would have made perfect sense.

First and most obviously, there is regal Rome. It is not necessary, and it is in fact extremely dangerous, to think of regal Rome in the way in which it appears in the literary tradition, that is, as a fully developed state, with all the appropriate appendages of a state. The Senate for instance, as T. J.

30   But cf., for instance, Richardson 2008a, 630 and n. 11.
31   See n. 17 above, although the wording in both instances may well be late.
32   Cf. Strachan-Davidson 1888, 80: 'It is to be noticed that the oath "Jovem lapidem" was taken only in the case of the First Treaty. The other instances of this ceremony relate to oaths made by private persons. It may be conjectured that originally the Fetials employed this as the most solemn form of oath known to them; but that, as there might be a question whether the vengeance was to fall on the swearer personally, or on the State as represented by him, it was afterwards discarded in public business in favour of the pig-smiting ceremony, where the two are kept distinct, and the curse is expressly imprecated on the Roman People.' But the change may instead have been the result of the development of the very idea of the Roman people or perhaps of the *res publica*. Nor was there, it would seem, any room for the fetials in the oath sworn *per Iovem lapidem* (unless their role in proceedings was significantly different); cf. Wissowa 1924, 780, 782. The fetial college was said to have been invented during the regal period, but that is likely no more than an unhistorical assumption; if Polybius' evidence is good and early, as it appears to be, then it is reasonable to conclude that the ritual performed and the oath sworn when a treaty was made must have changed; see Richardson 2017, 264–73 for an attempt to trace the development of the rituals performed by the Romans when making a treaty.
33   On these comments, see below.

Cornell has plausibly argued, may not have originally been the comparatively fixed and independent public body that it is presented as being in the literary tradition. It may, until the passing of the *lex Ovinia* in the fourth century, have been something much more akin to an individual's *consilium*.[34] And the *comitia centuriata*, or what became the *comitia centuriata*, may have once consisted of nothing more than the (or, possibly better, an) army gathered together as a largely undifferentiated body.[35] There is some useful archaeological evidence too.

In 1977 archaeologists from the Dutch Archaeological Institute in Rome discovered an inscription at the temple of Mater Matuta near Satricum. The stone on which the inscription was written had been reused in the construction of the temple and that reuse provides a *terminus ante quem* of about 500 BC. The inscription commemorates a dedication made to Mamars by the companions (*suodales*) of an individual called Poplios Valesios. The inscription therefore provides good evidence for a group of individuals who defined themselves not as citizens of some city, but instead as the companions of one particular individual.[36]

As it happens, the literary tradition of early Rome contains a number of stories that seem to presuppose similar circumstances. The historical value of many of these stories is questionable, but the evidence does have a certain cumulative force. So, for instance, there is Attus Clausus, the Sabine who migrated to Rome, and who took with him all his clients.[37] Similarly, Tarquinius Priscus left Etruria and moved to Rome with all his attendants and his considerable wealth.[38] Then there are the Vibenna brothers,

---

34 Cornell 2014a. For the *lex Ovinia*, see Fest. 290L.
35 Cf. Cornell 1995, 183–97; it is generally accepted that the complex system of multiple classes and numerous centuries developed later and no doubt over a period of some time; see, for example, Drummond 1989, 199–201; Momigliano 1989a, 92–3, 103–4; Forsythe 2005, 111–14; Fronda 2015, 48–51; Mouritsen 2017, 39–41; that certainly applied in the case of the tribes, see p. 35 n. 49; and see pp. 71–2 on the *curiae*. On the anachronistic nature of the literary evidence, see p. 29 n. 25.
36 Versnel 1980, 108–21; Bremmer 1982; Momigliano 1989a, 96–9, 104; Cornell 1995, 143–50; Forsythe 2005, 198–200.
37 Perhaps not unexpectedly, Cornell 1995, 144, 157, 174–5 treats the story as though it were historical. See Wiseman 1979b, 59–65 on the evidence.
38 The story may well be historical, cf. Zevi 2014.

Aulus and Caeles, and their army, and there is also Caeles' faithful companion Mastarna; he too was said to have moved to Rome.[39] It has been suggested that the career of Cn. Marcius Coriolanus should be viewed in this context as well.[40] And, although it is a calque of the story of the 300 Spartans at Thermopylae, it is worth mentioning the expedition of the 300 Fabii against Veii.[41] All these episodes envisage a single leader and a band of adherents, men who appear to have owed their allegiance only or primarily to their leader and, with the exception of the 300 Fabii (the tradition of whose expedition has obviously been reinterpreted), not to any particular city. That must be why these men were prepared to follow their respective leaders and move elsewhere. They were presumably not citizens, or at least they did not think of themselves as citizens, and so had no strong or binding allegiance to any state; and, if the concept of citizenship was not fully developed, then that is perhaps also why it was so easy for them to settle in another city.

All this is, then, good evidence of a time when concepts such as the state and citizenship were in their infancy, and when allegiances could still be owed to individual leaders before anything else. It is surely against this background that the early stages of the conflict of the orders should be viewed. Law-codes and the practice of creating and keeping documents – and note that it was the plebs that was said to have kept records from an early age – are the things of a state.[42] The plebeian movement was perhaps

39   See Alföldi 1965, 212–31; Pallottino 1987; Cornell 1995, 133–41, 144–5; Richardson 2015, with further bibliography.
40   Cornell 1995, 144; Cornell 2003, 86–91.
41   See Heurgon 1973, 181–2; Richard 1990a, 245–62; Cornell 1995, 144, 290–1, 311; Smith 2006b, 290–5, etc. On the parallels with Thermopylae, see Scapini 2011, 186–202; Richardson 2012, 139–42; Pais 2014.
42   Cf., for example, Wiseman 2004, 66–8; Momigliano 2005, 178–9; note as well in this context the idea that the role of inscriptions was primarily symbolic, see Williamson 1987; Wiseman 2008, 2–4. This is why the *leges regiae* are almost certainly unhistorical. The argument that the *leges regiae* contain seemingly archaic language and so must be authentic (e.g. Gaughan 2003, 331–2, developing the comments of Cloud 1971, 3) is facile and needs no refutation (cf. Oakley 1998, 485–6 on Livy's account of the prayer used for a *devotio*); the argument that they were preserved in the pontifical records (e.g. Watson 1972, 103–4) supposes that such records must have been kept in the regal period, but that is highly unlikely. Livy, in

then at first an attempt to force these individual warlords – for such they undoubtedly were, at least in origin – to adhere to the idea of a state. In this context of warlords and emerging ideas of a state, or at least ideas of a state to which not everyone subscribed, the oath sworn *per Iovem lapidem*, an oath that was binding on only one individual and that did not presuppose the existence of a state, would have fitted extremely well.[43]

Naturally a reconstruction such as this implies a rather different context from that found in the literary tradition for, most obviously, the Twelve Tables (another early document the authenticity of which no one seriously doubts). But the degree to which the literary tradition is based on serious misconceptions about the nature of early Rome is, in this instance, easily illustrated. The Romans noticed that there were Greek elements in the Twelve Tables. They devised two stories to explain the presence of these elements. According to one, before they drafted their law-code, the Romans sent embassies to various Greek cities to collect the best of their laws, and to Athens to collect Solon's.[44] According to the other, Hermodorus of Ephesus, wandering in exile, by chance happened to arrive at Rome just in time for the decemvirs to be able to take advantage of his advice.[45] Although it seems that there are some who still wish to claim that these stories are to a certain degree historical, it is quite obvious that they are both aetiological.[46] They are both also simply unnecessary. There is a good body of archaeological evidence that shows that, from the very outset, the Romans

---

any case, did not think that the *leges regiae* were preserved in the pontifical records; he clearly distinguishes those records, which he says were lost in the Gallic fires (Livy 6.1.2), from the *leges regiae*, certain of which were, he implies, recovered after the Gauls' departure (Livy 6.1.10). See also pp. 149–50, 188–9.

43   See also Richardson 2017, 265–6; and pp. 28–46 above.

44   Livy 3.31.8; Dion. Hal. *Ant. Rom.* 10.51.5–52.4; Jerome *Chr.* on 452 BC, 112H; Lyd. *De mag.* 1.34; Pompon. *Dig.* 1.2.2.4; Zonar. 7.18.

45   Strabo 14.1.25; Plin. *HN* 34.21; Pompon. *Dig.* 1.2.2.4.

46   For example, Cornell 1995, 275 who draws attention to the appearance of the loan-word *poena* in the Twelve Tables; but the word's appearance need be evidence of nothing more than the use of Greek loan-words; it is certainly not evidence of an embassy to any Greek city. Both stories are late inventions; see Ruschenbusch 1963; Ogilvie 1965, 449–50; Siewert 1978.

were exposed to, and heavily influenced by, Greek culture.[47] A Greek influence on the Twelve Tables is not therefore at all unexpected. It was for those Romans who lived at a much later date, but that was only because they believed – wrongly – that the arrival of Greek culture at Rome was the result of Rome's expansion into the Greek east. They were simply unaware of the early influence that Greek culture had had on their city, and so naturally they found it necessary to invent stories to explain the presence of the various Greek elements that were discernible in the Twelve Tables.[48] So here, as elsewhere, a distinction needs to be made between what the few pieces of contemporary evidence imply about the nature of archaic Rome, and what Rome's historians, who were writing in considerably later times, imagined about their distant past.

II

The wealth that Tarquinius Priscus took with him when he migrated to Rome may have played a role in developing his new place of residence into a major city.[49] That physical development need not have been accompanied by widespread development of, or subscription to, ideas concerning the Roman state. And naturally it cannot be assumed that the concept of a *res publica* to which, perhaps by definition, all Romans belonged simply sprang into existence the very moment Tarquinius Superbus was expelled from the city. Exactly how Superbus' rule was brought to an end is unclear, but the possible involvement of Lars Porsenna, the king of

---

47 See, for example, Wiseman 1994, 26–9; Cornell 1995, 86–92, 147–8, 162–3; Wiseman 1995, 35–42; archaeological evidence in Cristofani 1990.

48 See, most famously, Hor. *Ep.* 2.1.156–63. Not surprisingly, straightforward acceptance of the literary tradition concerning the Twelve Tables can lead to some rather awkward results; see Watson 1992, for instance, who argues that the plebeian movement in this instance resulted in a patrician victory.

49 Cf. Wiseman 2004, 38–40; Zevi 2014; but note also Hopkins 2017.

Clusium,[50] may raise doubts about the extent to which Rome became a *res publica* at that time. And even if the expulsion of Superbus is believed to have secured the liberty of Rome and the Roman people,[51] that need not necessarily imply the establishment of any sort of republican regime either (the removal of the tyrant alone may have been enough to liberate the city), and certainly not of anything along the precise lines of what the sources imagine.[52]

Polybius claims that the first treaty with Carthage was made in the first year of the republican period, when Brutus and Horatius were consuls. That claim is extremely difficult, and not just because of the problems with Brutus and Horatius. No less problematic is the idea that Brutus and Horatius were *consuls*. Livy was well aware that, after the kings had been expelled, Rome had not at first been led by two consuls. The chief magistracy of the state had been the praetorship, and Livy also found good evidence for a magistrate called the *praetor maximus*.[53] Livy seems to have supposed that what was involved was merely a change in name (the consuls had once been called praetors); but, since he was unable to exploit this information in any way whatsoever, Livy instead simply claimed that Brutus and his colleague (Tarquinius Collatinus in his version), and their numerous successors had been elected to the consulship.

50 See Plin. *HN* 34.139; Tac. *Ann.* 3.72; Alföldi 1965, 72–7; Gjerstad 1969; Heurgon 1973, 156–65; Momigliano 1989a, 93–4; Cornell 1995, 217–18; Forsythe 2005, 148–9; Wiseman 2008, 317–18; for surveys of the evidence and arguments, see Ridley 2015 and Ridley 2017.

51 Cf. Richardson 2008a; also Wiseman 2008, 136–9 on Liber and the Liberalia.

52 On what the sources imagine, cf. for instance n. 34 above on the Senate or n. 35 on the development of the army and the classes; on the unhistorical approach of ancient historians see p. 29 n. 25; see also Chapter 5.

53 Livy 3.55.12; see also Fest. 249L; Zonar. 7.19; *praetor maximus*: Livy 7.3.5. Much has been written about the *praetor maximus*; cf. variously, and with discussion of earlier work, Staveley 1956, 94–8; Momigliano 1989b, 171–81; Giovannini 1993, 89–93; Cornell 1995, 227–9; Oakley 1998, 77–80. There is little to be gained by offering yet another hypothesis about the precise nature of the constitution of early Rome; modern reconstructions are inevitably highly fragile as the evidence is just too sparse and difficult. It is sufficient simply to say that this evidence is enough to show that Rome was, after the expulsion of the kings, not originally led by dual consuls. See Chapters 5 and 6.

Many modern scholars have followed Livy in all this: the change from
the praetorship to the consulship is generally treated as a change in name
only, and the evidence for the early praetorship is by and large simply set
aside in favour of the literary tradition.[54] But magistracies often derive
their names from their duties. Praetors presumably went in front (*praeire*),
that is to say, they led, while consuls presumably consulted (*consulere*).[55]
'Consulting' implies that there is someone to consult or someone whose
interests should be consulted. Ancient tradition claims that it was the
people whom the consuls were to consult, although the Senate is often
mentioned as well, or that the consuls were to consult the interests of the
state.[56] On the other hand, since collegiality was a fundamental feature of
the dual consulship, it is not impossible that the person with whom it was
imagined the consul would consult (even if only ideologically speaking)
was his colleague.[57] After all, it is not necessary to have a dual magistracy
to consult the Senate or the citizens, or the interests of the state; but it is
necessary to have at least two equal magistrates if those magistrates are to
consult one another.

The title 'leader', in contrast, does not require or presuppose the existence of a colleague, but it may presuppose a quite different relationship
with the people; and a magistrate known as the *praetor maximus* clearly

54 For example, Ogilvie 1965, 231; Scullard 1980, 78, 118, 465 n. 1; Cornell 1995, 226;
    Lintott 1999, 104; Forsythe 2005, 151–3; see also various works cited in the previous
    note. See Chapter 6.
55 See Varro *Ling.* 5.80, 5.87, *De vita pop. Rom.* fr. 67 Pittà (= Non. 35L) with Riposati
    1939, 173 and Pittà 2015, 277–9; Cic. *De or.* 2.165, *Leg.* 3.8 with Dyck 2004, 457–8;
    Livy 22.1.14; Dion. Hal. *Ant. Rom.* 4.76.2; Quint. *Inst.* 1.6.32; Plut. *Rom.* 14.3; Flor.
    1.9.2; August. *De civ. D.* 5.12; Pompon. *Dig.* 1.2.2.16; Isid. *Orig.* 9.3.6; cf. De Martino
    1972, 246, 249; Wiseman 1995, 103; Stewart 1998, 114–16; Forsythe 2005, 151.
56 See the previous note. If the Senate was long akin to a magistrate's *consilium*
    (see n. 34 above), then it would naturally have been consulted by the executive
    magistrate(s) of the community; that is, the consultation of the Senate is presum-
    ably not something to be connected specifically with the consulship. The idea that
    consuls in particular were to consult the Senate is doubtless due to the etymology
    of the name and also the role of the Senate.
57 The tradition of course came to connect the duality of the consulship with the
    desire to preclude monarchy (cf., most explicitly, Eutr. 1.9.1); but that ideology is
    probably anachronistic, see Richardson 2008a and Chapter 5.

must have been superlative in some sense (and the very use of the superlative stands in stark contrast to the ideology of the two consuls, whose power was shared, balanced and equal). If the model of independent warlords has been overstated, is simply flawed or should only be adopted for an earlier era,[58] then here is another possible context in which the oath sworn *per Iovem lapidem* would have made good sense. If the community was led by perhaps a single leader, or by a leader who could be described as the 'greatest' of however many leaders there may have been, then that leader may have been responsible (or just more so) for the community. He may also have been responsible for ensuring that the terms of any treaty were adhered to; that, certainly, is what the use of the oath *per Iovem lapidem* when the first treaty with Carthage was struck would seem to suggest. The employment of that particular form of oath implies that only one individual took the oath, that only that one individual was to be held accountable, should the terms be violated, and presumably therefore that it was up to that one individual to ensure that the clauses of the treaty were honoured.

There is a further piece of evidence that should be considered in this context, and that is the *foedus Cassianum*. This treaty was said to have been struck in the consulship of Sp. Cassius and Postumus Cominius (493 BC). The text of the treaty was apparently inscribed on a bronze column that was set up in the Forum, near the Rostra, and it may be that the text included the name – if it included any names at all – of only one individual, Sp. Cassius.[59] Certainly the treaty was associated with Sp. Cassius alone (hence, obviously, its name), and this was clearly something that Livy at least felt required some explanation.[60] Caution is needed here, however;

58　Although note, for instance, Harris 1990, 500–1 (on naval activity), also 505 and 508. See Chapter 1 as well.

59　For the sources, see Broughton 1951, 15. There were, it would appear, no names on the treaty with Carthage; Ogilvie 1965, 318 seems certain that Cassius' name 'stood in the treaty', although Ogilvie goes on to say: 'but perhaps in his capacity as fetial rather than consul'. The idea that Cassius made the treaty as a fetial and not as a consul contradicts the ancient tradition; the idea is presumably Ogilvie's own solution to the problem that only one name was associated with the treaty, but see Livy 9.5.4: Livy imagined that the names of *two* fetials would be preserved when a treaty was made.

60　Livy 2.33.4, note also 2.33.9; so too perhaps Dion. Hal. *Ant. Rom.* 6.91.1. See Richardson 2017, 267–70.

much of the tradition regarding the *foedus Cassianum* is highly questionable, and the possibility that this treaty may have actually been struck at a
considerably later date, a date in the fourth century, or even in the third,
has been entertained.

The *foedus Cassianum* has in the past been used by some as evidence
that, in the early fifth century, Rome was ruled not by two consuls, but
instead by a single magistrate.[61] That is an idea that fits extremely well in
the present context. The sources for the *foedus Cassianum* say nothing specific about the form of oath that was employed by Sp. Cassius,[62] but the
mere fact that the Cassian treaty was associated with only one individual
suggests that it could very well constitute further evidence of precisely the
same circumstances that the use of the oath *per Iovem lapidem* for the first
treaty with Carthage implies. That is, that the city of Rome was at that
time led by one individual, or that one individual held a position in the
city that meant that he could somehow represent the entire community, or
at least the dominant part of it. Needless to say, whether or not the *foedus
Cassianum* does in fact constitute evidence of circumstances such as these
naturally depends on whether or not the evidence for the *foedus* itself is of
any value in the first place.

The suggestions made here about what the employment of the oath
per Iovem lapidem seems to imply about the nature of the early Roman
state and constitution obviously do not fit at all well with what the much
later literary tradition has to say about the nature and constitution of the
early Republic, and they do not fit with modern reconstructions that are
closely based on that later tradition. But good, contemporary evidence
should never be discarded, especially in favour of a literary tradition composed centuries later by historians who clearly did not fully understand the

61 Cf., for example, Hanell 1946, 172–5 (with arguments in favour of the traditional
    date); Alföldi 1965, 114–15 (although Alföldi doubts the authenticity of most of the
    tradition). Much is also made out of the tradition concerning M. Horatius (cf. e.g.
    Hanell 1946, 170–2; n. 7 above); since the argument hinges on his dedication of
    the temple of Jupiter Capitolinus, rather than on any oath, the matter is beyond the
    scope of this chapter.

62 Only Dion. Hal. *Ant. Rom.* 6.95.3 says anything about the oath, but his comment is
    far too vague to be of any use and is probably his own contribution.

early history of their city, who had only a limited awareness of processes of change and development, and whose aims and purposes often differed quite significantly from those of the modern historian. Instead, the later literary tradition, and those reconstructions that are heavily dependent on it, must give way before the good, contemporary evidence. Although suspicions have been raised about the value of the evidence for the *foedus Cassianum*, there is no good reason at all to doubt what Polybius has to say about the oath sworn by the Romans when they made their first treaty with Carthage. And, of course, to doubt Polybius' evidence *because* of what it implies about archaic Rome is to treat the evidence in precisely the same manner that Procrustes treated his guests.

CHAPTER 4

Rome's Treaties with Carthage: Jigsaw or Variant Traditions?

I

It was in the consulship of L. Iunius Brutus and M. Horatius, according to Polybius, that the Romans struck their first treaty with the Carthaginians. The terms of this treaty Polybius found inscribed on a bronze tablet and, although observing that the Latin in which they were written was archaic and not easily understood, he nonetheless provided his readers with a translation.[1] For present purposes it is sufficient to note that the terms that Polybius records seem to support his claim that the treaty was indeed early, as do his comments about the language in which they were written.[2] More difficult, however, is Polybius' precise date for the treaty: the year in which Brutus and Horatius were consuls, that is to say, the very first year of the republican period. It has been well noted that the names of these consuls do not come from the text of the treaty itself but presumably from some other source, while, according to later tradition, Brutus was never consul alongside Horatius.[3] Brutus is, in any case, almost certainly unhistorical, so his name can hardly have appeared in the treaty.[4]

---

1   Polyb. 3.22.
2   Cf., for example, Cornell 1995, 211–12; Oakley 1998, 255–6. As does also the nature of the oath that was sworn when the treaty was made, see Chapter 3 and also Richardson 2017.
3   Walbank 1957, 339; see section IV below.
4   Cf. Welwei 2000; Wiseman 2014 who dates Brutus' membership of the *gens Iunia* to the fourth century; there is also the fact that the name Brutus is a *cognomen*; see p. 145 and n. 36.

The treaty may well have been early, but Polybius' precise date for it is unacceptable.[5]

Sometime later, Polybius claims, the Romans struck a second treaty with Carthage. Polybius does not provide a date for this treaty but he does, as with the first, offer a translation of it.[6] And it was, Polybius implies, this second treaty that was renewed when King Pyrrhus of Epirus was campaigning in Italy. New clauses for dealing with the king were, however, added to the agreement at this time, and Polybius provides a translation only of these.[7] Finally, Polybius notes that Philinus of Agrigentum claimed that the Romans struck a treaty with the Carthaginians in which they agreed to stay out of Sicily and in which the Carthaginians agreed to stay out of Italy, a treaty that the Romans, Philinus alleged, broke when they crossed to Sicily in 264 BC. But Polybius could not himself find any evidence to support Philinus' claims and, well aware that Philinus was as biased in favour of the Carthaginians as Fabius Pictor was in favour of the Romans, decided to reject them outright and deny that any such treaty had ever been made.[8]

Further evidence for Rome's treaties with Carthage is found in Diodorus. According to him, in 348 BC the Romans struck a treaty with the Carthaginians;

5   It is simply not enough to say, as Serrati 2006, 116: 'Brutus was slain in battle during his consulship, while Horatius abdicated, yet this does not discount the treaty, as they probably still gave their names to the year.' According to later tradition at least, Brutus and Collatinus were the eponymous consuls; it was Collatinus who famously abdicated; Horatius was just one of three suffect consuls. Serrati adds: 'Of course ... the beginning of the Republic is now variously dated from 509–501.' This however is mysteriously supported with references (in n. 10) to Gjerstad 1967, Werner 1963 and Wiseman 1995, 103–7. But Gjerstad and Werner both famously put the beginning of the republican period much later, in the fifth century, while Wiseman's discussion in his *Remus* is concerned with the establishment of the dual consulship (which Wiseman dates to 367) rather than with the date at which the republican period commenced.

6   Polyb. 3.24.1–13.

7   Polyb. 3.25.1–5.

8   Polyb. 3.26; for Polybius' opinion of Philinus, see Polyb. 1.14.1–15.12.

and this treaty, Diodorus asserts, was the first ever to be made between the two states. Diodorus also records that the Romans struck a treaty with the Carthaginians after Pyrrhus had come to Italy.[9]

Like Diodorus, Livy too claims that a treaty between Rome and Carthage was struck in 348. Unlike Diodorus, Livy does not explicitly say that this was the first, but he records no earlier treaty and so, not surprisingly, his evidence has at times been taken together with Diodorus' claim that the treaty of 348 was the first.[10] At 9.19.13 Livy does have Rome and Carthage bound *foederibus vetustis* [by ancient treaties], and this may suggest that he was aware of earlier agreements; but the reference is clearly imprecise and *vetustus* is a relative word. Livy also records that the Romans received a Carthaginian embassy in 343. He does not say that any treaty was made or renewed at this time, although some have supposed that this was the case. Livy does claim that the treaty with Carthage was renewed in 306, however, but he says that it was renewed for the *third* time. A renewal for the third time would require, if reckoned inclusively, two previous agreements, but three, if exclusively.[11] Finally, in the *Periocha* of book thirteen, the renewal (for the fourth time) of the treaty at the time of Pyrrhus' expedition is recorded.[12]

---

9   Diod. 16.69.1: ἐπὶ δὲ τούτων Ῥωμαίοις μὲν πρὸς Καρχηδονίους πρῶτον συνθῆκαι ἐγένοντο [In this year the first treaty was made between the Romans and the Carthaginians]; 22.7.5.

10 Livy 7.27.2: *et cum Carthaginiensibus legatis Romae foedus ictum, cum amicitiam ac societatem petentes venissent.* [At Rome a treaty was struck with the Carthaginian ambassadors, who had come seeking friendship and an alliance.] Note Oros. 3.7.1–2, who does refer to the treaty as the first (*numerandum etiam inter mala censeo primum illud ictum cum Carthaginiensibus foedus* [I consider that that first treaty struck with the Carthaginians is also to be reckoned among Rome's misfortunes]), and also the change in Livy's vocabulary: here (at 7.27.2), *foedus ictum* [the treaty was struck], but subsequently (see n. 12 below), *foedus renovatum* [the treaty was renewed].

11 That is, *foedus ictum, renovatum* (2), *renovatum* (3); or *ictum, renovatum* (1), *renovatum* (2), *renovatum* (3).

12 Livy 7.38.2 (343); 9.43.26 (306): *cum Carthaginiensibus eodem anno foedus tertio renovatum* [in this year the treaty with the Carthaginians was renewed for the

II

This evidence, it is widely supposed, is sufficient both in quality and in quantity to allow for the complete reconstruction of the history of Rome's alliances with Carthage prior to the First Punic War.[13] So, for example, one recent study offers in essence the following: Polybius' date for the first treaty, despite the difficulties involved, is accepted;[14] Polybius' undated second treaty is equated with the treaty that Diodorus in fact unequivocally says was the first, that is, the treaty of 348 which Livy also records;[15] since the terms, as related by Polybius, of this second treaty would have been out of date by the time of Pyrrhus' expedition, when the treaty was again renewed and when extra clauses for dealing with the Epirote king were added, it is supposed that there must have been another revision of the treaty, sometime after 348, but before 279/8; Livy's evidence for a renewal in 306 is therefore brought into play, and it is further supposed that Livy's treaty of 306 was the same as the treaty that Philinus alleged had existed,[16] despite the fact that that treaty would have constituted an entirely new agreement rather than the simple renewal recorded

---

third time]; *Per.* 13 (279/8): *cum Carthaginiensibus quarto foedus renovatum est* [the treaty with the Carthaginians was renewed for the fourth time].

13   The bibliography on this subject is immense; indeed, as long ago as 1979, Badian could claim that it was now impossible to make an original contribution to this 'well-worn subject' (161). For references up to the 1960s, see Werner 1963, 304 n. 1; Alföldi 1965, 350 n. 2; cf. further Walbank 1957, 337–8; Oakley 1998, 262; Eckstein 2010, 406 n. 3; Scardigli 2011.

14   Serrati 2006, 116.

15   Serrati 2006, 119: 'Polybius again does not date the treaty, but we know from Diodorus (16.69.1) and Livy (7.27.2) that the year was in fact 348.'

16   Serrati 2006, 120–9, cf. esp. 129: 'I believe the strongest objection to Polybius [who presented the 279/8 treaty as a renewal of his second agreement] rests on the argument that without a treaty in 306, the treaty of 279–8, as a renewal of that of 348, allowed the Carthaginians to seize cities within Latium, and this is quite simply an impossibility.' The arguments in favour of Philinus' terms were clearly set out long ago by Cary 1919. It appears to have become fashionable in some quarters to support Philinus, see the bibliography in Eckstein 2010, 406 n. 3; see also Ameling 2011, 55–6; Beck 2011, 231–3; Scardigli 2011, 32–4.

by Livy; finally, in 279/8, after Pyrrhus had invaded, the treaty then in force, that is the treaty of 306, was renewed, which must mean, on this reconstruction, that the terms recorded by Philinus were renewed,[17] even though this cannot have been the case because Polybius saw the treaty struck at the time of Pyrrhus' expedition but could find no evidence for Philinus' terms.[18]

It is fair to say that, despite the several and often quite significant problems, all this represents an entirely orthodox reconstruction. Indeed, many of the prevailing arguments on the subject appear on the whole simply to have been reproduced and there is certainly nothing original in this particular attempt to establish the history of Rome's treaties with Carthage. Nonetheless, it is worth noting a few alternatives to parts of this reconstruction, because they are not uncommon, or because they have at least enjoyed some currency in the past.

Since Polybius' precise date for his first treaty is clearly of little value, this treaty has been taken by some to be the same as Diodorus' first, and so it has been assigned to 348, despite the fact that the terms that Polybius records are not altogether appropriate for the mid-fourth century.[19] Another date is therefore needed for Polybius' second treaty, and the year 343 has sometimes been chosen,[20] even though Livy records only that a Carthaginian embassy came to Rome in this year, and even though only a few years had passed since the treaty had supposedly been made in the first place. Others have opted for Livy's date of 306 for Polybius' second treaty, although that does not fit with Livy's claim that the treaty was renewed for the third time in this year, unless it is to be supposed that there was another treaty, one struck sometime between Polybius' first and second.[21] There

17   Serrati 2006, 129: 'The terms of the 306 treaty [i.e. the Philinus treaty, according to Serrati] were renewed [in the 279/8 treaty], and additional clauses, all concerning military co-operation, were added.'

18   As Badian 1979 showed. Serrati 2006 offers no solution to this and chooses instead not even to acknowledge Badian's argument.

19   Cf. most notably, Mommsen 1859, 320–5; De Sanctis 1960, 239–40. This was an important part of Alföldi's (1965, 350–5) revised history of early Rome, but Alföldi's reconstruction has rightly been dismissed.

20   For example, Alföldi 1965, 354–5.

21   Mommsen 1859, 320–5; cf. Walbank 1957, 346; Oakley 1998, 258 and n. 20.

are also obviously grave problems with the idea that the treaty recorded by Philinus existed, and the only extant source for it, Polybius, who had investigated the matter of Rome's treaties with Carthage as thoroughly as he could, denied that it ever did so. There is every reason to believe that he was right.[22] Livy's treaty of 306, which Livy in any case says was only a renewal, cannot therefore be equated with Philinus' treaty.

It is not necessary to rehearse all the various other arguments and possible combinations thereof here. The important point is that, however the evidence for Rome's treaties with Carthage is merged together, the basic assumption behind all the numerous reconstructions is that the evidence *can* be so merged. And despite all the disagreements about the details, and about which of the various arguments should be adopted and which rejected, the basic methodology employed is essentially always the same. Arguably, however, both the methodology and the assumptions that lie behind it are deeply flawed.

It is best to begin at the beginning. The Carthaginians made a treaty with Rome; subsequently, and perhaps periodically, that treaty was renewed. At least twice the terms of it were altered, so that they were in accordance with contemporary conditions (Polybius' second treaty), and to make arrangements for dealing with Pyrrhus, but they may well have been altered on any number of other occasions. Three treaties between Rome and Carthage were apparently preserved (in the treasury of the aediles, according to Polybius),[23] for Polybius claims to have found and read them. Whether or not some other record of these events was ever made is simply unknown. The pontiffs might have put together some account,

22   See Badian 1979; Hoyos 1985; Oakley 1998, 258–62; Eckstein 2010.
23   Polyb. 3.26.1, with Walbank 1957, 353–4. There is no need to discuss the problems of this building here. The idea that the Romans secreted away or destroyed the evidence for the treaty that Philinus claimed existed (as Serrati 2006, 123 suggests, although he is not the first to do so) seems only to be evidence of desperation; the idea will not work in any case, as Oakley 1998, 261 n. 1 shows; see also Eckstein 2010, and n. 29 below. On the usual reconstruction, which Serrati follows, not only would the Philinus treaty itself need to have been removed, but so too would the treaty struck at the time of Pyrrhus' expedition, since, on that same reconstruction and given what Polyb. 3.25.2 says, the terms of the Philinus treaty would have also been included in that later treaty.

perhaps,[24] but there was certainly no native Roman historian working at this early date.[25] Later, Polybius related the contents of those three treaties and also the substance of a fourth, evidence for which he could not find himself, but for which Philinus of Agrigentum presumably could, if, that is, Philinus had not simply fabricated the whole thing outright. Later still, Diodorus found in some unknown source the claim that Rome's first treaty with Carthage was made in 348 and that another was made in 279/8. Livy, too, found evidence for treaties in 348 and 279/8 but, in addition to that, he also found evidence for a renewal in 306 and, for what it is worth, an embassy in 343. Like Diodorus', Livy's sources too remain elusive.

To suppose that all this evidence can be pieced together like some jigsaw puzzle and thus the history of Rome's alliances with Carthage recovered is to suppose that the contemporary evidence for the sequence of events became fragmented (if it was not already so to begin with), that Philinus, Polybius, Diodorus and Livy each preserve different fragments of that original evidence and also that what they preserve is for the most part of equal value. Various unhistorical details need to be cleared up, of course, and a few creases ironed out along the way, but once all that has been done, the different fragments need only to be put in order, and thus the complete history of Rome's alliances with Carthage can, it is assumed, be recovered.

This supposition not only requires that a good record was made of Rome's treaties with Carthage, but it also requires that only certain pieces

---

24 If they did, the chaotic state of the evidence may support the argument that Rome's historians did not consult their records (Rawson 1991, 1–15; Richardson 2011), or the argument that they were not easily consulted (Bucher 1987 [1995], 38). Wiseman 2018, V–VII has recently defended the old idea (Beloch 1926, 94) that the pontifical records only began to be kept after 300 BC, that is, following the passing of the Ogulnian law (for an even later date, see Rüpke 1993); see Frier 1979 and Wiseman 2018, X–XIII on their later publication. See also Richardson 2018 on Valerius Antias, and Chapter 6.

25 It is worth drawing attention to Livy 8.40.5: *nec quisquam aequalis temporibus illis scriptor exstat quo satis certo auctore stetur.* [Nor is there extant any writer contemporary with those times on whose authority it would be sufficient to depend.] Livy's comment was prompted by the presence of several major variant traditions concerning the events of 322.

of that record were available to Philinus, Polybius, Diodorus and Livy, and, in addition, that those pieces that were available to Philinus, for instance, were not available to Polybius, and that those pieces that were available to Polybius were not available (at all, or to the same extent) to Livy (or better, to his sources), and so on. By a stroke of incredible good luck, however, it must be supposed, these various authors have somehow managed between them to preserve a complete account. That does seem improbable.

There are further difficulties. The various arguments used to make all the evidence fit together not infrequently depend on the assumption that some part of each piece of the evidence is of value and that some part of it is not, that the different parts can be separated out and can stand independently of one another, and, on top of all that, that the good part can then be distinguished from the bad. So, for example, concerning Livy's claim that Rome's treaty with Carthage was renewed for the third time in 306, it is supposed that the date of 306 can be accepted as good, but that, if this treaty is to be equated with the one that Philinus recorded, the claim that the treaty was simply renewed in this year must be rejected; or, if the treaty is to be equated with Polybius' second, then it is the claim that it was renewed for the third time that must be jettisoned. But can Livy's notice that the treaty was renewed in 306 really stand independently of his claim that it was renewed for the third time in this year?

The same applies to Diodorus' evidence. It is often supposed that the date of 348 can be separated from the claim that the treaty struck in that year was the first, and that it is the date that is the good piece of evidence, rather than the claim of primacy (that is to say, and it is certainly less likely, that some good record that Rome's first treaty was struck with Carthage was not mistakenly dated to 348). Yet it is perfectly possible that it is both the date *and* the claim of primacy that are of no value. They could both very easily be part of the same flawed account and so cannot be separated from one another.

Anyone who wishes to adopt this sort of approach must also lay claim to being able to distinguish between those parts of the evidence that are good and those that are not. All too often, however, it seems to be the case that, in the end, it is only those parts of the evidence that fit the desired reconstruction that are accepted as good, while those that do not are discarded. The whole approach appears quite often to be entirely subjective and not infrequently circular in nature too.

III

Polybius states explicitly that Rome's first treaty with Carthage was struck in the consulship of M. Horatius and L. Iunius Brutus, that is to say, in 509.[26] Diodorus, in contrast, states explicitly that the first treaty with Carthage was made in the consulship of M. Valerius Corvus and M. Popilius Laenas, that is, in 348.[27] One possible way out of this impasse is to suppose that Diodorus' source was simply unaware of the treaty struck in the first year of the republican period and so innocently assumed that the treaty of 348 must have been the first.

This solution is not without problems of its own. If Diodorus' source had been one of those several historians, Q. Fabius Pictor, L. Cincius Alimentus, A. Postumius Albinus, C. Acilius, M. Porcius Cato or possibly even L. Cassius Hemina,[28] who wrote before Polybius had completed the final revision of his work, then potentially Polybius could have come across the claim that Rome's first treaty with Carthage was made in 348 while he was still writing. Had he done so, there is every reason to suppose that he would have mentioned it in his discussion of Rome's treaties with Carthage. Polybius certainly had no qualms about drawing attention to the errors of his predecessors; and, in fact, his discussion of the treaties is in part designed to disprove Philinus' claims.[29] This is, of course, an

---

26   Or 508/7 on Polybius' chronology, cf. Walbank 1957, 340.

27   Diod. 16.69.1; cf. Broughton 1951, 129–30.

28   See Walbank 1957, 27–9 on Polybius' Roman sources.

29   See Polyb. 3.26.2, where Polybius comments on the ignorance of Romans and Carthaginians about the treaties; this is presumably good evidence for his knowledge of what others said or had written about the topic. His comments are, of course, a further complication for those who maintain that the Romans had removed or destroyed the evidence for the Philinus treaty (see n. 23 above).

argument from silence, but to it can be added the conclusion of A. Klotz, who demonstrated long ago that Diodorus relied on late annalists for his Roman material.[30] The tradition that Rome's first treaty with Carthage was struck in 348 in all likelihood came from the work of someone who wrote after Polybius. If it did, there are two immediately obvious ways in which Diodorus' version may be explained.

First of all, Diodorus' source may, again, have simply been unaware (despite Polybius' extensive discussion of the matter) of the earlier treaty and so assumed that the treaty of 348 must have been the first. If this were the case, it would certainly not reflect all that well on the calibre of his source. Polybius' work was influential on later Roman historiography. His dictates concerning the requirements of the genre were evidently taken up by serious historians like Sempronius Asellio and perhaps also Cornelius Sisenna, while his account of later events was often closely followed by Livy, and for the very reason that Livy knew Polybius to be a good source.[31]

To this it can be added that, if Diodorus' source failed to include one treaty, then his source could very easily have failed to include more than one. An argument that requires that a source is flawed because it has omitted something must certainly be prepared to acknowledge the possibility that that source may have omitted more than one such thing. If Diodorus' claim that it was the first treaty between Rome and Carthage that was struck in 348 is to be rejected, then the treaty allegedly struck in that year could just as easily be the third or the fourth as it could the second. After all, Livy's claim that the treaty was renewed for the third time in 306 presupposes a number of earlier agreements. This is a possibility that needs to be emphasised. Modern reconstructions all suppose that no single extant source preserves a complete record of Rome's treaties with Carthage. Even if the sources are good in so far as what they do preserve, there must always remain the possibility that the extant evidence is *in sum* similarly incomplete. Indeed, the extant evidence for early Rome is so sparse

30   Klotz 1937.
31   Cf. Asellio *FRHist* 20 F1–2 (= Gell. *NA* 5.18.7–9); Badian 1966, 17–18; Frier 1979, 218–20; Rawson 1985, 218, 221–2; Rawson 1991, 373–4; Beck and Walter 2004, 88–9, 242; Briscoe 2013b, 308; Pobjoy 2013, 276; for his assessment of Polybius, see Livy 30.45.5, 33.10.10.

and difficult that it would be rather extraordinary if, somehow, a full and complete record of Rome's alliances with Carthage *had* been preserved.

The alternative explanation is that the claim that the first treaty was struck in 348 is simply a straightforward variant tradition. And, if that is the case, then it is impossible to reconcile Polybius' and Diodorus' evidence, because incompatible variant traditions, by definition, cannot be reconciled. Not surprisingly, given the state of the existing evidence, it is simply not possible to tell which of these causes is responsible for the disagreement in the sources concerning the year in which Rome's first treaty with Carthage was made. Having said that, however, if the variant traditions concerning the date of the first treaty are precisely that, variant traditions, rather than flawed reconstructions based on partially good and partially faulty evidence (which, in any case, must in themselves therefore constitute variant traditions), then it should not be surprising if significant and substantial parts of the rest of the evidence are also incompatible, and that is precisely what they are.

Polybius' second treaty is not dated by him. His third and only other treaty dates to 279/8. Diodorus records only two treaties, one in 348 and one in 279/8. Livy has a treaty in 348, another in 306 that presupposes two or even three earlier agreements and one more in 279/8. The only point therefore on which Polybius, Diodorus and Livy all agree is that a treaty was made between Rome and Carthage during the course of Pyrrhus' campaigns. About everything else, there is almost no consensus: Diodorus has only the one treaty struck prior to 279/8; Polybius has two; Livy also has two but, since he claims that the treaty was renewed for the third time in 306 and for the fourth in 279/8, he must in effect have three treaties (counting inclusively) or four (counting exclusively) struck before 279/8. The Philinus treaty is worth considering in this context too. Although Polybius does not say to which year Philinus assigned the treaty, or even if he provided a date for it at all, the content of it alone clearly constitutes in itself a variant tradition.

Important questions also need to be asked about the evidence for the treaties of 348 and 306: where does it come from,[32] and why did Polybius,

---

32   The claim that such material is 'pontifical' does not provide an easy escape, nor do recent arguments about Valerius Antias; see n. 24 above. On the treaty of 348, note p. 186.

who investigated the matter so carefully, seemingly not find any trace of
one or possibly even both of these agreements? Diodorus used late annalists and Livy tended to rely on them as well. Is their evidence really worthy
of all the trust that has been put in it?

What all these discrepancies and problems suggest is that Philinus,
Polybius, Diodorus and Livy do *not* in fact merely preserve different parts
of the same reliable account of events, as is generally supposed, but instead
pass on material drawn from a range of different sources, material that is
in some instances simply unreliable and in others incompatible too. It is
worth repeating that, by definition, mutually incompatible accounts cannot
simply be merged together. Polybius certainly records valuable material,
and Diodorus and Livy possibly do so as well, but the manner in which
their evidence is so often forced together into a single sequence is extremely
problematic, astonishingly simplistic and almost certainly unhistorical.

IV

Polybius claims that the Romans made their first treaty with Carthage
in the very first year after the expulsion of the kings. The identity of the
consuls of that year should pose no difficulties. L. Iunius Brutus, the in-
stigator of the conspiracy that deposed Tarquinius Superbus and the man
responsible for establishing the new republican regime, had to be one of
the pair, and he needed but a single colleague. According to Polybius,
that colleague was M. Horatius. In the more prevalent tradition, however, Brutus' colleague was instead L. Tarquinius Collatinus, although,
according to Cicero, Valerius Maximus and the Elder Pliny, P. Valerius
Publicola was one of the first consuls.[33] Only two names were required,
but the Romans managed to come up with five: L. Iunius Brutus,
L. Tarquinius Collatinus, P. Valerius Publicola, Sp. Lucretius Tricipitinus

---

33   Cic. *Flac.* 25; Val. Max. 2.4.5, 4.4.1; Plin. *HN* 36.112.

and M. Horatius Pulvillus. A solution to this problem was eventually found in a rather contrived and convoluted story. Brutus and Tarquinius Collatinus were accepted as the first consuls of Rome. Subsequently Tarquinius either abdicated, or was forced into exile, on account of the odium of his name, and Valerius Publicola was elected to replace him. Brutus then died, killed in battle, and so Lucretius replaced him, but only briefly, for he in turn conveniently passed away, just a few days after taking up office, thus allowing for his replacement by Horatius.[34]

It is obvious that this story represents an attempt to formulate a single, coherent narrative in which the various rival traditions could all be accommodated. But the attempt could only ever result in a compromise. The different traditions were simply incompatible. In Polybius' version, Brutus' colleague was Horatius but, in the later version, Brutus and Horatius did not even hold office together.

The point of this digression is, firstly, to give some brief indication of how prevalent and significant variant traditions can be.[35] Writers like Livy and Dionysius of Halicarnassus dominate the modern reception of the Roman historiographical tradition, but both were writing in the late first century BC and both were literary artists who sought to provide their readers with a single, unified and coherent narrative. As a consequence, it is all too easy to underestimate the extent and significance of variation in the tradition.[36] This discussion of Rome's first consuls is also useful because it illustrates well the dangers involved in attempting to reconcile variant

---

34 Sources in Broughton 1951, 1–3; cf. Wiseman 2008, 306–19; Wiseman 2014, 135–6; see also pp. 166–8 below.

35 Examples of variant traditions abound; to pursue only and briefly the theme of office-holding: see Livy 2.18.6–7 and Fest. 216L for the variant tradition that Rome's first dictator was M'. Valerius; and *De vir. ill.* 20.2 for the variant tradition that the first plebeian consul was Licinius Stolo; for uncertainty concerning the details of various magistracies, cf. Livy 4.7.10–12, 4.13.7, 4.20.5–11, 4.23.1–3, 7.42.3–7, 8.30.7, 9.44.15, 9.46.3, etc. See further Ridley 1983; Oakley 1997a, 13–15, 79–83, 108; Forsythe 1999; and Chapters 6 and 7.

36 It is worth quoting here Finley 1985, 9: 'The ability of the ancients to invent and their capacity to believe are persistently underestimated. How else could they have filled the blatant gaps in their knowledge ...? Or how could they contest an existing account other than by offering an alternative ...? No wonder that, even in

traditions. The evidence for Rome's treaties with Carthage is certainly better than the evidence for those who held office in the first year of the republican period, but the method used to reconcile the various variant traditions and to produce a coherent account of Rome's alliances with Carthage from those traditions is little different from that used by those Romans who, two millennia ago, sought to make sense of the various traditions of events immediately after the expulsion of the kings, and no one would today wish to accept as historical the results of *their* endeavours.

---

the hopelessly fragmentary state of the surviving material on early Rome, there is a bewildering variety of versions, a variety that continued to increase and multiply as late as the early Principate.'

CHAPTER 5

Ancient Historical Thought and the Development of the Consulship

I

For the first two and a half centuries of its existence, as far as the Romans were concerned, their city had been ruled by kings. The seventh, and the last, of these kings was the odious 'Tarquin the Proud'. He had been a cruel tyrant, and he and his family had abused their position. Inevitably a conspiracy had formed, and the Tarquins were shut out of the city and sent into exile.[1]

The rule of kings had, in the end, proved to be disastrous. A new system of government was clearly needed. Since the kings' authority had been total and without restraint, it was decided by the Romans that henceforth two men holding equal power should govern the state. With two men in office each could provide a check on the behaviour of the other. And, since each king's reign had lasted until the king had died or been deposed, it was further decided that the two men appointed to govern the state should hold office for just one year, after which time they should step down and return to private life.[2] Thus the dual consulship was created, and thenceforth, a few periods of disruption in the fifth and early fourth centuries BC aside,[3] the Romans elected two consuls every year to govern their state.

Told like that – and that is essentially how the Romans told it – the transition from monarchy to Republic seems both logical and natural. The last

1   Livy 1.49–60; Dion. Hal. *Ant. Rom.* 4.41–85, etc.
2   Sall. *Cat.* 6.7; Livy 2.18.8; Dion. Hal. *Ant. Rom.* 4.73.4; Plut. *Publ.* 1.4; Tac. *Ann.* 1.1; Flor. 1.9.2; Eutr. 1.9.1; August. *De civ. D.* 5.12; Wirszubski 1950, 22–3; Cornell 1995, 226; Wiseman 1995, 103.
3   See section III below.

king was expelled from the city and an office designed specifically to prevent the crimes that had been perpetrated by him from ever happening again was immediately set up. But unfortunately, nothing is ever quite so straightforward, and it has long been acknowledged that the tradition in fact contains a number of rather serious difficulties. Most notably, individuals from plebeian families appear among the early consuls (L. Iunius Brutus, the leader of the conspiracy to oust Tarquinius Superbus and one of the very first consuls, was himself from a plebeian family), even though tradition claimed that the first plebeian consul was not elected until as late as 367 BC. Prior to that date, plebeians were, supposedly, ineligible to hold the state's highest magistracy.[4] No less damaging to the tradition is the likelihood that Superbus may not even have been forced out of the city by those Romans who could endure his abuses no longer, but instead by the military operations of a rival king, Lars Porsenna of Clusium, who appears to have captured Rome.[5]

Despite the existence of these sorts of problems many have nonetheless sought to defend the tradition. Perhaps plebeians had been allowed to hold the consulship in the early years of the republican period, before the patricians had monopolised power, or perhaps, because the distinction between patricians and plebeians was probably not really or quite so readily applicable in the early fifth century BC, members of families subsequently classed as plebeian had previously been able to attain the state's highest office?[6] As for Lars Porsenna, if he captured Rome, that does not mean that Tarquinius Superbus was not a tyrant, or that Roman citizens were not involved in his expulsion from the city; and who knows what Porsenna's motives were if, in fact, he did expel Superbus?

---

4   Livy 7.1.1–2; further, Broughton 1951, 114; on the problems in the tradition, cf.,
      for example, von Fritz 1950; Billows 1989; and also the works cited in nn. 6 and 7
      below. On Brutus, see also Chapter 8.
5   See p. 99 n. 50.
6   Cf., for example, Cornell 1983; Drummond 1989, 175–6; Cornell 1995, 251–8;
      Forsythe 2005, 160–6. Note that, while Cornell is prepared to reject what ancient
      tradition has to say about the patrician and plebeian orders (1983) and also what
      it has to say about the Senate (1995, 247–8; see n. 23 below; Cornell 2014a), the
      idea that consuls followed the kings, and the consular *fasti*, are treated as absolutely
      sacrosanct.

In contrast to this, some have instead used these and other difficulties in the evidence as an opportunity to demolish the entire tradition and to offer alternative, and sometimes really quite elaborate, reconstructions of their own. The problem is, such reconstructions are inevitably unverifiable and, since they are modern, they are usually of less value than the original tradition itself. The result is that the predominant reaction now seems to be a broadly conservative one, with the majority, or so it would seem, either defending the ancient tradition or at least being happy to accept it largely as it stands.[7]

But, if elaborate modern reconstructions of Rome's early constitution are ultimately unpersuasive, does it follow that the ancient tradition should therefore be accepted by default, especially when there is good reason to suspect that it too is a reconstruction?

II

The Romans believed that their city was founded by Romulus and that Romulus was their first king. As the founder and first king, he established the insignia of the monarchy, and he gave the Romans a law-code. He set up the Senate and the patrician order. He divided the population into three tribes and thirty *curiae*, and he enrolled Rome's first army. He built Rome's first walls too and the first temples.[8] Rome certainly did

---

7   See, for example, Beloch 1926, esp. 9–22 on the early consular *fasti*; Werner 1963, esp. 264–79 on the consular *fasti*; Alföldi 1965, 80–4 (see also 80 n. 1 for further references); for an overview of scholarly reactions to the *fasti*, see Ridley 1980. For other reconstructions, see, for example, Mazzarino 1945; Hanell 1946; Gjerstad 1962; De Martino 1972; discussion in Momigliano 1989b, 171–6; Cornell 1995, 226–30. For the conservative reaction, note Heurgon 1973, 245–6.

8   Insignia: Livy 1.8.2–3; understood at Dion. Hal. *Ant. Rom.* 2.57.2, cf. 3.61; Plut. *Rom.* 26.2; law-code: Livy 1.8.1; Dion. Hal. *Ant. Rom.* 2.9.1, 2.10, 2.24–9; Plut. *Rom.* 22.3; Senate and patrician order: Livy 1.8.7; Dion. Hal. *Ant. Rom.* 2.8, 2.12, 2.47.1; Plut. *Rom.* 13; tribes and *curiae*: Dion. Hal. *Ant. Rom.* 2.7.2–4; Plut. *Rom.* 20.1–2;

not appear fully formed, as Athena from the head of Zeus, but it did in many ways simply appear, as did many of its oldest and most important institutions. That, at least, is what the Romans believed. Archaeological evidence, however, has revealed that Rome actually began life rather differently, both much earlier than the Romans generally imagined and in a less centralised and organised manner. Rome, after all, was not founded by one person at one precise moment and in one precise location; instead, it developed over a period of some considerable time.[9] It is a reasonable assumption that many of the institutions said to have been established by Romulus similarly evolved over time, but, as with the evolution of the city itself, there is little genuine appreciation of such developments in the literary tradition.

After Romulus came Numa Pompilius. He was a pious man and, according to the Romans, it was he who established all the city's major priesthoods and priestly colleges. He appointed the first pontiffs, the first Vestal virgins, the first flamens, the first augurs, the first Salian priests and so on.[10] Although many of these priestly colleges grew in size as the number of priests appointed increased over time, and although the criteria for admission and the method of appointment changed,[11] there is little to no sense in the tradition that the colleges and priesthoods themselves developed in any real way. Numa's priests and priestly colleges were in essence created fully formed, and they do not appear to be fundamentally different from those of later times. But again, a process of development can reasonably be assumed. The family unit at least necessarily precedes the state; priests of some kind and many of the duties performed by them almost certainly

curiae and centuries: Livy 1.13.6–8; army: implicit at Livy 1.10.4, etc.; Dion. Hal. *Ant. Rom.* 2.16.2, 2.33.2, note 2.37.5; Plut. *Rom.* 13.1; public works: Livy 1.7.2, 1.7.3, 1.8.4–5, 1.9.9, 1.10.7; Dion. Hal. *Ant. Rom.* 2.3.1, 2.18.2, 2.34.4, 2.37.1, 2.50.2–3; Plut. *Rom.* 10.1, 27.5. It is worth noting here also Alföldi 1965, 131–40.

9   See Chapter 1.

10   Livy 1.20; Dion. Hal. *Ant. Rom.* 2.64–73; Plut. *Numa* 7.4, 9–13. Some did claim that the cult of Vesta was established by Romulus (cf. Dion. Hal. *Ant. Rom.* 2.64.5–66.1; Plut. *Rom.* 22.1) but, given the nature of the cult, that is not surprising. The same circumstances apply in the case of the augurs (compare Cic. *Rep.* 2.16 with Livy 4.4.2).

11   Overview in Beard 1990, 20–1.

predate the existence of the state too; and many of Rome's priesthoods will, in any case, have developed over time, as will have their various duties and functions. The idea that they were almost all created at one moment in time and by one individual is entirely unhistorical.

Romulus was said to have created the first tribal system. The system was believed to have been archaic, so it was reasonable to hold Rome's founder and first king responsible for it. But Rome's citizens were later organised according to a quite different system, a system that (eventually) consisted of thirty-five tribes (of which four were urban and thirty-one rural) instead of Romulus' three, and of 193 centuries; and, rather than imagining that the later system might have evolved, perhaps in some way from the earlier, the Romans by and large preferred to credit the new system in its entirety to the reforms of just one individual.[12] That individual was Servius Tullius, Rome's sixth king.

Although the sources agree that it was Servius who established the new tribal and centuriate system, they disagree over how many tribes he actually set up. These discrepancies provide important evidence. Livy records the creation of fourteen new rural tribes from 387 to 241 BC.[13] That proves that the system that Servius was said to have established changed and expanded significantly over a lengthy period of time. And, if the total of thirty-five tribes was not reached until as late as 241, then Servius must have set up considerably fewer tribes. Yet, according to Fabius Pictor,[14] this king not only created the four urban tribes, but twenty-six of the rural tribes too; that is to say, Pictor thought that Servius had created a total of thirty tribes. The figure cannot be correct. Livy does not record the creation of the thirtieth tribe until 318.[15] The Elder Cato also believed that Servius must have created some of the rural tribes alongside the urban; perhaps wisely

12   It is still widely maintained that the Servian tribes simply replaced those of Romulus (Cornell 1995, 173, 185; Rix 2006, 167; Smith 2006b, 188; Capogrossi Colognesi 2014, 46; Fronda 2015, 48, etc.); Romulus' centuries were, in contrast, said to have been incorporated into Servius', see Livy 1.43.8–9 (although compare Dion. Hal. *Ant. Rom.* 4.18.1).

13   See p. 35 and n. 49.

14   Pictor *FRHist* 1 F9 (= Dion. Hal. *Ant. Rom.* 4.15.1).

15   Livy 9.20.6.

he did not say how many he believed Servius had actually created, but he too clearly assumed that the basic system of four urban tribes together with some number of rural tribes must have been set up by this king.[16] Worst of all, however, Vennonius claimed that Servius had actually established all thirty-one rural tribes alongside the four urban ones.[17] Since that gives a total of thirty-five tribes, it is obvious that Vennonius must have simply assumed that the conditions of his own day had existed from the very beginning. Fabius Pictor, perhaps remembering or perhaps finding evidence for the creation of five tribes, reduced the number that Servius had supposedly established, while Cato assumed only that Servius had created some rural tribes. Ultimately, however, their different approaches are as unhistorical as Vennonius', simply because the only change of which they can conceive is a quantitative one.

Precisely the same difficulties can be found in the evidence for the centuriate organisation. According to both Livy and Dionysius, Servius divided the citizen population into 193 centuries according to wealth and, in some instances, occupation.[18] But that was the system that existed in much later times and it is highly unlikely that Servius had actually arranged the people in such an elaborate and complicated way. In fact, it has been plausibly argued that, in the earliest form of the centuriate system, Rome's citizens were divided into just two groups, a single class and those who fell below it.[19] The system that consisted of 193 centuries presumably evolved from this considerably simpler version, although there is not one hint of this process in the literary tradition. Again, it has been assumed that the conditions that existed in much later times had existed in earlier, and that the centuriate organisation had been established in its mature form by Servius Tullius.

16   Cato *FRHist* 5 F17 (= Dion. Hal. *Ant. Rom.* 4.15.1).
17   Vennonius *FRHist* 13 F2 (= Dion. Hal. *Ant. Rom.* 4.15.1).
18   Livy 1.43; Dion. Hal. *Ant. Rom.* 4.16–18; musicians and engineers were enrolled in centuries of their own, Livy 1.43.3, 1.43.7; Dion. Hal. *Ant. Rom.* 4.17.3.
19   Cornell 1995, 183–6; cf. Gell. *NA* 6.13.1–2. See further p. 95 n. 35.

What these several stories serve to illustrate is just how unhistorical the ancients could be in their approach to the past. It is a well-recognised fact that Rome's historians tended to assume that the conditions of their own day had existed in earlier times.[20] Nor was it just historians who approached the past in this manner. Artists could equally present historical figures in the costume and style of the present.[21] What was lacking was not just an appreciation that the past could be profoundly different from the present, but also an appreciation that things naturally change and develop over time. The Senate, for instance, was created at that one moment in time in which Romulus invented it; so too was the college of the pontiffs created at that precise moment in time in which Numa invented it. Neither had existed previously in any prior form, and both were effectively created fully formed. It was only really the numbers of senators and pontiffs that ever changed. Indeed, the only change that was recognised, if any was recognised at all, was usually quantitative in nature; only rarely were other types of change noted.[22] And, if the past is viewed in such a way, how could the dual consulship *not* have existed from the very beginning of the republican period?

20   See p. 29 n. 25. Differences could be stressed, but for literary and political purposes, rather than in the attempt to reconstruct the past, cf. the comments of Wiseman 1979b, 42; Wiseman 2008, 125–7.

21   Small 1991, 247–50; 247–8: 'It never occurred to them [i.e. the Romans and the Etruscans] that the past was *physically* different from the present. It might be morally better or worse, but its accoutrements were contemporary ... If one could not literally see the past and how it was different, what grounds would one have for knowing that it was different?' Cf. Richardson 2017, 250–63.

22   Luce 1977, 234–9 argues that Livy was to a certain extent aware of the idea of historical development. But Livy's model is still, by modern standards, essentially unhistorical. Livy's Senate (one of Luce's examples, p. 240), for instance, develops in stages as individual kings add new members; the changes that take place are consequently only in size and membership; the fundamental nature of the Senate itself (i.e. what it is and what it does) does not alter.

III

After the kings came the Republic, and with the Republic came the consuls. But is that really how it happened? Just as there was a Senate, numerous priestly colleges, thirty-five tribes and 193 centuries when Rome's historians were working, so there were also two consuls elected every single year. Is it possible therefore that the idea that the dual consulship was created immediately after the last king was expelled is an assumption, an assumption greatly reinforced by the belief that the dual consulship was central to the definition of the free Republic,[23] but an assumption nonetheless, and one just as unhistorical as the idea that Romulus established the Senate, that Numa set up the major priestly colleges or that Servius Tullius created all the tribes and centuries? As it happens, just as there is good evidence that shows that Servius did not set up thirty-five tribes and 193 centuries, so there is also good evidence that shows that the state's chief magistracy likewise changed and that the dual consulship was developed at a later date.

Livy knew that the consuls had not always been called consuls; previously they had been known as praetors.[24] The difference is important because the change in name suggests a change in the ideology of the state's chief magistracy, if not an outright change in the magistracy itself. As far as the meaning of these names goes, a praetor was simply one who led, but a consul was one who consulted, or who took council, and that implies a sense of equality that the name praetor simply does not.[25] Livy also found good evidence for an early magistrate called the *praetor maximus*.[26] The

---

23   Compare Cornell's remarks (1995, 248) on the Senate: '[the sources] presuppose the existence of a permanent Senate from the earliest times; but this may be based on no more than the unthinking assumption, which came naturally to the annalists and to conservative political thinkers such as Cicero, that the Senate had always been an important part of the Roman political system.' The same could just as easily apply to the consulship.

24   Livy 3.55.12; also Fest. 249L; cf. Oakley 1998, 77–9.

25   See p. 100 n. 55.

26   Livy 7.3.5; note also Fest. 152L; cf. Heurgon 1964; also Wiseman 1979b, 45; Oakley 1998, 81.

title, and the context of Livy's notice, suggest that the *praetor maximus* was a magistrate of some considerable authority, and the office is quite probably to be connected in some way with those praetors who were once Rome's chief magistrates before the consuls took over, rather than with the better known praetors of later times, for the later type of praetorship was not established until 367 BC.[27] Since the use of superlative adjectives in Latin could be flexible, no conclusion about the number of these early praetors can be drawn from the word *maximus* alone.[28] Nonetheless, the use of the superlative makes it quite clear that parity was not the defining characteristic of the *praetor maximus*; and yet parity *was* one of the defining characteristics of the dual consulship. All this is, therefore, either evidence of development in the state's highest magistracy or evidence of significant change; but, either way, the sources ultimately know nothing of the process whereby the early praetors were replaced by, or evolved into, the consuls.

If the dual consulship was indeed central to the definition of the Republic and of republican liberty, as tradition claims, it is rather surprising that on several occasions the Romans were more than prepared to forego the election of consuls, and that they were even prepared to appoint a single magistrate who not only held supreme authority but who also quite obviously held it alone.

It was only a few years after the expulsion of Tarquinius Superbus, or so the Romans believed, that monarchy (that is, the rule of one man) returned to the city. In the very late sixth century BC or in the very early fifth (the sources disagree on the precise date),[29] the Romans appointed their first dictator, a single magistrate who held absolute power.[30] According to one tradition, the dictatorship was created precisely so that one man would, by virtue of the absolute power that the office conferred on him,

27   Cf. Livy 6.42.11, 7.1.2.
28   Momigliano 1989b, 177; Oakley 1998, 79–80.
29   Livy 2.18.1–5; Dion. Hal. *Ant. Rom.* 5.70.4–73.1; see Werner 1968, 61–4 on the relative chronologies behind the different dates.
30   Dion. Hal. *Ant. Rom.* 5.70.3: the dictator possessed powers equivalent to those of a tyrant and was above the law; by agreeing to the creation of this office, Dionysius claims (5.70.4), the people lost their freedom. See also Cic. *Rep.* 2.56; Livy 8.32.3; and Dion. Hal. *Ant. Rom.* 5.71–75.3.

be able to circumvent the appeal laws, laws that had supposedly been designed to prevent the sort of abuse that had occurred under the last king.[31] Another tradition claimed that the dictatorship was created to help prevent the exiled Superbus from regaining his throne: the rule of one man was restored (even if temporarily) to prevent the restoration of the rule of one man.[32] Neither tradition is especially compelling, and both traditions, along with the actual dictatorship itself, plainly subvert the anti-monarchic ideology that had supposedly led to the creation of the dual consulship in the first place. All this, incredibly enough, was said to have happened barely a decade after the very creation of the consulship itself.

About half a century later, in 451, the consuls said to have been elected for that year only came to office briefly, if they did so at all, and the election of consuls for 450 was suspended completely. Instead, in both years, a board of ten men was appointed. Their task was to draw up a law-code for the city, but they were given executive powers too.[33] Just a few years after that the consulship was – intermittently at first, but soon with some regularity – once again suspended. Henceforth the consuls were replaced with teams (of varying size) of military tribunes with consular power.[34] Since the patricians had been unwilling to allow plebeians to hold the consulship, this new executive office, according to one version of events, was created so that plebeians could gain access to the state's highest magistracy. The explanation does not seem very convincing, not least because so very few plebeians were ever elected to the consular tribunate.[35] An alternative

31   Dion. Hal. *Ant. Rom.* 5.70.2–5; Livy 2.18.8; cf. Cornell 1995, 226 on the appeal laws. Since Dionysius cites Licinius Macer (*Ant. Rom.* 5.74.4 = *FRHist* 27 F15) and criticises Sulla (*Ant. Rom.* 5.77.4–6), it is a reasonable guess that this explanation for the dictatorship comes from Macer; cf., for example, Musti 1970, 116–17; Drummond 1989, 191; Oakley 2013d, 429.

32   Livy 2.18.3–4; cf. Ridley 1979, 308. For the dictator as a tyrant appointed to oppose tyranny, see Dion. Hal. *Ant. Rom.* 5.70.2.

33   See Broughton 1951, 45–7.

34   See Broughton 1951, 52–113; overviews in Ridley 1986, 462–5; Oakley 1997a, 368.

35   Livy 4.6.8; cf. also 4.7.1, 4.7.7–9, 4.16.6, 4.25.1–2, etc.; Dion. Hal. *Ant. Rom.* 11.53–61, esp. 11.56.3; von Fritz 1950, 8, 37; Ogilvie 1965, 539–40; Ridley 1986, 462–5; Drummond 1989, 193–4; Cornell 1995, 335–7; Oakley 1997a, 373–6; Forsythe 2005, 235, 238–9.

explanation maintained that the consular tribunate was created for military reasons: sometimes two consuls were not sufficient to meet the demands of the day. But this explanation is no more convincing, since consular tribunes were often elected in peaceful years, while the dictatorship was still employed for military purposes when consular tribunes were in office.[36]

The consular tribunate could be evidence of development in the chief magistracy of the state, or it could be evidence of complete change, but the Romans, since they assumed that the consulship had existed from the very beginning of the republican period, could only ever present the election of consular tribunes as an interruption to the normal practice of electing consuls, and it is for this reason that they were then forced to concoct the various explanations found in the tradition for why the consulship was laid to one side and for why the consular tribunate was used in its place. If these explanations have proved to be unsatisfactory (and they certainly have), that is not just because the explanations themselves are inadequate, but it is above all because the whole premise on which they are based (namely that the consular tribunate replaced the dual consulship) is quite probably unhistorical.

The existence of the dictatorship, of the decemvirs and of the consular tribunes is enough, wrote T. P. Wiseman some twenty-five years ago, 'to invalidate the idea that from the start the Republic simply *was* the consulship'.[37] When the tradition of the dual consulship is assessed in the context of a discussion of the unhistorical way in which the ancients thought about the past, and the unhistorical assumptions that they made about their past, Wiseman's conclusion seems inescapable. There is evidence for other systems

---

36   Livy 4.7.2, but this is contradicted at 4.17.6–7 and 4.25.14–26.1; note also 4.31.2; Ogilvie 1965, 540; De Martino 1972, 247; Drummond 1989, 194; Cornell 1995, 337; Oakley 1997a, 373–6; cf. also Ridley 1986, 446–7 for the dictators appointed while consular tribunes were in office, and esp. 457–9 on the military achievements of the consular tribunes; Ridley concludes (459): 'It is hard to imagine a military command more ineffective or with a sorrier record.' None of the consular tribunes appears to have triumphed, cf. Degrassi 1947, 66–7 (although the *fasti triumphales* break off after 437 and only begin again with 367); Zonar. 7.19.5. This does not read like the history of a magistracy established for military purposes. See further Chapter 6.

37   Wiseman 1995, 104.

of government and there is evidence for change. If the ancients failed to recognise this evidence for what it is, and if they simply assumed that the consulship must have existed from the outset, that is to be expected. They were after all only adopting their usual approach to the past.

IV

When Vennonius claimed that Servius Tullius had set up thirty-five tribes, he was clearly assuming that the system as it existed in his own day had not changed since it was first established, and he was clearly also assuming that it had been established in its fully developed form. Vennonius may be an extreme example, but he is far from being an isolated one. Naturally no one today would ever accept Vennonius' evidence, simply because there is other, better evidence that shows that the tribal system had in fact evolved over the course of several centuries.

There is just as much good evidence that the dual consulship developed over time as there is that the tribal system did. If few are prepared to treat this evidence as proof of change and development, that is because most have adopted without question the ancient view that the dual consulship was established in its mature form the very moment the monarchy was abolished. The rule of the decemvirs and the appointment of military tribunes with consular power are, therefore, still treated as nothing more than interruptions to the usual practice of appointing consuls; and Livy's comment that consuls were once called praetors is still effectively discarded as unimportant.[38] But the modern historian who maintains that the Romans began to elect two consuls each year immediately after they had expelled their kings is in danger of defending an assumption that may be no more historical than Vennonius' claim that Servius Tullius had established thirty-five tribes.

38   Cf. Cornell 1995, 226.

So when might the dual consulship have been developed, if not in the late sixth century BC? Considerable caution is necessary. Modern reconstructions must inevitably contradict ancient tradition and so can scarcely be based on any direct evidence.[39] There may be some indirect evidence however. Tradition maintained that, following the 'interruption' of the consular tribunes, the dual consulship was reintroduced in 367 BC. It has very plausibly been suggested that the dual consulship may have instead been simply introduced in 367.[40] This suggestion fits extremely well with the argument so far. Since the Romans came to believe that the consulship was created at the same time as the Republic, they could naturally only ever conceive of the election of consular tribunes as an interruption to the usual practice of appointing consuls, and so, in turn, they could only conceive of the subsequent introduction of the consulship as the restoration of that office. But if that initial belief about the creation of the consulship is discarded as the product of unhistorical thinking, and if the evidence for change in the state's chief magistracy is taken for what it actually is, then it can only be concluded that this part of Rome's constitution must also have changed over time (just as the tribal and centuriate systems did), and that the dual consulship must have been created at a later date (just as the total of thirty-five tribes and 193 centuries was reached at a later date).

A date in the mid-fourth century provides the perfect context for the creation of a dual magistracy. Such a date means that the development of the consulship can be put in the context of the conflict of the orders (as the reintroduction is by the ancient sources, a fact that does rather undermine the idea that the dual consulship was really all about preventing the sort of abuses that can happen under a monarchy). The conflict of the orders

39   The approach of simply removing plebeian and other problematic names from the consular *fasti* (see works cited in n. 7 above) is flawed. The consular *fasti* are a late document, and a document put together in the belief that the Romans had always elected two consuls following the expulsion of the kings. The earlier part of the consular *fasti* is best dismissed in its entirety, cf. Wiseman 1995, 104–5; Wiseman 2014, 135–6; Chapter 6.

40   De Martino 1972; Wiseman 1995, 106–7; Welwei 2000, 49–50. Note also Kraus 1991 on the striking parallels between the stories of Lucretia and Fabia Minor, stories that are connected with the expulsion of the kings and the opening up of the consulship to the plebs respectively; Richardson 2012, 153–9.

is of course the struggle in which, in its later stages at least, the plebeians sought to gain access to high office and political power. One consul could come from the plebs and the other from the patricians, and thus the new system allowed for both orders to be represented at the level of the state's highest and most prestigious magistracy.[41]

But if the dual consulship arose out of social conflict and was an institution designed to facilitate power-sharing between the two orders (or indeed if the dual consulship was established at almost any time and in almost any context other than that which the tradition claims), then the anti-monarchic ideology with which it was associated must represent a subsequent development. When might this change have taken place? Such a radical shift in ideology would be unlikely to occur until the original ideology that had led to the creation of the office in the first place had lost its significance (or had been forgotten), and until circumstances required that a new one be adopted. There are two immediately obvious and plausible contexts for the development of an ideology for the consulship that was hostile to kings. First, in the early third century BC, when King Pyrrhus of Epirus invaded Italy and went to war with the Romans. It has been convincingly argued that it was also at about this time that the Romans were organising and developing many of their historical traditions.[42] And second, in the late third century and in the early second, when the Romans clashed with the kings of the Hellenistic east and even dismantled the oldest Hellenistic kingdom of them all, the kingdom of Macedonia. The Romans replaced the Macedonian monarchy with a series of republics and, by doing so, or so they claimed, they bestowed liberty on the Macedonian people.[43] An important component of this liberty was the

41 See the works cited in the previous note. Cornell 1995, 228 labels the idea 'attractive' but rejects it nonetheless, simply because plebeian consuls were not regularly elected until 342; but it is easy to imagine that, for instance, there was a concerted patrician effort to dominate the new office.

42 Gabba 2000, 11–23; note Wiseman 2014 on the development of the myth of L. Brutus, and Sordi 1972, 62–5 on the battle of Lake Regillus (in which Tarquinius Superbus was finally defeated by the Romans).

43 Polyb. 36.17.13 and Walbank 1979, 467, 681–2; Diod. 31.8.1–9; Livy 45.18.1–6, 45.29.1–10, 45.30.1, 45.32.1–2; Plut. *Aem.* 28.6, 29.1. Compare Livy 2.15.3: *non in regno populum Romanum sed in libertate esse* [the Roman people were not ruled

election of annual magistrates;[44] and the dual consulship was of course the annual magistracy of Rome *par excellence*. If the anti-monarchic ideology of the consulship did not already exist, then here is the perfect context in which it might have developed.

If the dual consulship was indeed introduced in 367, then by the end of the third century it would have been the chief magistracy of the Roman state for over 150 years. After such a long period of time the belief that it was inseparable from the Republic could easily have become well entrenched, and so with it the assumption that the election of consuls must have begun when the Republic did. It was also at the end of the third century and during the course of the second that Rome's first historians were writing. Since they wrote in Greek it is reasonable to assume that they expected or were at least open to the possibility of a Greek audience.[45]

---

by a king, but were free] with Livy 45.29.12: *omnibus dare libertatem pronuntiavit, qui sub regno Persei fuissent* [[Aemilius Paullus] announced that freedom was being given to everyone who had been under the rule of King Perseus]. Note also Richardson 2013.

44 Compare Livy 2.1.1 (after Superbus' expulsion from Rome): *liberi iam hinc populi Romani res pace belloque gestas, annuos magistratus, imperiaque legum potentiora quam hominum peragam* [From now on I shall be describing the exploits of the free Roman people in peace and in war, annual magistrates and the rule of laws more powerful than men] with Livy 45.29.4 (after King Perseus had been defeated): *omnium primum liberos esse iubere Macedonas, habentes urbes easdem agrosque, utentes legibus suis, annuos creantes magistratus* [[the Senate and Paullus] ordered, first of all, that the Macedonians were to be free, having the same cities and lands, enjoying their own laws and electing annual magistrates]; see Gruen 1984, 143–57 on Rome's adoption of the Greek rhetoric of liberty; the inclusion of annual magistrates as a prerequisite of liberty is a new, and Roman feature of that rhetoric (obviously no Hellenistic king could ever have moved in this direction), and the possible implications of this for the history of the consulship are obvious.

45 Cf., for example, Badian 1966, 3–6; Momigliano 1989b, 403–4; Bispham and Cornell 2013, 168 on Fabius Pictor. The idea has been challenged, on the grounds that there is no evidence that Pictor ever found a Greek audience, and that Latin historiography did not yet exist (e.g. Gruen 1984, 254), but Pictor was certainly read in Tauromenium (cf. *FRHist* 1 T7), while people like Livius Andronicus evidently found the absence of Latin texts no hurdle to using that language for literary purposes (cf. Momigliano 1989b, 398; Bispham and Cornell 2013, 169), nor did it stop the Elder Cato.

Rather than telling how Rome's highest office had arisen out of domestic strife – assuming they were even aware that it had, and they probably were not – they may well have preferred to pass over those problems, to present an image of a united Rome,[46] and to claim that the consulship had arisen in opposition to the abuses of kings and for the defence of liberty.[47] The political value of such an ideology for Rome in the second century would have been considerable. This is not to suggest that the idea that Rome was liberated when Tarquinius Superbus' rule was brought to an end is late, or equally that Roman dislike of monarchy is necessarily late, but simply that the precise anti-monarchic ideology with which the dual consulship was so specifically associated represents a further development of that office (as would inevitably have to be the case if the consulship had originated in the conflict of the orders). The sources are of course unaware of any such developments, but that should come as no surprise.

46 As Polybius appears to have done, cf. Momigliano 1975, 26–7. Rome's earliest historians produced short works and handled affairs after the foundation of the city and before their own times in a summary fashion (cf. Dion. Hal. *Ant. Rom.* 1.6.2). In how much depth could they have covered domestic affairs, especially of the fourth century?

47 Cf. Billows 1989, 127–30, also 131–2 on patterns in office-holding; the ideal of shared power (as a way of avoiding monarchy) would suit the pattern of office-holding discernible in the second century B C much better than that in earlier centuries.

CHAPTER 6

The Roman Nobility, the Early Consular *Fasti* and the Consular Tribunate

In his well-known and influential paper, 'An Interim Report on the Origins of Rome', A. Momigliano observed that '[n]othing was remembered of what the Fabii had done during the monarchy.' In the accompanying footnote he suggested that this may say something about the honesty of Fabius Pictor, Rome's first historian, for, he said, Pictor 'must have known ... that the Fabii were as old as Romulus.'[1] According to the story that the founder of the *gens* was a child of Hercules, conceived during the hero's visit to the site of Rome,[2] the Fabii were much older than that. More importantly, they must have been influential from an early date too, if the naming of one of the so-called 'Servian' tribes after them is any indication.[3]

---

1   Momigliano 1963, 118, and n. 97 which reads: 'This is perhaps not irrelevant if one tries to assess Fabius Pictor's honesty as a historian: to the best of our knowledge he did not attribute any role to his family in the monarchic period, though he must have known (from the Luperci Fabiani) that the Fabii were as old as Romulus.' See also Momigliano 1990, 104–5; 105: 'the striking thing about our tradition on the Fabii is that it is silent about their activities, if any, in the monarchic period. This means, of course, that no authentic recollection had been preserved of the prerepublican Fabii, but it also means that Fabius Pictor did not try to remedy the deficiencies of the tradition by inventions of his own.' More recently, see Bispham and Cornell 2013, 176.

2   Sil. *Pun.* 6.627–36; Plut. *Fab.* 1.1; Paul. Fest. 77L.

3   Cf. Cornell 1995, 173–9; Wiseman 2004, 56; Taylor 2013, 4–6, 35–7. As Momigliano notes (n. 1 above), one of the two teams of *Luperci* was similarly named after the Fabii. The antiquity of that is uncertain, however, despite the connection with Remus; if a third group of *Luperci* could be added in Iulius Caesar's day, and even projected back to Romulus' and Remus' time (Dion. Hal. *Ant. Rom.* 1.80.2 = *FRHist* 38 F3), there is no reason why the *Luperci Fabiani* must have been

The first Fabii to be found in the evidence, however, are the three brothers, Quintus, Kaeso and Marcus, who allegedly held in succession one of the two consulships from 485 to 479.[4] Their father, Kaeso, must (in theory) have lived during the regal period, as must they, but if he did anything, there is no trace of it. Kaeso's name is only found in the evidence because his sons held political office in the republican period;[5] had they not done so, there would be no evidence even for that. As for the rest of Kaeso's family, there is not one word.[6] And the same is true for most of the other *gentes* that ought to have had members alive at Rome in the regal period.[7]

Momigliano's argument, that Fabius Pictor must have been honest because the Fabii are absent from the regal period, obviously requires that there was no evidence for the Fabii who lived at that time and thus no one was able to write anything about them. Had anyone done so, this would necessarily have been dishonest. It is fair to say that Momigliano could have drawn a comparable conclusion about any number of other *gentes*, including those that did not produce historians.[8] Nothing much, if anything at all, was said about them, because there was simply no evidence.

---

primordial. See Wiseman 1995, 80, 86, 126–7; Wiseman 2008, 73–4, for the suggestion of a late fourth-century context for the creation of the *Luperci Fabiani*.

4 The consuls of 485 were Ser. Cornelius and Q. Fabius; of 484, L. Aemilius and K. Fabius; 483, M. Fabius and L. Valerius; 482, Q. Fabius and C. Iulius; 481, K. Fabius and Sp. Furius; 480, M. Fabius and Cn. Manlius; 479, K. Fabius and T. Verginius; for the evidence, see Broughton 1951, 21–5; for a discussion of the evidence, see Richardson 2012, 65–77.

5 Dion. Hal. *Ant. Rom.* 8.83.1: Καίσων Φάβιος Καίσωνος υἱός [Kaeso Fabius, the son of Kaeso]; 8.87.2: Μάρκος Φάβιος Καίσωνος υἱός [Marcus Fabius, the son of Kaeso]; 8.90.5: Κόιντον Φάβιον Καίσωνος υἱὸν [Quintus Fabius, the son of Kaeso]. In each instance, Dionysius is giving the names of the new consuls (for 484, 483 and 482 respectively).

6 Jerome does have Remus killed with a spade by a certain Fabius (Jer. *Chron.* p. 152 Fotheringham); Wiseman 1995, 10 notes in this context the story that the Fabii got their name from their alleged practice of digging pits to catch animals (Plut. *Fab.* 1.2 ['Fodii' from *fossae* [ditches] and *fodere* [to dig]]; Paul. Fest. 77L); Jerome's variant could be a learned inference, from the use of spades; it is, in any case, of no historical value.

7 See Wikander 1993, 88.

8 As, indeed, he does in his contribution to the second edition of the *Cambridge Ancient History* (1989a, 89–90) where, alongside the Fabii, he also discusses the

In contrast to this, it has been said more recently that Rome's nobility has been 'more or less wholly written out' of the traditions of the regal period.[9] That obviously implies that Rome's nobility was once there, in the literary tradition, but that it was later removed for some reason. This is a much more difficult proposition, and it seems better to say not that Rome's nobility was 'written out', but that it was never 'written in'. That would be in keeping too with the general trend for historical works at Rome to get longer and fuller (this is the phenomenon that E. Badian memorably called 'the expansion of the past');[10] although, significantly, even then, the nobility was not written in. It would seem that there was no reason for them to be written into the traditions of the regal period, and that was, presumably, because there was nothing to be gained by doing so.

It is, however, an entirely different story when it comes to the republican period, especially after the emergence in the mid-fourth century of the office-holding nobility for whom office-holding was, naturally enough, so very important. By then, there *was* something to be gained by being 'written in', that is, at least, by being written into the traditions of the Republic. For Rome's office-holding nobility, ancestors from the regal period just did not matter, since they did not hold political office. They could not, because, the position of king aside, there was none for them to hold (which is why Momigliano's argument about Pictor's honesty does not really work).[11]

Valerii, the Claudii, the Marcii and the Trojan families that came from Alba Longa. See also Cornell 1995, 10; Bispham and Cornell 2013, 176.

9   Smith 2011b, 36; Smith's comments are worth quoting in full: 'A nice side question of course is 'where is the Roman aristocracy for the so-called regal period?' They are more or less wholly written out. We may well wonder about the processes by which this may have happened, but it does seem to me at least a surprise that a historical tradition which allegedly is forged by elite families managed to be on the one hand so self-effacing as to omit themselves from the first two hundred years of their history, and on the other hand so accommodating as to allow the Tullii, Marcii, and Hostilii to insert themselves in the fifth, fourth, and third centuries, as Wiseman suggested.' For Wiseman's suggestions about the Tullii, Marcii and Hostilii, see n. 11 below.

10   Badian 1966, 11.

11   Wiseman 2008, 315 suggests that the kings Servius Tullius, Ancus Marcius and Tullus Hostilius may be inventions, of the Tullii, Marcii and Hostilii in, respectively, the fifth century, the late fourth century and the late third century. The

For the office-holding nobility, only ancestors from the republican period mattered, and above all those ancestors who had held the consulship, for that office in particular was, as F. E. Adcock succinctly put it decades ago, 'the hallmark of their rank'.[12]

So the issue is not so much the absence of the Fabii and all the various other *gentes* from the traditions of the regal period, although that absence is certainly important evidence. The issue is really the sudden and almost full appearance of the Roman nobility in the traditions of the earliest Republic, and even more so since the nobility generally appears with the consulship. In the first year alone (509 BC), individuals from no fewer than eight different *gentes* can be found in the evidence, and that is just in terms of office-holding and priesthoods. Five of these eight *gentes* allegedly produced consuls in this year.[13] In the first thirty years of the republican period (509–480), as many as twenty-five different *gentes* supposedly made their first appearance with the consulship.[14] That is almost a new *gens* a year. This is, moreover, to note only the first appearance of each *gens* in

number of positions available was, of course, capped at seven. The idea that quaestors had existed in the regal period (see Tac. *Ann.* 11.22; Ulp. *Dig.* 1.13.1.*pr.*) is hardly of any historical value; the position was a junior one in any case, cf. pp. 173–4.

12 Adcock 1957, 13; more recently, Forsythe 2005, 167; this is, however, to simplify somewhat; cf. Hölkeskamp 1993 for something more nuanced. See Wikander 1993, 79–80 for an analysis of the numismatic evidence, which shows a similar trend: little interest in ancestors from the regal period, but a clear interest (more than two thirds of the evidence, according to Wikander) in ancestors who lived after 367 (in which year the Licinio-Sextian legislation was passed, legislation crucial for the establishment of the consulship and the formation of the office-holding nobility).

13 Evidence in Broughton 1951, 1–4; on the first year of the republican period, see Wiseman 2008, 306–12 and pp. 166–8 below. The word *gens* is used here and in the following discussion purely for convenience; whether or not it can rightly be used of plebeians is not a consideration (on that question, see Oakley 2005b, 112–16).

14 Following Broughton 1951, 1–24: Iunius, Tarquinius, Valerius, Lucretius, Horatius (509 BC); Postumius (505); Menenius (503); Verginius, Cassius (502); Cominius (501); Sulpicius, Tullius (500); Aebutius (499); Cloelius (498); Servilius (495); Geganius (492); Iulius, Pinarius (489); Nautius, Furius (488); Aquillius (487); Cornelius, Fabius (485); Aemilius (484); Manlius (480).

the evidence for magistracies, other offices and priesthoods; and a number of further *gentes*, including some the members of which also reached the consulship in this same period, appear for the first time in positions other than the consulship.

If the evidence, which is problematic and sometimes extremely so, for those other magistracies and posts is included, a further seventeen *gentes* can – according to the material collected in T. R. S. Broughton's *The Magistrates of the Roman Republic* – potentially be added to the total for this thirty-year period.[15] Of these seventeen *gentes*, six produced consuls in these same years too (the Herminii, in 506; the Larcii, also in 506; the Veturii, in 499; the Minucii, in 497; the Sempronii, in 497 too; and the Claudii, in 495) and, given the great difficulties with the evidence for junior positions, it may well be that all six could have originally appeared for the first time with a consulship. The Claudii, for instance, may have first appeared with a quaestorship in 496 (the story of their arrival at Rome aside), although it is only a conjecture that they did. In any case, Broughton dismisses the evidence; the quaestorship, he says, is 'hardly authentic'.[16] Without it, the Claudii would have appeared for the first time with a consulship in the following year (495). The same could very easily apply to any of the other *gentes* in this same position. There are two more quaestors,[17] one prefect of the city,[18] and two men who appear as tribunes of the soldiers and as legates, or so Broughton suggests.[19] If any of these

15   Broughton 1951, 3–25: Minucius, Veturius (quaestors, 509); Herminius, Larcius (legates, 508); Sempronius (prefect of the city, 499); Claudius (quaestor, 496); Albinius, Licinius, Sicinius, Viscellius [Icilius?] (tribunes of the plebs, 493); Decius, Icilius (envoys, 493); Rabuleius, Mucius (tribunes of the plebs, 486); Maenius (tribune of the plebs, 483); Pontificius (tribune of the plebs, 480); Siccius (legate, 480).

16   Broughton 1951, 12.

17   M. Minucius and P. Veturius were quaestors in 509; Broughton 1951, 3. The Veturii reached the consulship for the first time in 499 and the Minucii in 497; Broughton 1951, 10, 12.

18   A. Sempronius in 499; Broughton 1951, 11. The Sempronii reached the consulship for the first time in 497; Broughton 1951, 12.

19   T. Herminius and Sp. Larcius in 508; Broughton 1951, 5. The Herminii and the Larcii both reached the consulship for the first time in 506; Broughton 1951, 6. On both, see Forsythe 2005, 154.

should prove to be later inventions, and it is highly likely that they all are, the total number of *gentes* to appear for the first time with a consulship in the years 509 to 480 could potentially have been as high as thirty-one. This would mean that, on average, a new *gens* appeared each year in the first three decades of the republican period with the consulship alone.

In contrast, if the evidence, which is likewise problematic, for priesthoods is included as well, just two more *gentes* can be added, although there may be a third, if F. Münzer's suggestion that M. Laetorius was *decemvir sacrorum* in 495 should happen to be right (although it is most unlikely).[20] That brings the total number of *gentes* to appear, in the context of magistracies, priesthoods and other positions, in the period from 509 to 480 up to forty-four (or forty-five, if Laetorius is included). This means that, again on average, a new *gens* and a half appeared each year during this time.

It is reasonable to suppose that most, if not all, of those who held an office or priesthood in the first few decades of the Republic would have been born in the regal period, although there is scarcely any evidence for them in the traditions of that period. Members of Rome's nobility do appear in regal times, but not in great numbers and not in circumstances that encourage much faith in the historicity of the evidence.[21] In any case, the nobility goes from conspicuously absent (hence the discussions of Momigliano and others) to conspicuously present (and excessively so, in the case of 509 BC) in a very short period of time, and, just as significantly, for the most part, the nobility appears with the consulship.[22]

20   In 509, C. Papirius was *pontifex maximus*, while M'. Papirius was *rex sacrorum*, see Broughton 1951, 4; Rüpke 2008, 826 deems both fictitious; on these early Papirii, see also pp. 187–90 below. For the Vestal Oppia, see Broughton 1951, 23; Rüpke 2008, 822 and n. 3 on her identity. For Laetorius, see Münzer 1920, 90; Broughton 1951, 13; Rüpke 2008, 757 and n. 8 ('Münzer's surmise that he was *decemvir sacrorum* is without foundation').

21   For a list of individuals who appear in the regal period and the evidence for them, see Wikander 1993, 88–9 (Wikander concludes: 'many of the names are certainly fictitious, some presumably rest on genuine tradition, but extremely few seem deliberately interpolated in order to enhance the glory of the mighty, Late Republican nobility').

22   So too Smith 2006b, 302: 'Before the lists of magistrates began to be kept, in other words, before the creation of the Republic, [the patricians] are silent and invisible

It is probably fair to say that most scholars are not that distrustful of this evidence for the nobility, because it is widely maintained, firstly, that consuls were indeed elected immediately after the expulsion of the kings, and secondly, that a list of the names of the men who had held that office was made, if not from the very outset, then at least early enough to ensure that an accurate record was preserved.[23] So much faith has been placed in this hypothesis – and a hypothesis *is* all that it is – that the appearance of an individual in the consular *fasti* is apparently enough to prove that he really existed. Thus G. Forsythe, for example, accepts that L. Iunius Brutus, the founder of the Republic and one of the very first consuls, must be historical, effectively because his name appears in the consular *fasti*, while T. J. Cornell has used essentially the same argument with reference to M. Furius Camillus.[24] Moreover, the early consular *fasti* are also crucial for a range of modern reconstructions, including, most famously, the idea of the 'closing' of the patriciate.[25]

But are the *fasti* really worthy of such extraordinary trust? The means by which the names of the earliest consuls were preserved is entirely a matter of conjecture. The most common hypothesis is that the names were kept in the pontifical records.[26] No one knows when those records began to be kept, and an early date for a written document in an essentially oral

---

actors. As soon as the Republic begins, they are the most powerful interest group in Roman society.'

23   For optimistic views about the creation of the consulship at the end of the sixth century and the consular *fasti*, see Ogilvie 1965, 230–1; Momigliano 1969, 14–15, 18–20; Drummond 1989, 173–6, 186–8; Cornell 1995, 13–15, 218 (13: 'the practice of recording the names of the men who held the chief magistracy must go back to the very early years of the Republic, and it is certain that continuous lists were kept in written form'); Forsythe 2005, 151–6; Kvium 2008, 273: 'the reliability of the listed gentile names [in the consular *fasti* from 509 to 367] is not – and should not be – a serious subject of discussion any longer'! For earlier discussions (presumably serious), see the overview in Ridley 1980. See also n. 26 below.

24   Forsythe 2005, 154; Cornell 1995, 319: Camillus' 'importance in Roman public life ... is proved by the *Fasti*.'

25   See, for instance, Cornell 1995, 252–6; Forsythe 2005, 162–6.

26   For example, Badian 1990a, 216; Ridley 1990, 553; Cornell 1995, 13–15; Oakley 1997a, 39–40 (but focusing on later times); Forsythe 2005, 71, 155–6; Smith 2006b, 4–5; Rich 2013a, 157.

culture may seem unlikely.[27] Besides, if these priestly records contained the names of the chief magistrates of the state, it is just as likely that they would have also contained the names of the chief priests of the state, at the very least when they died and replacements were appointed.[28] But the nobility appears with the consuls, not with the priests, for whom the evidence is almost entirely lacking.[29] This is the case even though nobility was at first supposedly based on patrician status, and not primarily on the holding of office (that allegedly depended on patrician status); priesthoods, like magistracies, were supposedly the special preserve of the patricians too; and the grounds for excluding the plebs from the consulship included religious

27   For an overview of the various arguments, see Rich 2013a, 148–51; Rich argues against a later date (see 149–50) because he thinks that, had the records really begun in the late fourth or early third century, some memory of their creation would have survived; this is not at all a persuasive argument, not least because this is not the sort of thing Roman historians are likely to have been interested in (hence they did not note the records' creation in the fifth century, or at whatever other earlier date happens to appeal). Rüpke 1993, for example, argues that the records began in 249 BC, that is, in a period for which the evidence is really quite difficult; the argument from silence is therefore even weaker in this case, but it carries absolutely no weight anyway. See further p. 111 n. 24.

28   As in Livy 2.42.11, for the unchaste Vestal Oppia; Ogilvie 1965, 349 believes this would have been recorded in the *annales*; or Livy 3.7.6, for the death of two augurs; Ogilvie 1965, 407–8 assumes that this information came from the *annales*; Livy 3.32.2–3: two priests died as a result of plague and famine; concerning the plague, Ogilvie 1965, 451 says 'from the Annales'; Livy 4.44.11–12, on the Vestal Postumia; Ogilvie 1965, 602 says: 'The record is pontifical and reliable.' If Ogilvie is right, and all this material did come from the *annales maximi*, the paucity and inconsistency of it are extremely significant.

29   For the period from the time of Romulus and Remus down to 301 BC (so some four and a half centuries, if Romulus and Remus are placed in the mid-eighth century), Rüpke 2008, 69 lists just fifty religious officials, and that list includes such figures as Romulus, Remus, Tarpeia and Attus Navius; Rüpke's list of religious officials for the subsequent four and a half centuries fills about 200 pages (of Oxford University Press' translation of Rüpke's work). The same argument applies equally for other priestly books; see, for instance, Giovannini 1998 who thinks that 'les livres auguraux contenaient une véritable histoire de la constitution romaine' (110) as well as the names of the members of the college (111); but Giovannini's views are simply not supported by the evidence (indeed, they are somewhat undermined by his own discussion of it).

considerations.[30] And yet, despite all this, there is scarcely any evidence at all for priesthoods. The special focus *specifically* on office-holding and the holding of the consulship in particular was a distinctive feature of the office-holding nobility, since that nobility's status was based above all on the holding of office, and also on the things achieved while in office. But the office-holding nobility developed at a later date. For the early patrician nobility, holding office was undoubtedly still important, but it does not appear to have been entirely fundamental to their status, which was based first of all on being patrician and all that came with that.

The precise nature of the earliest Roman nobility is of course highly uncertain; but, whatever it may have been, it is necessary to believe that the Romans were apparently capable of preserving a complete list of the names of the consuls, but were seemingly incapable of doing the same for all the other offices and all the priests, even in documents made by priests.[31] This point is potentially also valid for the various other means of preservation that have been put forward: why record just the names of the consuls, but virtually nothing else?

The obvious difference is that the consuls were eponymous, but it is highly unlikely that the consulship was *created* as an eponymous magistracy.[32] That would require not only the significant political change that came with the creation of annually elected magistrates, and with the introduction of power-sharing and collegiality (all of which were new ideas, since

30   See, for instance, Momigliano 1963, 118; Linderski 1990; Hölkeskamp 1993, 21; Cornell 1995, 251–2 (252: 'the patriciate was essentially a class defined by religious prerogatives'); Forsythe 2005, 167–70; Smith 2006b, 258–74 (271: 'The only stated reason for the patrician control of the magistracies lay in their argument that the *auspicia* could only properly be in the hands of patrician magistrates.') Note also the theories of Mitchell 2005.

31   For Rich 2013a, who believes that the record of the *pontifex maximus* originated in the fifth century BC, this is a serious problem. He is forced to resort to the really rather desperate argument that Livy must have just chosen not to include this material (the consuls aside, of course); he claims, for instance (157): '[Livy] gives prodigy reports in only twenty of the year-narratives in books 2–10; he could surely have included more if he had chosen.' But why did he choose not to include more? And why did he later choose to start including more?

32   Assumed nonetheless by, for example, Ogilvie and Drummond 1989, 17–18; Cornell 1995, 13, 219.

Rome had previously been ruled by monarchs); it would also entail the creation of appropriate systems of record-keeping (also inevitably new) as well as significant changes in the very means by which time was measured (or, better, events dated). This requires radical and wide-ranging transformations in several areas of Roman life and, when it comes to the idea of a 'consular year', it is highly unlikely that any such concept could have developed until the consuls were in office for a regular period of time and for a period of time that reasonably equated to a year.[33] Moreover, comparative evidence – such as for lists of Olympic victors, archons, the priestesses of Argos and the like – suggests that these sorts of lists were assembled at a later date and not even then necessarily for dating purposes.[34] There is no good reason to believe that the circumstances of the consulship were any different.

Instead of revisiting all the various hypotheses about how the consular *fasti* may have been preserved, because they are after all only hypotheses, it is better to focus first on the evidence of the *fasti* themselves. Two arguments in particular are commonly used in defence of the earliest consular *fasti*.

First, there is the appearance in them of what have been called 'rare' or 'obsolete' names, and there is also the appearance of 'foreign' names, and names such as these, it is argued, cannot have been invented at a later date.[35] The difficulty with this argument, however, is that, if the evidence from which early lists were made was compiled, created and modified over a period of time, which is not at all an unreasonable assumption (note,

33 See Feeney 2007, 171–2. Livy's straightforward equation of consuls and years from the outset is clearly anachronistic (see e.g. Livy 2.16.1: *consules M. Valerius P. Postumius. eo anno* ... [The consuls were M. Valerius and P. Postumius. In this year ...]; 2.34.1: *consules deinde T. Geganius P. Minucius facti. eo anno* ... [The consuls elected next were T. Geganius and P. Minucius. In this year ...]; 2.43.1: *Q. Fabius inde et C. Iulius consules facti. eo anno* ... [Q. Fabius and C. Iulius were then made consuls. In this year ...]).

34 See Möller 2001; Hedrick 2002; Möller 2004; Feeney 2007, 85.

35 For example, Ogilvie 1965, 230–1: 'the most remarkable feature about [the early *fasti*] is the record of families who subsequently decline into complete oblivion ... These must be genuine'; Ridley 1980, 296: 'It is now widely agreed that one useful criterion of reliability is the relative unimportance of early consular families especially where they later died out and could exercise no influence over interpolation'; Drummond 1989, 176 on rare, obsolete and Etruscan names.

for instance, the inclusion of *cognomina* in the names of the earliest consuls which may very well be evidence of later intervention),[36] it is simply impossible to know what pressures were exerted on it, when and from what sources, and it is not known how the early lists of names were put together in the first place anyway. What counts as a rare or obsolete name can so often only be measured by office-holding, since the names of the magistrates make up so much of the evidence, and this inevitably distorts things. Those families whose members were holding the highest offices of the state, which are the families that are most clearly visible, were conceivably the ones with less pressing need to bolster their position with invented achievements and fictitious magistracies, and their names are not usually rare either. On the other hand, any fictitious claims made by such families are less likely to look unexpected or out of place. It is, however, those families that are no longer visible, the ones that were reaching perhaps only junior magistracies – for which there is seldom any evidence – and were just outside the inner circle that may have felt the need to resort to other means of acquiring prestige.[37] Besides, what really constitutes a rare or obsolete name in the fifth, fourth, third, second or even first century BC? It is generally impossible to know.[38]

The other argument that is very frequently used to defend the list of the early consuls is to note the general uniformity of it in the different sources,[39] but that is a difficult argument to make when the extant evidence

36 See the discussion in Smith 2006b, 18–20; earlier, Kajanto 1965, 19–20.

37 Since Rome's nobility long assimilated aristocrats from elsewhere (see the evidence collected a century ago by Münzer 1920, 46–97; this is, note, necessarily the evidence only for successful, and hence visible, individuals), it is not unreasonable to expect that there were numerous ambitious 'foreign' men looking to establish themselves, and not just in the early fifth century. Cf. also Wikander 1993, 80 on the numismatic evidence.

38 See Wikander 1993, 81–2 for the 'large group of families who presumably lived on unnoticed for generations, outside political life'. All this means, obviously enough, that traditional prosopographical methods cannot really help with the assessment of the early consular *fasti*.

39 For example, Ogilvie and Drummond 1989, 18–19; Cornell 1995, 13, 218; Oakley 1997a, 39–40 (but with a focus on later times); Forsythe 2005, 155–6 argues for a common source for the evidence and so has to play down the differences in that

is so very late, and it is even more difficult to make, if it were the case – as may seem likely enough – that some sort of list, or lists, of consuls already existed in Fabius Pictor's day, or soon thereafter.[40] Such a list, or one such list, may then have been used and developed by subsequent historians, irrespective of what other claims and stories were in wider circulation.[41] Even if the uniformity in the different accounts is evidence that the names of the consuls ultimately come from a single source, it is entirely an assumption that that source is an early one. This single source need be no older than the late third or second century BC. But, even then, the matter is not quite so straightforward.

In a number of places in his work, Livy notes that there were problems concerning the consuls and other magistrates of the state (and this was the case after more than a century and a half of historical writing and research). Two passages in particular are especially significant. About a third of the way into his second book, Livy comments that there are so many uncertainties about chronology, because the order of the magistrates in different works varies, making it impossible to know which consuls followed which, or what was done in any given year.[42] By this stage in his work, Livy has already noted a couple of problems, and later in the same book, he notes

---

evidence; Smith 2006b, 4–5: the 'striking degree of uniformity ... suggests a single source'; Armstrong 2016, 27 and n. 50.

40 See, for example, Bispham and Cornell 2013, 175, although the idea that Pictor may have had access to a list of consuls is hardly controversial; for arguments against this idea, however, see Wiseman 1979b, 9–26; Wiseman 2008, 235 who argues that the lists of early consuls were first put together in the second century BC; only the list of consuls from 366 onwards was authentic; and Rüpke 1995.

41 Cf. Flower 2009 on the marginal place of historiography in Roman society.

42 Livy 2.21.4: *tanti errores res implicant temporum, aliter apud alios ordinatis magistratibus, ut nec qui consules secundum quos, nec quid quoque anno actum sit, in tanta vetustate non rerum modo sed etiam auctorum digerere possis.* [There are so many uncertainties involving matters of chronology, with the magistrates ordered differently in different works, that the great antiquity not only of the events but even of the authorities means you cannot set out which consuls followed which or what was done in any year.]

further difficulties,[43] but it is especially clear from his comments about the different sequences of magistrates and the great number of uncertainties that there were considerable problems, and it may be that those problems that Livy does discuss constitute only the tip of a potentially large iceberg. Naturally Livy does not dwell on these problems, because that would have resulted in a different sort of work from the one he was writing, and such an approach would certainly have destroyed his narrative as well.[44] It is quite clear, however, that Livy just did not have access to a single list of magistrates that he could actually trust.[45]

Later, at the end of his eighth book, Livy addresses the origins of these problems in a brief but important passage. The record, he suggests, has been corrupted by funeral speeches and false claims made in *tituli*, the inscriptions that accompanied the *imagines* and that evidently detailed individual careers, as families dishonestly claimed for themselves great deeds and honours (which must include magistracies). The result is that individual careers (so again, the record of magistracies) and the public records have become confused.[46] This is no momentary observation either; elsewhere in his work Livy mentions the problems with *tituli* and he also notes discrepancies between claims made in funeral speeches and other sources.[47]

What Livy says was not without precedent. Cicero had noted earlier, in his *Brutus*, that claims made in funeral speeches had made Roman history somewhat faulty. Many things, he said, that had not happened had been included in those speeches: spurious triumphs, multiplied consulships, false genealogies and transitions to the plebs. Cicero offered an example of the sort of claims that were made: it would be, he said, as if he (M. Tullius

---

43   Livy 2.8.5, 2.18.4–7 (albeit on the first dictator), 2.21.3 (the immediate context of Livy's comment), 2.54.3; see Forsythe 1999, 24–39 for a collection of the relevant evidence in books 2–10 of Livy's work.

44   Even as it is, Quint. *Inst.* 2.4.19 can comment that *Livius frequentissime dubitat.* [Livy is very frequently in doubt.] By modern standards, Livy's expressions of doubt could barely even be described as *infrequent.*

45   The same conclusion is reached by Ridley 1980, 297–8.

46   Livy 8.40.3–5 (see p. 7 n. 16).

47   Livy 4.16.3–4, 4.34.6–7 on *tituli*; for problems with funeral speeches, see Livy 27.27.12–14 on the death of Marcellus.

Cicero) were to claim to be descended from Manius Tullius, the patrician consul who held office alongside Ser. Sulpicius (500 BC).[48]

It is unclear if, by 'false genealogies' (*genera falsa*), Cicero was referring to claims to be descended from gods or heroes, or that sort of thing. Such claims could certainly be put forward in funeral speeches, as Iulius Caesar's speech for his aunt shows, although whether or not this was a long-standing practice is another matter.[49] If Polybius' famous account in his sixth book is any indication, the focus of noble funerals and funeral speeches was clearly on office-holders and their achievements.[50] It may be that Cicero meant only false genealogies along the lines of the example he offered: descent from patricians and consuls. That would certainly make sense, since such claims were after all more useful for a nobility whose standing was based on office-holding, and since office-holding (according to tradition, at least) had originally required patrician status.[51]

A further piece of evidence can be included in this context as well. According to Plutarch, a certain Klodios claimed that the ancient records had been lost when the Gauls sacked Rome; what was on display, he said, was forged, made up to please those who wished to claim descent from leading families and illustrious houses.[52] This is obviously comparable with

48   Cic. *Brut.* 62 (see p. 7 n. 16). On the comments of Livy and Cicero, see, for example, Ridley 1983; Oakley 1997a, 30–3; Jones 2016, 196–7. Smith 2011a, 26 follows Taylor 1951, 72 in arguing that Cicero's comments about M'. Tullius show that Cicero actually had confidence in the reliability of the consular *fasti*; but this is wilful distortion: Cicero is making a different point, one to which the historicity of the *fasti* is simply not relevant; and Cicero's comments about M'. Tullius can hardly be used to refute his own earlier comments about there being too many consuls.

49   Suet. *Iul.* 6.1; cf. Hölkeskamp 1999, 19–20; Flaig 2003, 72, 96–7.

50   Polyb. 6.53.1–54.3. See the discussion in Flaig 2003, 51–4; on p. 72 Flaig claims 'Keine *pompa funebris* der republikanischen Zeit enthielt jemals einen Vorfahren, der nicht römischer Magistrat gewesen war', but it is impossible to know for certain.

51   Cf. Hölkeskamp 1999, 12–20. Kvium 2008, 270 thinks that Cicero has more in mind, but then has to explain why he does not include more; Cicero does not mention claims to be descended from kings, Kvium thinks, because he did not want to cause offence. But, even as they are, his comments have the potential to do that.

52   Plut. *Numa* 1.1: ἀλλὰ Κλώδιός τις ἐν ἐλέγχῳ χρόνων (οὕτω γάρ πως ἐπιγέγραπται τὸ βιβλίον) ἰσχυρίζεται τὰς μὲν ἀρχαίας ἐκείνας ἀναγραφὰς ἐν τοῖς Κελτικοῖς πάθεσι τῆς πόλεως ἠφανίσθαι, τὰς δὲ νῦν φαινομένας οὐκ ἀληθῶς συγκεῖσθαι δι' ἀνδρῶν

what Cicero had to say in his *Brutus* about transitions to the plebs and false genealogies. The idea that the earliest records of the city were destroyed in the Gallic fires was long a staple argument of the sceptical historians, those who denied the historicity of the literary evidence for early Roman history.[53] The lack of archaeological evidence for widespread destruction of the city at this time may, at first sight, seem to make that argument untenable. But, if there was no fire to destroy the city's records, why should ancient writers have claimed that those records had been lost? The most obvious explanation is that the story of their destruction is aetiological. It was invented to explain the general lack of documents, which later writers clearly assumed must have been made. But that assumption was simply anachronistic.[54]

That lack of documents presumably extended to the putative list of consuls. Like Klodios, Livy also says that documents were lost at the time of the Gallic sack, and he mentions in particular the pontifical records; however, Livy adds that some effort was subsequently made to recover Rome's treaties and laws, such as the Twelve Tables and certain laws of the kings.[55] It is reasonable to suspect that Livy (or his source) claims that documents of precisely that kind were recovered, simply because documents of that

---

χαριζομένων τισὶν εἰς τὰ πρῶτα γένη καὶ τοὺς ἐπιφανεστάτους οἴκους ἐξ οὐ προσηκόντων εἰσβιαζομένοις. [But a certain Klodios in his *Critique of Chronology* (for that is what the book is called) insists that those ancient records were lost when the city was sacked by the Gauls and that those that are now on display were put together fraudulently by men gratifying certain people who were trying to force their way into the first families and the most distinguished houses, with which they had no connection.] (Plutarch's Klodios has often been identified as Claudius Quadrigarius; recently a case has been made for Paulus Clodius, see Briscoe 2013c; for the present argument, his identity makes little difference.) Note also Plin. *HN* 35.8, for the indignation of the elder Valerius Messalla and the younger, concerning the misuse of *imagines*; note Pliny's reaction: *sed ... etiam mentiri clarorum imagines erat aliquis virtutum amor multoque honestius quam mereri ne quis suas expeteret.* [But ... even laying a false claim to the masks of famous men showed some love of excellence and was much more honourable than deserving that no one should aim to get masks of their own.]

53   Perhaps most famously, Pais 1899, 97–8, 725–8; Pais 1913, 3–7.
54   Wiseman 2008, 14, 235; Richardson 2012, 126–7.
55   Livy 6.1.2, 6.1.10.

kind were still extant, or believed to be so, in Livy's (or his source's) day. If that is the case, the fact that Livy does not have anything else recovered, other than laws and treaties, is extremely significant.

This evidence, of Livy and Cicero, and Klodios too, is absolutely un-equivocal, and it cannot simply be dismissed, nor is it easy to explain away (indeed, it would require a deliberate and concerted effort), although anyone who has confidence in the early consular *fasti* inevitably must do one or the other. Such an approach, however, means that the modern belief that the *fasti* are reliable is effectively being treated as better than explicit ancient evidence to the contrary.

Consular ancestors mattered, and the effects of this importance are perfectly predictable – multiplied, that is, too many, consulships, says Cicero – and when so many potentially stood to benefit (individually and collectively), and when perhaps many may have been making exaggerated, if not simply fictitious claims, it is difficult to imagine that Rome's nobles were busy reining in each other's inventions and deriding each other's distortions and fabrications, as has sometimes been suggested, when it comes to historiography in particular.[56] Of course, some individuals – people like Cicero and Livy – may have expressed concern or disapproval, but their comments, where they happen to survive, only really serve to show what was actually going on, and also that such expressions of disapproval were clearly not inhibiting anyone.

To argue that Rome's nobles were engaged in some sort of exercise in collective self-censorship is to assume not only that they would have wanted to do this, but also that they even knew who had been consul in

---

56   Cornell 2005, 49; Oakley 1997a, 31 ('two factors militated against the general ac-
     ceptance of any fantasy which a family might wish to ascribe to its ancestors: the first
     was the need for there to be a historian who believed it or recorded it; the second
     was the jealousy of other families, who would hardly encourage the acceptance of
     such claims'), 39–40 ('it is inconceivable that the Roman aristocracy ... would allow
     wholesale invention or fabrication to pass unchallenged.') To what extent does this
     involve imposing modern assumptions and standards on the ancient Romans? (Cf.
     Richardson 2012, 47–52.) To what extent did the collective needs of the nobility as a
     whole outweigh the need for veracity in individual claims, especially when exagger-
     ated claims may have been commonplace, and also to the advantage of the nobility
     as a whole?

any given year, or how many consuls a family had produced, and this may be unlikely, certainly for the distant past. Livy had problems, and he was writing after nearly two centuries of historiographical work and, presumably, with various texts directly in front of him. Beyond the achievements of their own ancestors (who may not always have been entirely familiar),[57] at the forefront of many nobles' minds may have merely been the stock of exemplary tales that they used during the course of their day to day political activities.[58]

Although the consuls were eponymous, their names were associated with specific events, not with numbers, and that inevitably will have made the fabrication of early consuls (and their achievements) much easier to effect and much more difficult to detect than it would otherwise have been, had the consuls' names been associated with an ordered and continuous sequence of numbered years, as they are today.[59] It would only have been after the consuls' names were first placed into an ordered sequence (and one of a precise length too) that so many of the problems would have become apparent, and it is in this context that comments such as Cicero's about there being too many consulships (*plures consulatus*) should probably be understood. (Hence, too, Cicero can only talk of *false* triumphs, alongside the *plures consulatus*; triumphs only took place irregularly, so the same criterion could not so readily be used in their case.)[60]

To all this, it can be added that the consulship itself appears to have been projected into the past – even some of the most optimistic historians

---

57   Cf., for example, Nep. *Att.* 18.3–4 on the genealogical works that Atticus was asked to put together; or Cic. *Fam.* 9.21.2–3, *Att.* 6.1.17–18.

58   On the range of exemplary tales available from noble funerals, note Flaig 2003, 87: 'In der alltäglichen politischen Kommunikation war nur ein winziger Ausschnitt davon zu gebrauchen. Ganz einfach, weil ein *exemplum* nur wirkte, wenn die Zuhörer es gut kannten.' On Cicero's use of historical *exempla*, note Rawson 2014, 260.

59   Cornell 1995, 401: 'the important thing to remember about Roman dates is that events were associated in the first instance with the names of the consuls of the year in which they took place. Locating that year in any general scheme of chronology ... is a secondary and necessarily somewhat artificial process.' Note also Flaig 2003, 59–60, 69–70 on the concertinaed chronology of the funeral procession.

60   See p. 7 n. 16 for Cicero's comments.

accept that[61] – and it must have been so in an entirely anachronistic way. Livy knew that the consuls had once been called praetors.[62] Yet, after the Tarquins had been expelled and the Republic established, Livy has Brutus and his colleague elected to the consulship, not to the praetorship.[63] By Livy's day the consulship and the Republic went together, and it was clearly impossible for him to write an account in which Brutus, his colleague and their successors in office were praetors.[64]

Anyone who wishes to maintain that the early consular *fasti* are reliable must necessarily suppose that the change from praetors to consuls, whenever that happened, was largely just a change in name, and certainly did not affect the number of magistrates appointed each year.[65] Consequently, when those early praetors were anachronistically relabelled as consuls, nothing other than the name of the magistracy was affected. That is not impossible, of course, but changes in name usually do reflect more than just a change in name; rebranding is a modern phenomenon, and even rebranding normally involves considerably more than changing only the name. Moreover, any argument for such continuity also has to explain why one of the new magistracies said to have been introduced in 367–366 BC was the praetorship. The use of that particular name for what was believed to have been a new magistracy (whether or not it was is another matter)

61 For example, Cornell 1995, 226: 'It seems that [the consuls'] original title was prae-tors ... and only later that they came to be known as consuls (but the more familiar term will be used here to avoid confusion).' This is then followed with a discussion of the *consulship*. See also n. 65 below.

62 Livy 3.55.12, see also 7.3.5; Fest. 249L.

63 Livy 1.60.4: *duo consules ... creati sunt, L. Iunius Brutus et L. Tarquinius Collatinus.* [Two consuls were elected, L. Iunius Brutus and L. Tarquinius Collatinus.]

64 Wiseman 1979b, 45; Wiseman 2008, 15, 299, 310, 318: 'The story was something [Livy] had inherited from his predecessors; odd bits of evidence that were incompatible with it just had to be passed over.'

65 Cf., for instance, Momigliano 1969, 14–15: 'Roman historians thought that when the Tarquins were thrown out the Romans began to elect two magistrates every year with powers equivalent to those of the old king. These magistrates were called *praetores* or *consules*, and the latter name prevailed ... why should the Romans say that two yearly *praetores* or *consules* replaced the king, if that was not the truth?' Ogilvie 1965, 231; Cornell 1995, 226 (see n. 61 above); Oakley 1997a, 39 n. 89; Forsythe 2005, 151.

may tell against any sort of straightforward continuity between the earlier praetorship and the consulship.[66] If there was any continuity involved, it may be easier to look for it between magistracies that had the same name.

It has been shown time and again that Roman thinking was often unhistorical, as the conditions of the present were frequently assumed to have existed in the past.[67] That is almost certainly part of the explanation for why the consulship appears immediately after the expulsion of the kings, that is, at the earliest possible date for its existence. Something similar applies in the case of the Senate, which was likewise assumed to have existed from the earliest possible moment, which was Romulus' day.[68] Something similar applies to so many of Rome's priesthoods too, although they usually go back to Numa rather than Romulus, because of the way that king was viewed.[69] And something similar applies to the Servian tribes, the creation of even all thirty-five of which could be attributed to Servius Tullius, even though there was – and still is – plenty of evidence to the contrary.[70] No one today would argue that Servius Tullius had established all thirty-five tribes, because there is good evidence to the contrary; and yet, it is still quite widely maintained that the consulship was established immediately after the expulsion of the kings, even though there is good evidence to the contrary.[71]

To this anachronistic thinking can be added the importance of the consulship itself for a family's standing. From the mid- to late fourth century

---

66   Cf. Drogula 2015, 15, 19.

67   See above, p. 29 n. 25.

68   For example, Livy 1.8.7; Dion. Hal. *Ant. Rom.* 2.12; Plut. *Rom.* 13.1–5.

69   For example, Livy 1.20; Dion. Hal. *Ant. Rom.* 2.63–73 (although note 2.21–2 on Romulus' measures; but on this evidence see Wiseman 2009, 81–98); Plut. *Numa* 7.4–5, 9–13.

70   See Dion. Hal. *Ant. Rom.* 4.15.1, especially for the account of Vennonius (*FRHist* 13 F2), who claimed that Servius Tullius had divided the land into thirty-one rural tribes alongside the four urban tribes; Fabius Pictor (*FRHist* 1 F9) apparently had Servius establish thirty tribes, a number that is doubly problematic, since it is also even. For the creation of fourteen new tribes from 387 to 241, see p. 35 n. 49.

71   This is undoubtedly another very good example of the 'will to believe'; on which, see p. 4 n. 8.

BC onwards,[72] having an ancestor who had reached only the praetorship meant something else: success, but falling short of the consulship. It is, then, no surprise at all that the consulship appears as soon as it possibly can, that the nobility that generally based its standing on the holding of that office in particular by and large appears along with it, and that the memory of the early praetorship was almost entirely lost. Since the consulship could not be projected back any earlier than 509, it is also no surprise that the nobility barely appears before that date; appearing earlier just did not matter. If prestige and influence depended on the holding of office, why should anyone have been concerned about the regal period? It is quite clear that no one seriously was.

If the early consulship was indeed an anachronistic, and even tendentious, reconstruction, that would also accord nicely with, and may even help to explain, some of the confusion surrounding the mysterious consular tribunate that was allegedly introduced in the mid-fifth century and subsequently dispensed with in the mid-fourth. The confusion surrounding this magistracy is really quite considerable, although the usual approach is generally to seek to solve it,[73] rather than simply recognise it for what it is and what it reveals. It may very well be that this is because, once the full extent of all the different problems is properly acknowledged, the possibility that the historical reality may be recoverable from the extant evidence starts to look extremely remote.

First of all, there is the date. The first consular tribunes supposedly held office in 444 BC, although, according to one version of events, they

---

72   Or conceivably later still: as Drogula 2015, 41–2 notes, on existing evidence, it is technically possible that the title 'consul' was not used until as late as the early third century BC. It is, however, easier to suppose that the consulship was created in 367; the context is plausible (see pp. 131–2), and there is then also no need to find some other moment for the consulship's creation.

73   Given the many problems, the bibliography on the consular tribunate is considerable; see von Fritz 1950, 37–41; Staveley 1953; Adcock 1957; Boddington 1959; Sealey 1959; Ogilvie 1965, 539–41; Ridley 1986; Drummond 1989, 192–5; Richard 1990b; Sohlberg 1991; Richard 1992; La Rosa 1994; Cornell 1995, 334–9; Oakley 1997a, 367–76; Walt 1997, 313–18; Stewart 1998, 53–94; Brennan 2000, 49–54; Forsythe 2005, 234–9; Urso 2005, 123–34; Oakley 2005b, 502–7; Holloway 2008; Drogula 2015, 25–7; Armstrong 2016, 192–9, 210–11.

did so only briefly. They were apparently forced to step down and were replaced by consuls.[74] Some sources, however, evidently had only consuls in this year.[75] For the next five years, consuls allegedly held office, with the consular tribunate only reappearing in 438.[76] It is possible that, in those sources that had only consuls in 444, the consular tribunes of 438 were the first, although, according to a tradition found in Eutropius, the first consular tribunes did not hold office until as late as 389.[77]

Second, there is the name of the magistracy, which is variously reported. This seems an unlikely situation, if records had been made at the time.[78] Livy alone uses a very wide range of terms (*tribuni militares consulari potestate*, *tribuni militum consulari potestate*, *tribuni consulari potestate*, *tribuni militum consulares*, *tribuni militum pro consulibus*, *tribuni militum pro consule*, *tribuni consulares*, *tribuni militares*, *tribuni militum* and *tribuni*); the shorter of these can probably be attributed to convenience, given that the fuller ones are cumbersome, but even still, the variation is striking and it does not inspire any confidence in Livy's (and his sources') knowledge of what was supposedly happening.[79]

---

74   Livy 4.7.1–3, 10–12; Dion. Hal. *Ant. Rom.* 11.62.1–3.

75   Dion. Hal. *Ant. Rom.* 11.62.3: πλὴν οὐκ ἐν ἁπάσαις ταῖς Ῥωμαϊκαῖς χρονογραφίαις ἀμφότεραι φέρονται, ἀλλ᾽ ἐν αἷς μὲν οἱ χιλίαρχοι μόνον, ἐν αἷς δ᾽ οἱ ὕπατοι, ἐν οὐ πολλαῖς δ᾽ ἀμφότεροι. [However, both are not recorded in all the Roman annals, but in some the consular tribunes alone, in others the consuls, and in a few both.]

76   See Broughton 1951, 53–8.

77   Eutr. 2.1: *anno trecentesimo sexagesimo quinto ab urbe condita, post captam autem primo, dignitates mutatae sunt, et pro duobus consulibus facti tribuni militares consulari potestate.* [In the three hundred and sixty-fifth year after the foundation of the city, but the first after its capture [by the Gauls], the magistracies were changed and, instead of two consuls, military tribunes with consular power were elected.]

78   Adcock 1957, 9 n. 2 noted some time ago that the variation suggests that no contemporary documents with the magistracy's title on them survived. Solutions to this have been offered: for example, Ogilvie 1965, 541: 'The variation in their title might suggest that only the words *tribuni militum* were recorded in the Fasti and that the other words were added by historians anxious to create "an impression of orderly and legal development".' This reads like the suggestion of an historian anxious to do something comparable, and to save his own hypotheses; besides, the 'other words' do anything but 'create "an impression of orderly and legal development".'

79   For Livy's evidence, see Ridley 1986, 444–5; Oakley 1997a, 383.

Further variation in the name of the magistracy can be found in other sources, and some of the variation is extremely significant, as it directly affects the powers that the tribunes supposedly had. Several of the titles Livy uses credit the tribunes with consular *potestas*; at least two later sources, however, replaced the word *potestas* in the name of the magistracy with *imperium*. The Emperor Claudius called them *tribuni militum consulari imperio*, and Aulus Gellius, *tribuni militares consulari imperio*.[80] This may be nothing more than an attempt to smooth away apparent inconsistencies. Livy does say that, according to some writers, the tribunes possessed *imperium*;[81] besides, if they led the army, which they were said to have done, then they surely must have had *imperium*, or so it could very easily be assumed. Equally, however, it has been argued by some scholars that they simply cannot have had *imperium*.[82] So not only was the title itself a matter of some confusion, so too was the very nature of the power supposedly wielded by the consular tribunes.

80   Claud. *ILS* 212; Gell. *NA* 17.21.19.

81   Livy 4.7.2: *tribunos militum tres creatos dicant ... et imperio et insignibus consularibus usi sunt.* [They say that three military tribunes were created ... and possessed *imperium* and the insignia of the consuls.] Brennan 2000, 53 claims to be able to assert that these writers, whoever they were, 'are wrong'; as for Claudius, Brennan thinks that he 'may not have known the peculiar fact that the consular tribunes had only consular *potestas*, and not *imperium*' (53); but an approach that dismisses the evidence that does not fit with the desired reconstruction by claiming that the authors of that evidence are either mistaken or ignorant is hardly ideal.

82   So, for instance, Badian 1990b, 469: 'what they lacked was, precisely, *imperium*: the avoidance of that term [in their title] must have been deliberate.' Badian is followed by Brennan 2000, 51. Compare Ogilvie 1965, 541: 'They had *imperium* but evidently not the auspices, since no consular tribune celebrates a triumph.' Sealey 1959, 529 and n. 3, however, appears to use the very same evidence to conclude that they did not have *imperium*! Others have argued that their *imperium* was lesser or somehow impaired; see Richard 1990b, 780–8; Richard 1992. As for the auspices, which Ogilvie believes they did not have, Richard 1990b, 779 and Brennan 2000, 52 conclude the opposite; but, while Brennan 2000, 52 likes Versnel's idea (Versnel 1970, 350–1) that the curiate law was not passed for the consular tribunes, Richard 1990b, 779 argues that it was. Equally diverse and incompatible answers have been given to the question of whether or not consular tribunes could triumph; see Urso 2005, 130 n. 19 for a useful overview.

Next, there is the inconsistency in the numbers appointed. Although, in Livy at least, the election of six consular tribunes eventually (that is, after 405 BC) seems to become reasonably standard,[83] there is considerable fluctuation in the later fifth century.[84] Alongside this, there is also the intermittent appearance of consuls, most notably in the later fifth century.[85] If three or four consular tribunes were usually appointed at this time, is it possible that the election of two men may simply represent further fluctuation in the numbers, instead of the appointment of consuls? It would be natural enough for ancient writers to assume that the appearance of two names meant that consuls must have been elected. Be that as it may, the variation in the numbers remains completely mysterious.[86]

Finally, and most significantly, there is the question of why the consular tribunate was created in the first place. The impression that ancient writers did not possess much information about this magistracy and consequently did not really know what they were writing about seems to be confirmed, not just by the unpersuasive nature of their explanations for

83   See Oakley 1997a, 368 (exceptions are 403, 396, 387 and 385; consuls allegedly held office in 393 and 392). See Urso 2005, 131–2 on the idea that six were to be appointed from the outset.

84   Oakley 1997a, 368, also for the numbers in Diodorus and the *fasti Capitolini*.

85   In the period 444–367, consuls were said to have been appointed in 443, 442, 441, 440, 439, 437, 436, 435, 434, 431, 430, 429, 428, 427, 423, 421, 413, 412, 411, 410, 409, 393 and 392.

86   Von Fritz 1950, 39–40 points to changing administrative needs; also Drummond 1989, 194; Forsythe 2005, 236–7: behind the fluctuation in numbers lies 'a complex combination of Rome's increasing external-military and internal-administrative needs'; but this solution only really moves the problem elsewhere: why should Rome's needs have fluctuated so greatly, so that in some years only two men were required, while in others as many as six were needed? How could these changing needs have been predicted in advance? A steady increase in numbers would make this explanation more plausible. Drogula 2015, 37 suggests that increasing competition was responsible for the growth in numbers (although cf. p. 26), but that does not explain the fluctuation either, and competition never affected the number of consuls elected, which was kept at two, even when the number of praetors increased. Not surprisingly, procrustean solutions have been entertained, cf. Drummond 1989, 195.

the tribunate, but also by the fact that they ended up offering two very different explanations for it.

One of these was that the consular tribunate had been created to allow plebeians to have access to the state's highest office,[87] an explanation that is undermined by the fact that so very few plebeians appear to have held the office and by the lateness with which those few reached it. The other explanation is that it was created for military reasons, to ensure that there were more commanders available to lead Rome's armies.[88] That explanation, however, is undermined by the continued use of the dictatorship, the appointment of consular tribunes in peaceful years, the general lack of success of the consular tribunes in the field and so on. All these problems have received considerable attention over the years, and it has long been recognised that neither of the ancient explanations for the magistracy's creation is convincing. Nor, it must be said, has any convincing explanation been found since.[89]

Part of the problem is that ancient writers did not need just to devise an explanation for the creation of the consular tribunate. They also needed to come up with an explanation for why the consulship had been put to one side in favour of the consular tribunate.[90] This inevitably meant that the circumstances of the consulship set the terms for their explanation of the consular tribunate. The most prominent differences between these two magistracies, as they appear in the sources, are really just two. First, there is the difference in the number of men appointed each year, and second, there

87   Livy 4.6.8; Dion. Hal. *Ant. Rom.* 11.56.3, 11.60.5; Pompon. *Dig.* 1.2.2.25; Zonar. 7.19.
88   Livy 4.7.2, cf. also Livy 5.10.1–2, 5.16.2, 5.31.9 and Cass. Dio 40.45.4.
89   See Urso 2005, 127 n. 10 for an overview of various modern explanations for the magistracy. On the results, note Cornell 1995, 462 n. 17: 'this is the one topic in archaic Roman history where English-speaking scholars predominate (although the results of their efforts are not much of an advertisement)'; Oakley 1997a, 373: 'Despite much scholarly attention, the nature, origins, and demise of the consular tribunate await a satisfactory explanation'; 376: 'the consular tribunate remains enigmatic'; Walt 1997, 317: 'Die moderne Forschung ist also nicht zu einer eindeutigen Erklärung der *tribuni militum consulari potestate* gekommen'; Smith 2006b, 272: 'All attempts to give a rational explanation for the consular tribunate are disputed.'
90   Cf. above p. 129.

is the belief that plebeians could hold the consular tribunate, whereas they were supposedly ineligible to stand for the consulship.[91] It seems unlikely to be a coincidence that the explanations for the creation of the consular tribunate that were offered in antiquity were also just two in number, and that one of them was based on the number of the tribunes, and the other, on the idea that plebeians could hold this office. It looks suspiciously like these explanations are simply inferences made from the most obvious differences between the two magistracies.[92] If these explanations are unpersuasive (and they are), that is probably just because the initial assumption on which they are based, namely that the consular tribunate replaced the consulship, is entirely mistaken.

So ancient writers disagreed about when the consular tribunate had been created, and they quite clearly did not know why it had been created. They were uncertain about what it had been called, and about what powers were associated with it, and they do not seem to have known either why the numbers of tribunes appointed each year fluctuated or why consuls were sometimes still appointed (if they even were). So why should they have been better informed about the earlier period, from 509 down to the moment when the tribunate was supposedly introduced (whenever that was)? There is no reason whatsoever to believe that they were. The difference is that they thought that consuls had been elected in this period, and since consuls were elected in their own day, they knew about the consulship. It was easy for anyone in the third, second or first century BC to say

---

91   Cornell 1995, 335. Given all the confusion in the sources, even something as simple as this is contested: Drummond 1989, 193: 'In character ... and perhaps even in nomenclature the consulship and consular tribunate may have been identical ... The distinction drawn by Roman historians would then be a false deduction'; La Rosa 1994, 27: consular tribunes 'avevano gli stessi poteri dei consoli; la novità consisteva nel fatto che i *tribuni militum* erano eletti dal *populus*'; Oakley 1997a, 383: 'in most respects it is hard to distinguish between the powers of consular tribunes and consuls ... In one important respect, however, they did differ: no consular tribune ever triumphed'; Forsythe 2005, 236: 'the only apparent difference ... lay in the title of the office and their number.'

92   So too, for one of the explanations at least, Drummond 1989, 194: 'More probably the alleged later admission of plebeians to the consular tribunate created the notion that the office was introduced for that reason.'

something plausible about consuls. On top of that, spurious claims had helped to provide the necessary material: lots of consuls (indeed, *plures consulatus*) and – to stay with Cicero's complaint – false triumphs too, although the lists of early triumphators, unlike the lists of early consuls, have not won quite such extraordinary confidence in their historical value (after all, they begin with Romulus, while the consular *fasti* obviously do not; how differently would the consular *fasti* be perceived, if they did?). This is the case, even though the issues at stake are the same, and those issues are of course politics and power,[93] although not, perhaps, of the late sixth or fifth century B C. The politics and power that may have been most relevant to the earliest consular *fasti* may have been those of the later fourth and third centuries B C, that is, the period following the emergence of Rome's office-holding nobility and before the advent of historiography, although the advent of historiography certainly did not bring about an end to the making of spurious claims.

As for the realities of Roman government in the first century and a half or so of the republican period, there is simply insufficient reliable evidence to allow for anything approaching a certain answer. There is, of course, plenty of scope – indeed perhaps too much scope – for hypothesis and conjecture, although it is important to realise first that much of the extant evidence is similar in nature; that is to say, it too represents an attempt (or an amalgamation of different attempts) to reconstruct the past, and it too is equally based on various hypotheses, a good many assumptions, as well as some highly questionable methods.

---

93   The substance of this chapter was first presented at a conference on the theme of *Politics and Power in the Early Roman Republic (509–264 BC)*; hence the precise formulation.

CHAPTER 7

'Firsts' and the Historians of Rome

Until recently it was quite widely accepted that many of Rome's historians of the republican period sought to glorify their ancestors in their
works and that this sometimes even led to the outright invention of accomplishments of one kind or another. Many of the arguments used to
support this view were inevitably conjectural in nature, since the writings of Rome's republican historians no longer exist, but the general
case itself certainly did not lack evidence to support it. Moreover, the
case seemed to be in perfect accordance with what is known about the
highly competitive nature of Rome's nobility, the characteristics and
aims of that competition and the ways in which it was played out.[1]

This view has of late come under increasing amounts of criticism,
and it would seem that it is now starting to become unfashionable. It has
been noted in particular that there is little or no direct evidence in what
remains of the writings of Rome's historians to support it.[2] This argument

---

1   Election to office and the performance of services to the state (especially of a military nature) were common goals; Cicero (*Brut.* 62) and Livy (8.40.4–5; see p. 7
n. 16) both say that false claims about precisely these things were made in funeral
speeches, and that Rome's historical traditions had been corrupted as a result;
Livy also blamed the *tituli* which accompanied the *imagines* in the atrium of the
home (4.16.3–4, 4.34.6–7, 8.40.4); note, as well, the uses that Rome's moneyers
made of coinage in the late republican period to advertise family traditions (see e.g.
Hölscher 1984, 12–13). If funeral speeches, inscriptions and even coinage could be
used to put forward spurious claims of various kinds, then why not historiography
too? Plut. *Numa* 1.1, 21.2 (on which, see Forsythe 1994, 201–6) certainly provides
good evidence to suggest that historiography was indeed so used. Although more
general in nature, note the comments of Polybius at 1.14; Polybius is, of course, the
exception that proves the rule.

2   On Valerius Antias, who more than anyone else is held to have glorified his ancestors, see Cornell 1986, 77: 'there is no warrant for the contention that Valerius Antias
exaggerated the part played by the Valerii in the early history of Rome ... the theory

is an extremely difficult one to use, however, simply because the works of
Rome's republican historians have been lost, and the few fragments (which
generally consist of brief quotations, paraphrases and allusions in later
works) that do exist represent only the tiniest fraction of what there once
was. The amount of potentially useful material is somewhat further reduced
still. Many of Rome's republican historians wrote *ab urbe condita* [from
the foundation of the city], and so the early books of their works were usually dedicated to the stories of the origins and foundation of the city, and
after that, the stories from the regal period, and these are all stories from
which the noble houses of Rome are almost entirely absent. This situation

---

is not based on any evidence ... It would not be at all surprising if Valerius Antias'
account was favourable to the Valerii; after all, other historians certainly were, and
Antias may well have felt a vicarious pleasure in recounting the good deeds of the
great patrician clan whose name he shared. But nothing proves that he invented
any of the Valerian material, or even that it was invented by anyone'; Oakley 1997a,
91: 'there is no direct attestation of Antias thus glorifying his family, and the Valerii
certainly had a very prominent place in the tradition before Antias wrote'; Beck
and Walter 2004, 170–1: 'Bei der immer wieder konstatierten Verherrlichung der
gens Valeria, deren Ruhm allenthalben hochstilisiert worden sein soll, muss man
dagegen differenzieren. Diese Sichtweise kann sich auf überhaupt nur ein einziges
Fragment [of Valerius Antias' work] berufen (F 18). Selbst wenn man dies zum
Anlass für eine entsprechende Überhöhung nehmen wollte, greifen die dahinter
stehenden literarischen Verherrlichungsmechanismen keineswegs so einfach, wie
das gängige Interpretationsmuster suggeriert. Für Fabius Pictor hat sich gezeigt, dass
kaum mit einer rücksichtslosen oder gar unverhohlenen Lobpreisung der Fabier zu
rechnen ist'; see Beck and Walter 2001, 122 on Pictor; see also n. 116 below; Rich
2005, 155: '[Antias] may have used his inventive powers to enhance the prominence of the Valerii and to elaborate their role as champions of the people, but this
remains an unconfirmed assumption, without clear support from the evidence of
the fragments; the core elements of this tradition were probably established well
before Antias wrote'; Cornell 2009, 21: 'Although there is no direct evidence to link
Valerius Antias with this feature [i.e. the 'favourable light' in which the Valerii are
presented], and none to show that much (or indeed any) of it was invented by him,
it nonetheless remains probable that he was pleased to record the achievements
of the early Valerii, and that his account lies behind the adulation of the Valerii in
Livy and Dionysius'; 25: 'The role of historians such as Antias and Macer was to
exploit these pre-existing traditions and to elaborate them – negatively in the case
of the Claudii, and positively in those of the Valerii and Licinii (respectively)'; Rich
2013b, 302.

is further exacerbated, since it is often the case that more fragments tend to come from the first book of any given work than from subsequent ones.[3]

Although the evidence of the fragments may not support the traditional view (or, it must be said, disprove it), it is not true that there is no evidence for it. Livy says quite explicitly that the testimony of the historian Licinius Macer is less weighty, precisely because of the praise that he sought to bestow on his family.[4] There is no direct evidence of this praise in the fragments of Macer's work (which shows that any argument based on the silence of the fragments is nothing more than an argument from silence), but it would be extraordinarily perverse to try to disprove Livy's assessment on the basis of the fragments that happen to exist.[5] Livy could read Macer's work, which no one today can do, and there are no grounds for supposing that Livy was not in a position to be able to make a fair assessment of what he read.[6] If Licinius Macer praised his family and was unreliable as a result, it seems extremely unlikely that he was somehow unique in this.

It is not necessary to suppose that all of Rome's republican historians glorified their ancestors, that those who did were as blatant as Macer appears to have been, or that they sought to glorify their ancestors mendaciously. It is perfectly reasonable to assume that different historians wrote for different purposes and with different audiences in mind,[7] and it is reasonable

---

3   Cf. Cornell 2004, 117; Cornell 2009, 5. See Chapter 6 on the absence of Rome's nobility from the traditions of regal Rome.

4   Livy 7.9.5 (see p. 8 n. 18).

5   Nonetheless Smith 2011a, 28–31 essentially attempts to do just this; moreover, he argues (31) that 'this [i.e. Livy 7.9.3–6] is the passage on which the whole argument for Licinius' false insertion of his family into the history of Rome is based, and all told, it seems to me that Licinius is inaccurate, and perhaps tendentious, but not evidently for the sole purpose of falsifying or actively inventing the *Fasti*.' But how is it possible to know that Livy 7.9.3–6 is 'the passage on which *the whole argument* for Licinius' false insertion of his family into the history of Rome is based' (my emphasis)? This is only the point at which Livy offers his assessment, an assessment that could be based on any amount of material. How can Livy's assessment (or Macer's work) possibly be judged fairly on so very little evidence?

6   Cf. Livy's assessment of Polybius, 30.45.5, 33.10.10.

7   So Fabius Pictor, Rome's first historian, who wrote in Greek (and so presumably must have expected to have a Greek audience of some kind) at a time when Rome's influence beyond Italy and Sicily was first expanding almost certainly wrote with

to assume that those historians who did seek to glorify their families may have done so in a variety of different ways, with some prepared to distort or fabricate episodes and others content merely to add rhetorical embellishment. It is probably also the case that these different approaches and different levels of praise (and inventiveness) make the evidence of the few fragments even less helpful for detecting that praise.

The argument from silence is not, in the end, persuasive, and since Livy is explicit about Macer, the argument from silence simply collapses. Alongside this, there is also some resistance to the basic idea that Rome's historians were able to tamper with the literary tradition of Rome's past. T. J. Cornell, most notably and with some considerable influence (certainly in the English-speaking world), has stated quite firmly on a number of occasions his view that 'Roman annalists were not in a position to impose a fraudulent version of Rome's history on their contemporaries and on succeeding generations of historians.' This was because the 'main outline of political and military events was a matter of public knowledge in the later Republic' and so it is 'simply inconceivable that relatively late writers such as Valerius Antias could have departed radically from the received tradition and hoped to get away with it'. Equally, Rome's very first historian, Fabius Pictor was not in a position to make things up or modify them either; his contemporaries would have been 'familiar with the main elements of their historical tradition' and so presumably would have not tolerated any invention or distortion of the tradition of events on Pictor's part.[8]

The idea that Romans of the late Republic, and even more so of earlier times, were indeed familiar with the 'main outline of political and military events' may well be doubted. It does inevitably depend on what constitutes a 'main outline' (assuming that 'outline' is even the correct word to use; 'elements' or 'episodes' may be better), and the level at which the tradition may have been vulnerable to manipulation and alteration. The purpose of

---

different aims from someone like Licinius Macer, who wrote in the first century BC, when Rome's hegemony was established, and who wrote in Latin. It may be useful to compare the situation with the visual arts, and Rome's coinage in particular, cf., for example, Hölscher 1984, 12–13.

8   Cornell 2005, 49; see also Cornell 1986, 80; and his review of Wiseman 1979b, Cornell 1982, 206.

this chapter, however, is simply to compile some evidence that seems to support precisely the opposite position, namely that Rome's historians could, and did, tamper with the tradition, and that at least several of them did so with the intention of glorifying their ancestors. The evidence in question consists of a number of 'firsts' that can be found in the literary evidence for Rome's early history.[9]

As with many other cultures, and as is still the case today, it was considered prestigious to be the first to perform a particular deed, or to be the first to hold an important position.[10] The almost inevitable result is the existence of rival claims. Naturally these claims need not necessarily be associated with historians, as will be seen, and some, possibly even many, of them may have originated in contexts outside the literary tradition. Having said that, however, when a range of different 'firsts' from the tradition is brought together, a very clear pattern in their distribution quickly emerges. Not only is there a significant number of 'firsts' that are claimed by families that produced historians, but there also appears to be some evidence of rival claims made by these very same families, claims that appear to have been associated with just two in particular, the Postumii and the Valerii. Although it is only an inference that individual historians may have been responsible for the appearance of these claims in the evidence, the very distribution of them makes the inference a reasonably safe one.

The following list is not exhaustive by any means, not least because in many cases the identity of those individuals who first held a particular

9   Note that the following discussion is not limited only to those events that are explicitly identified as 'firsts' in the extant sources, but includes other achievements that may also constitute 'firsts'. While this may mean that some episodes have been included erroneously, as they may appear to be 'firsts' only because of a lack of evidence to the contrary, the approach should at least ensure that the argument is not unduly affected by the nature of the evidence that does exist. The approach should also help to reduce the effects of any interests or aims of those writers whose works survive (cf., for instance, Cornell 2009, 12 on Livy's handling of the first plebeian censorship and the first plebeian praetorship); as will be seen, the evidence for the patterns that can be found in the distribution of the 'firsts' comes from a range of different works, and this may imply that several common sources are behind these claims.

10   Note Sall. *Cat.* 7; cf. Wiseman 1985b.

position, or who first achieved a particular thing, is simply unknown. As will become clear, there is a predictable enough connection with prestige.

1. According to Polybius, the first consuls of Rome were L. Iunius Brutus and M. Horatius. Whether Polybius was transmitting a variant tradition, an early version that was subsequently modified, or was simply mistaken, it is impossible to say.[11] At any rate, in the later literary tradition, as exemplified most obviously by Livy, there were five consuls in the first year of the republican period and, although Brutus and Horatius were still numbered among them, Horatius had been deprived of his position as one of the first. He was now merely a suffect consul.[12] Moreover, Horatius was said only to have been appointed after the death of Brutus, and so in Livy's version of events he did not hold office, even as suffect consul, alongside the founder of the Republic. Brutus' first colleague was, according to Livy, L. Tarquinius Collatinus.[13]

It is clear that, in order to fit five consuls into just one year, numerous stories had to be devised, to make room for the several rival candidates, most of whom could obviously only be accommodated as suffect consuls. Hence Brutus died in office, as did Sp. Lucretius (appointed as he was at such an advanced age, that was all he managed to do), while Tarquinius Collatinus was subsequently exiled, once it had dawned on the Romans that he was in fact a Tarquinius, and so a member of the exiled royal house.[14] However unconvincing these stories may appear,[15] they were clearly necessary. There was no other way to accommodate so many rival claims.

11 Polyb. 3.22.1; cf. Walbank 1957, 339.
12 Livy 2.8.4–5. Detailed references for the consuls and traditions of events of 509 in Broughton 1951, 1–3.
13 Livy 1.60.4.
14 Brutus: Livy 2.6.9; Lucretius: Livy 2.8.4–5; Tarquinius: Livy 2.2.3–11.
15 In the case of Tarquinius Collatinus, note also Ogilvie 1965, 238–9; Scapini 2011, 156–64; Wiseman 2014, 137–9.

Even though these stories are self-evidently nonsense, it is worth noting that in year two there were only two consuls; there were only two consuls in year three as well, and in year four, year five and year six. In fact, the next suffect consul was not appointed until as late as 478 BC, although he is not to be found in the literary evidence; the next suffect consul actually found in the literary evidence was appointed in 460, after half a century of republican government (and after the consul P. Valerius Publicola had died fighting heroically to free the Capitol, which had been captured by the Sabine Ap. Herdonius).[16] Obviously the appeal of having a consular ancestor in year two or three or four of the republican period was just not as great. Suffect consuls abound in year one for a very good reason: primacy was prestigious, but it was only possible to have two first consuls. And the surfeit of consuls in year one must inevitably be evidence of rival claims, and so also evidence of attempts to impose a fraudulent version of Rome's history on contemporaries and succeeding generations.

The first year of the Republic provided room not only for the first consuls, but also, quite obviously, for the first suffect consul, and that, according to the more familiar tradition (again, as exemplified by the likes of Livy), was P. Valerius Publicola.[17] However, just like Horatius, Valerius appears to have also once held the more prestigious position of Brutus' first colleague. According to Cicero, Valerius Maximus and Pliny the Elder, Valerius Publicola was one of the first consuls at Rome.[18] But if, like Horatius, he

---

16   478: see Degrassi 1947, 25; Broughton 1951, 26; 460: Livy 3.18.8, 3.19.2; Dion. Hal. *Ant. Rom.* 10.17.1–3.

17   Livy 2.2.11.

18   Cic. *Flac.* 25; Val. Max. 2.4.5, 4.4.1; Plin. *HN* 36.112. As Wiseman 2014, 136 n. 26 has observed, Plut. *Publ.* 1.3–4 'seems to presuppose a rejected tradition of Valerius as the first consul'; see also Dion. Hal. *Ant. Rom.* 6.39.2, where Dionysius must be following a different source (Valerius Antias?). All this naturally has significant implications for the value of the early consular *fasti*; although it is often asserted that the *fasti* are reliable, this is clearly not the case; cf. Richardson 2012, 48–51, and Chapter 6.

too had simply been displaced by a rival candidate, he had at least managed to hold on to one 'first'.

It should be noted here that one of Rome's historians was Valerius Antias, and that he has often been suspected of writing up the history of the Valerii.[19] Although the precise date at which Antias worked remains a subject of some debate,[20] he certainly wrote after Polybius and before Livy.

2. The first plebeian consul was appointed, according to tradition, in 366 BC. He was L. Sextius.[21] But there appears to be evidence for a rival version of events. According to the author of the *De viris illustribus*, the first plebeian consul was actually C. Licinius Stolo.[22] As T. P. Wiseman has suggested, this variant may have been invented by the historian Licinius Macer.[23] Given Livy's comments about Macer, the suggestion seems perfectly plausible.

It was also in this same year, 366, that the first praetor held office. He was Sp. Furius Camillus, a patrician. The first plebeian to be elected to the praetorship was Q. Publilius Philo in 336. In 366 curule aediles also took up office for the first time. They were Cn. Quinctius Capitolinus and P. Cornelius Scipio.[24] The names of the first plebeians to hold this magistracy are not known,[25] but it was a minor one, and it would seem that the names of the

---

19   For example, Ogilvie 1965, 14 and *passim*; Wiseman 1998, 75–89. But see n. 2 above for views to the contrary.

20   See Rich 2005, 139–43; Rich 2013b, 294–6.

21   Livy 6.42.9, 7.1.1–2, 10.8.8; Plut. *Cam.* 42.5; Degrassi 1947, 33.

22   *De vir. ill.* 20.2: *primus Licinius Stolo consul factus.* [Licinius Stolo was the first to be made consul [*sc.* from the plebs].]

23   Wiseman 2009, 19.

24   Camillus: Livy 7.1.2; Philo: Livy 8.15.9, 10.8.8; Capitolinus and Scipio: Livy 7.1.2.

25   Livy 7.1.6 may suggest that plebeians should have held this office in 365. Fest. 436L records the name M. Popilius, who is usually assumed to have held office in 364; see Broughton 1951, 116. It did later become common for plebeians to hold this office in even years, and patricians in odd.

aediles of 366 are noted by Livy only because the magistracy itself was new in that year.[26]

3. According to Livy, the 'oldest writers' said that the first dictator of Rome was T. Larcius.[27] Livy, however, clearly found a variant tradition in which the first dictator was instead M'. Valerius.[28] It has long been suspected that Valerius Antias was responsible for the invention of this story.[29]

Livy claims that T. Larcius was appointed during the consulship of Postumus Cominius and T. Larcius (that is, in 501 BC),[30] but Dionysius of Halicarnassus put his appointment several years later, during the consulship of Q. Cloelius and T. Larcius (498).[31] Rome's second dictator, A. Postumius Albus, was appointed either, following Livy, during the consulship of T. Aebutius and C. Veturius (499) or, following Dionysius, during the consulship of A. Postumius Albus and T. Verginius (496), just two years later on either chronology.[32] J. Pinsent has suggested that '[the historian] Postumius Albinus might have made A. Postumius the first dictator instead of the second that he is in the developed tradition. He could easily have done this by putting the dictatorship of T. Larcius in 498V while keeping the battle of Lake Regillus, and so the dictatorship of A. Postumius, in 499V.'[33] The difficulty with this suggestion is that there appear to be two separate chronological sequences here, in both of which Postumius' dictatorship comes two years after Larcius.'[34] Pinsent's proposal would

26 Cf. Livy's comments at 7.1.1. Note as well the absence of any mention of the first plebeian aediles at Livy 10.8.8, where Livy has P. Decius Mus enumerate plebeian 'firsts'.

27 Livy 2.18.5.

28 Livy 2.18.6–7; also Fest. 216L.

29 For example, Ogilvie 1965, 282–3; Musti 1970, 116; Ridley 1979, 303; Wiseman 1998, 85.

30 Livy 2.18.1–4. See Broughton 1951, 9 and n. 3 for further references.

31 Dion. Hal. *Ant. Rom.* 5.70.4, 5.73.1.

32 Livy 2.19.1–3; Dion. Hal. *Ant. Rom.* 6.2.1–3.

33 Pinsent 1975, 32.

34 Cf. Werner 1968, 61–4.

require the blending of these two sequences, with the earlier date
for Postumius' dictatorship coming from one, and the later date
for Larcius' coming from the other. In any case, given that there
were clearly several rival traditions, and that there is considerable
disagreement and confusion in the evidence at this point,[35] it
would probably be unnecessary for anyone to have had to exploit
these particular difficulties in the chronology in order to put forward a rival claim. The confusion and various other problems are
in fact more likely to be the result of the existence of rival claims
than to have provided some opportunity for them to be made.
Nevertheless, it may be that there is perhaps some slight evidence
that may support Pinsent's suggestion.

In his account of Larcius' dictatorship, which he places in 501,
Although Livy places Postumius' dictatorship in 499, he was
well aware of the alternative tradition that Postumius was dictator
three years later, in 496.[36] However, it is evident that this alternative tradition, as Livy records it, was quite different from the version related by Dionysius. The consuls of 496 were A. Postumius
Albus and T. Verginius. According to Livy the loyalty of Verginius
fell into question, presumably because it was suspected that he was
a supporter of the ousted Tarquins. Postumius resigned, and was
then made dictator.[37] In the version related by Dionysius, however, Verginius' loyalty was never in doubt, and Verginius plays a
prominent role in Dionysius' account of the events of that year.[38]
The two versions are clearly different in several respects and are
mutually incompatible.

In his account of Larcius' dictatorship, which he places in 501,
Livy notes that there were variant traditions not only concerning
the identity of the first dictator, but also the year in which he was
appointed. Significantly, Livy comments at this point that there
was further disagreement in his sources concerning the loyalty of

35   See Livy's comments at 2.18.4 and 2.21.4.
36   Livy 2.21.3.
37   Livy 2.21.3: *A. Postumium, quia collega dubiae fidei fuerit, se consulatu abdicasse;
      dictatorem inde factum.* [A. Postumius, because his colleague's loyalty was in doubt,
      resigned from the consulship; he was then made dictator.]
38   Dion. Hal. *Ant. Rom.* 6.2.1–3, 6.4.3, 6.5.5.

the consuls.[39] Livy's comment implies that the issue of the consuls' loyalty – the same story that Livy later sets out when he notes the variant tradition concerning Postumius' dictatorship in 496 – was associated with the appointment of Rome's first dictator. Since the allegiances of Postumius' colleague were uncertain, and since Postumius was made dictator on account of this, this may conceivably be evidence of a tradition in which Postumius was Rome's first dictator. If it is, this would fit with Pinsent's suggestion, although the case is obviously not a strong one.

The first plebeian dictator was C. Marcius Rutilus; he was appointed in 356. Some five years later, C. Marcius became the first plebeian censor. Marcius also held the consulship on no fewer than four occasions (357, 352, 344 and 342). All this would seem to suggest that his was just an extraordinarily successful career, and the mid-fourth century date may be grounds for having at least some confidence in the general historicity of the evidence.[40]

---

39   Livy 2.18.4: *sed nec quo anno nec quibus consulibus quia ex factione Tarquiniana essent – id quoque enim traditur – parum creditum sit, nec quis primum dictator creatus sit, satis constat.* [But there is no agreement about the year or which consuls were mistrusted because they were from the faction of the Tarquins – for that too is related – or who the first dictator was.] Admittedly Livy does go on to note the variant tradition that M'. Valerius was the first dictator, but his phraseology certainly permits more than one variant. As Wiseman 1998, 85 notes, if the loyalty of both consuls was uncertain, then neither could safely be appointed dictator; this not only allows room for M'. Valerius, but conceivably also for Postumius (if, that is, the variation in the tradition did not extend to the identity of the consuls too). The idea that it was Verginius' loyalty only that was in doubt in 496 (following Livy's version) may simply be a way around this problem.

40   Livy 7.17.6, 7.22.7–10, 10.8.8. His dictatorship is, however, rejected by Beloch 1926, 71: 'C. Marcius ist der erste plebejische Censor gewesen; ist es wahrscheinlich, daß er auch der erste plebejische Dictator gewesen ist, und daß dann, nachdem einmal das Eis gebrochen war, 42 Jahre bis zur nächsten plebejischen Dictatur vergangen sein sollten?' Marcius' career appears to have been an exceptional one, so any gap may be of little significance; but, in any case, the total of forty-two years is only reached because Beloch also rejects the dictatorships of the plebeians Q. Publilius Philo (339), M. Claudius Marcellus (327) and C. Maenius (320), and retains only that of C. Maenius (314).

As for the first master of the horse, T. Larcius' *magister equitum* was Sp. Cassius, while A. Postumius' was T. Aebutius. The first plebeian *magister equitum* was C. Licinius (Stolo or perhaps Calvus).[41]

4. According to tradition, the first tribunes of the plebs held office in 493 BC. There is, however, considerable disagreement in the sources concerning both their number and their identity. As far as Livy was concerned, two were elected first, and then three more were subsequently added. The first two were C. Licinius and L. Albinius, after whom came L. Sicinius and two others whose identity was uncertain; in fact, Livy notes that some of his sources held that there were only two tribunes appointed in total.[42] Dionysius, however, believed that there were five: L. Iunius Brutus, C. Sicinius Bellutus, C. Licinius, P. Licinius and C. Visellius Ruga.[43] According to Plutarch, the first tribunes were Iunius Brutus and Sicinius Vellutus.[44] Asconius also recorded two names: L. Sicinius Velutus and L. Albinius Paterculus.[45] The one constant here is the involvement of a Sicinius, although it is possible that not every version that Livy found did include a Sicinius.

Given that there is evidence for a Licinius as the first plebeian consul (number 2 above), a Licinius as the first plebeian *magister equitum* (number 3 above) and a Licinius as the first plebeian consular tribune (see number 6 below), the idea that a Licinius (or two Licinii, according to Dionysius) was among the first plebeian tribunes is not at all surprising. The fact that these Licinii are mostly found in variant traditions, or in inconsistent or problematic ones, may suggest that their insertion into the tradition came quite late. Licinius Macer – who is the most obvious candidate for

41 Broughton 1951, 9, 11, 112. For Licinius, see Livy 6.39.3, 10.8.8; Plut. *Cam.* 39.5; Cass. Dio fr. 29.5; Degrassi 1947, 33; on his identity, see Oakley 1997a, 664, 692–3; Oakley 2005b, 534–5.

42 Livy 2.33.2–3, 2.58.1 (= Piso *FRHist* 9 F25).

43 Dion. Hal. *Ant. Rom.* 6.89.1; there are some textual difficulties with the last name, on which see Broughton 1951, 16 n. 1.

44 Plut. *Coriol.* 7.1. The same names are also found in the Suda, s.v. Δήμαρχοι.

45 Asc. 77C; he names as his sources Tuditanus, Atticus and Livy.

the inclusion, if not also the invention, of these claims – wrote in the first century B C.[46]

5. The origins of the quaestorship are extremely difficult. Some sources have the quaestorship established under the kings, but others, in the republican period. Some have quaestors elected by the people even during the monarchy, while others introduce popular elections at a later stage.[47] According to Plutarch, P. Valerius Publicola appears to have introduced the election of quaestors in 509, although Plutarch also appears to have had Publicola create the quaestors, at least as treasurers (i.e. the *quaestores aerarii*, if they are to be distinguished from the *quaestores parricidii*). Certainly, he says that Publicola established the temple of Saturn as the treasury. The first to be elected, Plutarch claims, were P. Veturius and M. Minucius.[48] Since the quaestorship was a junior magistracy, there may well have been more prestige associated with establishing it than holding it.[49] On the other hand, Tacitus says that the first quaestors to be elected by the people, rather than chosen by the consuls (this was in

---

46   Cf. Ogilvie 1965, 313; Forsythe 1994, 292; Wiseman 2009, 19, 60–3; Oakley 2013c, 327–8.

47   Tac. *Ann.* 11.22; Ulp. *Dig.* 1.13.1.*pr.*: *Gracchanus denique Iunius libro septimo de potestatibus etiam ipsum Romulum et Numam Pompilium binos quaestores habuisse, quos ipsi non sua voce, sed populi suffragio crearent, refert.* [Indeed, Iunius Gracchanus reports in his seventh book *On Powers* that Romulus himself and Numa Pompilius each had two quaestors, whom they appointed not by their own command, but by the vote of the people.] Pompon. *Dig.* 1.2.2.22–3, in contrast, has the quaestorship created in the fifth century B C; cf. also Livy 4.4.3. See Urso 2005, 37–43.

48   Plut. *Publ.* 12.2–3: ταμιεῖον μὲν ἀπέδειξε τὸν τοῦ Κρόνου ναόν, ᾧ μέχρι νῦν χρώμενοι διατελοῦσι, ταμίας δὲ τῷ δήμῳ δύο τῶν νέων ἔδωκεν ἀποδεῖξαι· καὶ ἀπεδείχθησαν οἱ πρῶτοι Πούπλιος Οὐετούριος καὶ Μινούκιος Μάρκος [he made the temple of Saturn a treasury, as it remains to this day, and granted the people the right of appointing two young men as treasurers (quaestors); the first to be appointed were Publius Veturius and Marcus Minucius]; cf. also Zonar. 7.13. On *quaestores parricidii* and *quaestores aerarii*, see Latte 1936; Lintott 1999, 133–4; also Urso 2005, 37–43.

49   The first plebeians to be elected as quaestors were Q. Silius, P. Aelius and P. Pupius (Livy 4.54.2–3), but the minor nature of the milestone may be suggested by the omission of it, by Livy at 10.8.8, from P. Decius Mus' list of plebeian 'firsts'.

446, according to Tacitus' chronology) were Valerius Potitus and Aemilius Mamercus.[50] Following one tradition, the magistracy may have been first established by a Valerius; following another, a Valerius may have been one of the first appointed to it by popular election.[51]

6. One tradition claims that consular tribunes were elected for the first time in 444 BC, although the men who were appointed allegedly held office for just a few months and were soon replaced by suffect consuls. They were A. Sempronius Atratinus, L. Atilius Luscus and T. Cloelius Siculus; the suffect consuls were L. Papirius Mugillanus and L. Sempronius Atratinus.[52] According to Dionysius, some of the authorities he consulted recorded only consuls in this year.[53]

Consular tribunes were supposed to have next been appointed in 438; these may have been the first, at least in those accounts that had only consuls in 444. They were Mam. Aemilius, L. Quinctius Cincinnatus and L. Iulius Iullus.[54] It has, however, been argued that consuls were in fact appointed both in 444

50   Tac. *Ann.* 11.22: *mansitque consulibus potestas deligendi, donec eum quoque honorem populus mandaret. creatique primum Valerius Potitus et Aemilius Mamercus sexagesimo tertio anno post Tarquinios exactos.* [The power of choosing quaestors remained with the consuls until the people began to bestow this honour too. Valerius Potitus and Aemilius Mamercus were the first to be elected, in the sixty-third year after the expulsion of the Tarquins.]

51   Note that the Valerii are often depicted as the people's champions, Livy 2.8.1–2, 3.18.6, 3.55, 7.32.13–16, etc. This depiction has been associated with Valerius Antias (see Walsh 1961, 88–9; Wiseman 1979b, 113–17), although it is not necessary to do so, cf. Richardson 2012, 17–55; indeed, the very fact that this particular pattern of behaviour was established for the Valerii may conceivably even help to explain the appearance of Valerii in evidence of this kind. Two further 'firsts' associated with Publicola's consulship that both seem to fit with this depiction can be added: the first law passed by the centuriate assembly (Cic. *Rep.* 2.53) and the first grant of citizenship to a freedman (Plut. *Publ.* 7.5).

52   See Broughton 1951, 52–3.

53   Dion. Hal. *Ant. Rom.* 11.62.3 (see p. 155 n. 75); Cic. *Fam.* 9.21.2; cf. also the discussion in Livy 4.7.10–12.

54   See Broughton 1951, 57–8.

and in 438, but it is impossible to know one way or the other. Another tradition claims that consular tribunes were only first appointed in 389; the men said to have been in office in that year were L. Valerius Publicola, L. Verginius Tricostus, P. Cornelius, A. Manlius, L. Aemilius Mamercinus and L. Postumius Albinus, although the earliest evidence for this college includes only four names (L. Valerius Publicola and P. Cornelius are not named).[55] Given these several difficulties, it is not at all easy to draw any firm conclusions about the identity of the first consular tribunes, and the creation of the consular tribunate is itself beset with major problems.

According to one version of events, the consular tribunate was created in order to allow plebeians to gain access to the state's executive magistracy. Members of the plebs could not stand for the consulship, as they were not eligible to hold that office, but they could supposedly stand for the consular tribunate.[56] Livy states explicitly that the first plebeian consular tribune to be elected was P. Licinius Calvus, and he held office in 400. The tradition is extremely problematic, as Livy has himself already recorded the election of men to that office who appear to have

---

55 444 and 438: Beloch 1926, 249, 260; Pinsent 1975, 32 suggests that the historian Postumius Albinus may have tried to claim that Sp. Postumius Albus, consular tribune in 432, was a member of the first ever college of consular tribunes; the argument is tenuous, since it requires that several colleges of consular tribunes were in fact of consuls. 389: Eutr. 2.1 (see p. 155 n. 77); the tribunes' names are not mentioned by Eutropius; see Broughton 1951, 96–7. The earliest evidence for them comes from Cassius Hemina and Cn. Gellius (*FRHist* 6 F23 and *FRHist* 14 F8 = Macrob. *Sat.* 1.16.21–4); Briscoe 2013a, 172 supplies the missing names, as if it were all a simple matter of fact; under the circumstances, some caution may be in order.

56 Livy 4.6.8, 4.7.1–2, 4.7.7–9, 4.16.6, 4.25.1–2, and so on; Dion. Hal. *Ant. Rom.* 11.53–61, esp. 11.56.3, 11.60.5; Pompon. *Dig.* 1.2.2.25; Zonar. 7.19. Note that there may be traces of a different tradition, one in which plebeians were not eligible to hold the consular tribunate (see Livy 6.34.9, on which see Kraus 1994, 269). On the consular tribunate, and the various difficulties associated with it, see Oakley 1997a, 367–76; Oakley 2005b, 502–6; Urso 2005, 123–36, all with further bibliography; see also Chapter 6.

been from plebeian families, and several of Licinius' colleagues in 400 were also plebeian (despite Livy's assertions to the contrary). The easiest solution is to suppose that Livy has simply reproduced a claim that he found in his source (presumably the history of Licinius Macer) without seeing any need to reconcile that claim with his own narrative; indeed, it is not impossible that he may have been oblivious to the inconsistency.[57]

According to a different version of events, the consular tribunate was created not for the sake of the plebeians, but instead to meet the military needs of the day. The several consular tribunes allowed for more armies to be put in the field than had been possible when just two consuls had been in charge. While this may seem like a perfectly plausible explanation for the creation of the office, it is in fact no less difficult than the alternative. Consular tribunes were sometimes appointed in peaceful years, may not have been able to triumph and were on occasion even superseded by a dictator, that is, by a single magistrate. Moreover, they appear to have long been ineffective in the field, sometimes allegedly even on account of their numbers.[58] Despite the increased number of commanders, it was not until 414 that a consular tribune actually campaigned with any success. That consular tribune was P. Postumius Albinus.[59]

---

57   Livy 5.12.8–9, note also 5.18.5; Ogilvie 1965, 539–40: 'It is well to notice that L. owes the political explanation [for the creation of the consular tribunate] directly to Licinius Macer and furthermore that the first plebeian alleged to have been elected to the office was P. Licinius (5.12.9). That is in fact false. L. Atilius in 444 and Q. Antonius Merenda in 422 were also plebeians', 666–7; Oakley 1997a, 372; Cornell 2009, 23; Oakley 2013c, 327–8.

58   Livy 4.7.2, but compare 4.17.6–7, 4.25.14–26.1, 4.31.2, 4.45.7; see the discussions in Oakley and Urso (n. 56 above); for the dictators appointed while consular tribunes were in office, see Ridley 1986, 446–7 and also 457–9 on the consular tribunes' military accomplishments. On the apparent inability of consular tribunes to triumph, see Zonar. 7.19, and also Urso 2005, 130–1, with an overview of earlier discussions in n. 19. See also Chapter 6.

59   Ridley 1986, 457: 'The first success, note, of the tribunes came in 414, when Postumius, "cum levibus proeliis" subdued the Aequi and captured Bolae (4.49).' The primacy of this is unsurprisingly not noted by Livy, who, like other sources, is

7. The first censors were appointed in 443, according to tradition. They were L. Papirius and L. Sempronius.[60] The historicity of this censorship has been questioned, but whatever its value may be, the tradition is fairly well attested.[61] Nonetheless, it may be worth mentioning the names of the next censors (who took up office in 435), although their censorship has equally been questioned. They were C. Furius and M. Geganius.[62]

8. A range of different individuals are recorded as being the first to hold various priesthoods. There is something of a spread, but some families do reappear.

After the expulsion of King Tarquinius Superbus, the position of *rex sacrorum* was established. According to Dionysius, the first *rex sacrorum* was M'. Papirius.[63] Dionysius also claimed to know the name of the *pontifex maximus* in office after the expulsion of the kings. It was C. Papirius.[64] Although he was obviously not the first to hold the priesthood, one M. Papirius was allegedly *pontifex maximus* in 449. So, at least, Asconius claims.[65] According to Livy, however, the *pontifex maximus* in 449 was Q. Furius.[66] The variation in the evidence is significant, in its own right, but also because the historicity of the priesthoods of M'. and C. Papirius

---

much more interested in the subsequent fate of Postumius; he was allegedly stoned to death by his own soldiers (on the sometimes negative depiction of the Postumii, see n. 86 below).

60 Cic. *Fam.* 9.21.2; Livy 4.8.7; Zonar. 7.19; cf. also Dion. Hal. *Ant. Rom.* 11.63.

61 Mommsen 1864, 116; Mommsen 1887a, 335 n. 1; Beloch 1926, 80–1, who draws attention to the surprising number of Papirii who were allegedly censors early on.

62 Livy 4.22.7, 4.24.4–9, 9.33.7–9, 9.34.9. This censorship was accepted by Mommsen 1887a, 334–5, but rejected by Beloch 1926, 80–1. For the first plebeian censor, see number 3 above; according to Livy *Per.* 13 the first plebeian censor to close the *lustrum* was Cn. Domitius (280 BC).

63 Dion. Hal. *Ant. Rom.* 5.1.4.

64 Dion. Hal. *Ant. Rom.* 3.36.4.

65 Asc. 77C.

66 Livy 3.54.5. It has been noted that both men may have been consular colleagues in 441; it is, however, impossible to know if this is the cause of the confusion.

has long been doubted, and J. Rüpke has recently deemed all three Papirii fictitious.[67]

While the origins of the fetial college are variously reported, the earliest fetial priest whose name is found in the literary evidence is M. Valerius. He was allegedly a fetial at the time of Tullus Hostilius, Rome's third king. It has been suggested that the historian Valerius Antias was responsible for his appearance in the tradition.[68] M'. Valerius Maximus was said to have been an augur, and to have been appointed before his dictatorship of 494. It is conceivable that he was one of the first augurs of the republican period.[69] The first priestess of Fortuna Muliebris was Valeria, and it was also she who began the rites for the first sacrifice. Valerius Antias has similarly been held responsible for her appearance.[70]

9. As celebrating a triumph was an extremely prestigious honour, it was perhaps inevitable that spurious claims to have held one should have been made.[71] While the honour of having celebrated the first ever triumph belonged either to Romulus or to Tarquinius Priscus,[72] there was still the first triumph of the republican period to be claimed. That honour went to P. Valerius Publicola.[73]

Publicola's triumph was celebrated in 509. The second was celebrated by M. Valerius Volusus in 505. P. Postumius Tubertus also triumphed in that year. Both men triumphed over the Sabines, although Dionysius later says that M. Valerius was the

67   Mommsen 1864, 116; Szemler 1972, 50–1; Rüpke 2008, 826; Bianchi 2010, 26 n. 68; see n. 124 below.

68   Livy 1.24.6; Ogilvie 1965, 14; Rüpke 1992, 70; Rüpke 2008, 934.

69   *Inscr. It.* 13.3.78 = *ILS* 50 = *CIL* I², p. 189; *Inscr. It.* 13.3.60; Broughton 1951, 14 and n. 1; Ogilvie 1965, 306–7, 407–8; Szemler 1972, 52–3; Rüpke 2008, 939.

70   Dion. Hal. *Ant. Rom.* 8.55.3–5; Rüpke 2008, 934 and n. 5: 'Valerius Antias was possibly the first to use the name.'

71   Cic. *Brut.* 62 (see p. 7 n. 16).

72   Romulus: Dion. Hal. *Ant. Rom.* 2.34.1–3; Degrassi 1947, 65; Ampolo and Manfredini 1988, 313–14. Priscus: Plut. *Rom.* 16.8; Eutr. 1.6.

73   Livy 2.7.3; Dion. Hal. *Ant. Rom.* 5.17.2; Plut. *Publ.* 9.5 (ἐθριάμβευσε δ' ἀπ' αὐτῆς Οὐαλλέριος εἰσελάσας τεθρίππῳ πρῶτος ὑπάτων [Valerius celebrated a triumph for his victory, and was the first consul to drive into the city on a four-horse chariot]), *Rom.* 16.8; Degrassi 1947, 65.

first to do so.[74] Valerius was also, according to some sources,[75] awarded a house on the Palatine, one that was entirely unique, because its doors opened outwards. Significantly, the story is found in a fragment of Valerius Antias' history, although Antias appears to have told it in connection with a Valerius Maximus.[76] The disagreement in the sources about the recipient of this honour aside, Valerius Antias must at the very least have related the story, if he did not actually invent it himself.

P. Valerius Publicola, M. Valerius Volusus and P. Postumius Tubertus celebrated their triumphs following consular campaigns. The first triumph celebrated by a dictator was that of A. Postumius Albus, after his victory in the battle of Lake Regillus (499/496; on the date, see number 3 above).[77]

Another Valerius, M'. Valerius Maximus, triumphed in 494. Along with the usual honours, Valerius was also awarded a place in the Circus from which to watch the games, as well as a curule chair. He was the first to receive such honours.[78] He was also the first to be called 'Maximus'; according to Cicero, he received this

---

74 Livy 2.16.1; Dion. Hal. *Ant. Rom.* 5.39.4 and 6.12.1 where Dionysius describes Valerius as the first to triumph over the Sabines (ὁ τὸν κατὰ Σαβίνων πρῶτος καταγαγὼν θρίαμβον); Plut. *Publ.* 20.1 (Plutarch mentions only Valerius' triumph); Eutr. 1.11; Degrassi 1947, 65.

75 Iulius Hyginus *FRHist* 63 F1 (= Asc. 13C): *Varronem autem tradere M. Valerio, quia Sabinos vicerat, aedes in Palatio tributas, Iulius Hyginus dicit in libro priore de viris claris* [However, in his first book on distinguished men, Iulius Hyginus says that Varro relates that a house on the Palatine was assigned to M. Valerius, because he had defeated the Sabines]; Dion. Hal. *Ant. Rom.* 5.39.4; Plin. *HN* 36.112; Plut. *Publ.* 20.2.

76 Valerius Antias *FRHist* 25 F21 (= Asc. 13C): *nam Valerio Maximo, ut Antias tradidit, inter alios honores domus quoque publice aedificata est in Palatio, cuius exitus, quo magis insignis esset, in publicum versus declinaretur, hoc est extra privatum aperiretur.* [For, as Antias related, among other honours, a house was built at public expense for Valerius Maximus on the Palatine, the door of which, so that the distinction would be greater, opened out towards the public domain, that is, it opened beyond his private space.]

77 Livy 2.20.13; Dion. Hal. *Ant. Rom.* 6.17.2; Degrassi 1947, 67.

78 Livy 2.31.3; Fest. 464L; and his *elogium* (see n. 69); also Dion. Hal. *Ant. Rom.* 6.43.1 for his triumph; Degrassi 1947, 67.

title for his role in restoring peace between the orders, but, according to Zonaras, he was called Maximus on account of his victory over the Sabines.[79] M'. Valerius Maximus was the second dictator to celebrate a triumph. As was discussed earlier (number 3 above), there exist variant traditions concerning the identity of Rome's first dictator and, according to one of these traditions, a M'. Valerius was the first to hold this magistracy. If this variant tradition – for which the evidence is extremely limited – happened to include a triumph for Manius, then he would have also been the first dictator to triumph.

The first *ovatio*, the lesser triumph in which the general entered the city on foot, was said to have been celebrated by P. Postumius Tubertus (in 503). He was also the first man to wear a myrtle wreath.[80]

In 431 the dictator A. Postumius Tubertus celebrated a triumph for his victory over the Aequi and Volsci at Mount Algidus. According to Ovid, Postumius triumphed using white horses.[81] He may have been the first to do so, at least in republican times (Propertius has Romulus triumph with white horses,[82] but the story could easily be late). The difficulty is that Plutarch says that M. Furius Camillus was the first to have white horses in his triumph (of 396). Camillus was also said to have lost favour and even, according to some sources, to have been sent into exile on

79   Cic. *Brut.* 54: *M. Valerium dictatorem dicendo sedavisse discordias eique ob eam rem honores amplissimos habitos et eum primum ob eam ipsam causam Maximum esse appellatum* [M. Valerius the dictator appeased their discord with a speech and, on account of this, was granted the most distinguished honours and, for the same reason, was the first to be called Maximus]; Plut. *Pomp.* 13.7; Zonar. 7.14 (Zonaras also calls him Marcus). Cf. also Wiseman 1998, 87.

80   Dion. Hal. *Ant. Rom.* 5.47.2–4 = Macer *FRHist* 27 F14; Plin. *HN* 15.125; Degrassi 1947, 65.

81   Diod. 12.64.3; Livy 4.29.4. Ov. *Fast.* 6.723–4: *unde suburbano clarus, Tuberte, triumpho / vectus es in niveis postmodo victor equis.* [Whence, Tubertus, you later rode as the victor on snow-white horses, illustrious in your suburban triumph.]

82   Prop. 4.1.32.

account of this, as white horses were believed to be the preserve of the gods.[83] There are several difficulties in the tradition concerning Camillus' exile and his use of white horses, and the tradition is quite probably late.[84] But equally, Plutarch could simply have made a mistake when he claimed that Camillus was the first to use white horses.[85]

Given the negative tradition of Camillus' triumph, if Ovid's story about Tubertus' horses is also late, it may be that it was intended to imply that Tubertus was likewise impious and overly proud, and certainly the Postumii are presented in this way on more than a few occasions.[86] On the other hand, if Ovid's story predates the hostile tradition of Camillus' triumph, then it may conceivably be free from such negative connotations.

10. When L. Iunius Brutus, the founder of the Republic and Rome's first consul, died, the eulogy in his honour was delivered by P. Valerius Publicola. Funeral speeches were customarily delivered by a member of the deceased's family.[87] Brutus, however, had executed his own sons, and his family had also suffered at the hands of Tarquinius Superbus. Whether or not Brutus had any living relatives was a matter of some considerable controversy, especially in

---

83   Plut. *Cam.* 7.1. Diod. 14.93.3, 14.117.6; Livy 5.23.4–6, 5.28.1; Cass. Dio 52.13.3; *De vir. ill.* 23.4; Zonar. 7.21.

84   The fact that Iulius Caesar triumphed with white horses has sometimes been thought to be potentially significant, Cass. Dio 43.14.3; as Weinstock 1971, 74 says, a 'post-Caesarian date would lead to an even simpler explanation: a friend justified, or an adversary condemned, Caesar's triumph by creating Camillus' precedent either as an exceptional privilege or as a sign of arrogance.' On this sort of approach to the traditions of the past, see also Chapter 8.

85   Plut. *Cam.* 7.1 states that Camillus was not only the first to use white horses, but he was also the last. As Weinstock 1971, 71 notes, this is either a mistake or evidence of Plutarch's use of a pre-Caesarian source. If the latter is the case, then this may suggest that Ovid's claim could be from a post-Caesarian source.

86   For example, Polyb. 39.1; Livy 4.44.11–12, 4.49.7–50.5, 10.37.6–12, *Per.* 11 (along with Bravo and Griffin 1988), *Per.* 19, 42.1.7–8 (a hostile re-working of the theme of the Postumian 'first'?); Dion. Hal. *Ant. Rom.* 10.33–41, esp. 10.41.5, 17/18.4–5; Cass. Dio fr. 36.32; Oros. 5.18.22.

87   Polyb. 6.53.2.

later times.[88] In any case, his funeral eulogy was said to have been given by Valerius Publicola. It was the first.[89]

11. It has been claimed that the first consultation of the Sibylline books in the republican period was carried out by A. Postumius Albus in 496.[90] This would be the case, were it not for an overlooked passage in Plutarch's life of Valerius Publicola, in which Publicola appears to have consulted the books in his fourth consulship (504).[91]

12. When P. Valerius Publicola died, he was honoured by being buried inside the city. According to Dionysius, Publicola was the only man ever to be so honoured. According to Cicero, however, P. Postumius Tubertus had been granted the same privilege.[92] Publicola's funeral was also paid for at public expense.[93]

13. On existing evidence, the first temple vowed during the course of battle in the republican period was the one promised to the Dioscuri by the dictator A. Postumius Albus at the battle of Lake Regillus.[94] Again on existing evidence, the *duumviri* (*sc. aedi dedicandae*) who dedicated this temple in 484 were the first to be appointed. One of them was A. Postumius Albus, the son of the dictator; the name of the other *duumvir* is not known.[95] According to Dionysius, Postumius Albus also vowed the temple to Ceres, Liber and Libera (following his consultation of the

88 See Chapter 8.

89 Dion. Hal. *Ant. Rom.* 5.17; Plut. *Publ.* 9.6–7; *De vir. ill.* 10.7.

90 Dion. Hal. *Ant. Rom.* 6.17.3; Gjerstad 1973, 266–7; Monaco 1995, 288; Orlin 1997, 78, 203.

91 Plut. *Publ.* 21.1.

92 Dion. Hal. *Ant. Rom.* 5.48.3; Cic. *Leg.* 2.58, who also mentions C. Fabricius; Plut. *QR* 79, naming only Valerius and Fabricius, *Publ.* 23.3.

93 Livy 2.16.7; Dion. Hal. *Ant. Rom.* 5.48.3; Val. Max. 4.4.1; Plut. *Publ.* 23.2; Apul. *Apol.* 18.10; *De vir. ill.* 15.6; Amm. Marc. 14.6.11; Eutr. 1.11.4; August. *De civ. D.* 5.18.

94 Livy 2.20.12, 2.42.5; cf. also Dion. Hal. *Ant. Rom.* 6.13.4.

95 Livy 2.42.5; Münzer 1953a. The first temple dedicated in the republican period was the temple of Jupiter; this was dedicated by M. Horatius, but either as consul or as *pontifex*, see Broughton 1951, 3–4; for other early dedications, none by *duumviri*, see Livy 2.21.2, 2.21.7, 2.27.5–6; Dion. Hal. *Ant. Rom.* 6.1.4, 6.94.3.

Sibylline books, number 11 above),[96] and the first votive games were said to have been vowed by him as well.[97]

14. The first military honours awarded after a battle were also awarded by A. Postumius Albus, following his victory at Lake Regillus. Pliny states explicitly that the first ever golden crown was awarded by Postumius.[98] There is a special significance to all this. The awarding of honours in recognition of achievement accords perfectly with the ideology of the newly established Republic. Previously, when kings had ruled Rome, prominence had been a source of suspicion and had only led to danger.[99]

15. On numerous occasions the Romans dispatched ambassadors on missions of one kind or another. Although it is inevitably difficult to single out any particular episode as a 'first', it may be useful nonetheless to draw attention to several of these embassies, and especially to those where the names of the ambassadors are recorded.

---

96 Dion. Hal. *Ant. Rom.* 6.17.2–4; although, at 6.94.3, Dionysius has Postumius make his vow on the commencement of the battle of Regillus. Wiseman 1998, 35–6 traces Dionysius' story back to the history of Postumius Albinus.

97 Cic. *Div.* 1.55: *omnes hoc historici, Fabii, Gellii, sed maxume Coelius: cum bello Latino ludi votivi maxumi primum fierent, civitas ad arma repente est excitata, itaque ludis intermissis instaurativi constituti sunt.* [All the historians have told this, Fabius, Gellius, but above all Coelius: when, during the Latin war, the greatest votive games were being held for the first time, the state was suddenly called to arms, and so, as the games had been interrupted, repeat ceremonies were ordained (following Wiseman 1979a, 142–4, reading *maxume* instead of *proxume*.)] For Postumius' vow, see Dion. Hal. *Ant. Rom.* 6.10.1, 6.17.2. Versnel 1970, 106, 113–14.

98 Plin. *HN* 33.38 = Piso *FRHist* 9 F23; Livy 2.20.12; Dion. Hal. *Ant. Rom.* 6.9.3–4, 6.14.1; Plut. *Coriol.* 3.2.

99 Cf. Forsythe 1994, 260; note also Wiseman 2008, 136–8 on Liber. Sall. *Cat.* 7.2: *nam regibus boni quam mali suspectiores sunt semperque eis aliena virtus formidulosa est* [For kings are more suspicious of good people than bad and the virtue of others is always frightening to them]; cf., for example, Livy 1.54.5–9; Dion. Hal. *Ant. Rom.* 4.56.1–4; Ov. *Fast.* 2.701–10; Zonar. 7.10 for the fate of the prominent citizens of Gabii.

In 507, T. Herminius and Sp. Larcius were sent by the consuls to the cities on the Pomptine plain in order to fetch grain, a task they carried out successfully. Some years later, in 501, M. Valerius was sent on a diplomatic mission to negotiate with the Latins, in the effort to prevent them from making war on Rome.[100] Of potentially greater significance is the embassy of 492. In this year P. Valerius, Publicola's son, and L. Geganius were sent to Sicily to purchase grain. Not only was this Rome's first embassy to Sicily, the episode is also noteworthy on account of the extraordinary chronological difficulties. Valerius and Geganius were said to have set out during the consulship of T. Geganius and P. Minucius (492) and to have returned in the following year. According to Dionysius, Cn. Gellius, Licinius Macer and many other Roman writers claimed that the ambassadors negotiated with Dionysius, the tyrant of Syracuse, but as Dionysius (the historian) points out, the chronology is completely wrong. The ambassadors would have dealt with Gelon. The tyrant Dionysius came to power almost a century later. Dionysius (the historian) suggests that the first Roman historian to record this episode may have simply made a mistake and that the rest had just followed him,[101] but the confusion, the involvement of a Valerius, and the significance of the embassy (Rome's first to Sicily) may be grounds for suspicion about the story as a whole. Note as well that Dionysius also says that ambassadors were sent at the same time and for the same reason to Etruria, Campania and the Pomptine plain, but that Dionysius does not have any names for these ambassadors,[102] whose missions were, of course, much less prestigious, by comparison, and also

---

100 Herminius and Larcius: Dion. Hal. *Ant. Rom.* 5.26.3–4; Valerius: Dion. Hal. *Ant. Rom.* 5.50.3–51.2.

101 Dion. Hal. *Ant. Rom.* 7.1.3–2.1, 7.20.3; Cn. Gellius *FRHist* 14 F25; Licinius Macer *FRHist* 27 F17.

102 Dion. Hal. *Ant. Rom.* 7.1.3; although it should be noted that Livy 2.34.3–7 records no names at all. Plut. *Coriol.* 16.1 is also silent, but he is not interested in the actual embassy itself.

because embassies of this kind had been sent to various regions in Italy before.

The historian Postumius Albinus was notoriously philhellenic. He was also a statesman of some success and, of the various duties that he performed during his political career, one is potentially relevant in the present context. In 146 Albinus went to Greece and, after the victory of L. Mummius, he served in the commission of ten men appointed to assist Mummius in the reorganisation of the region.[103] This may make the appearance of Sp. Postumius Albus in the embassy that was supposedly sent to Athens and other Greek cities in 454 to collect their laws, including those of Solon, a little suspicious.[104] Moreover, this was Rome's first such embassy to Athens. A few years later, after the embassy had returned, the Romans appointed a college of decemvirs to draw up their first law-code, the Twelve Tables. Sp. Postumius Albus was one of these decemvirs.[105] He was a member of the first college, which was said to have been just and fair in its rule, unlike the second, which was tyrannical (and of which no Postumius was a member). The other members of the first college were (following Livy)[106] Ap. Claudius, T. Genucius, P. Sestius, T. Veturius, C. Iulius, A. Manlius, P. Sulpicius, P. Curiatius and T. Romilius.

---

103 Postumius Albinus *FRHist* 4 F1 (= Polyb. 39.1; Gell. *NA* 11.8.2–3); Plut. *Cato Mai.* 12.5; cf. also Cic. *Acad. Pr.* 2.137, *Brut.* 81; embassy: Cic. *Att.* 13.30.2, 13.32.3; note also Veyne 1986. Walbank 1979, 726; Gruen 1984, 240; Northwood 2013, 185–6.

104 Livy 3.31.8; Dion. Hal. *Ant. Rom.* 10.52.4. His colleagues were A. Manlius and P. (so Livy, Dionysius calls him Ser.) Sulpicius Camerinus. It is, however, often argued that the tradition of the embassy to Athens was developed in the first century BC by L. Aelius Stilo, Ser. Sulpicius Rufus or Aelius Tubero; see Ruschenbusch 1963; Ogilvie 1965, 449–50; Siewert 1978, 341–3; cf. also Ungern-Sternberg 2005, 89–90. On the choice of Postumius, Münzer 1953b, 934: 'vielleicht unter dem Eindruck ähnlicher Missionen späterer Postumier', which does not necessarily preclude invention by Postumius Albinus; although cf. in this context Richardson 2012, 17–55.

105 Diod. 12.23.1; Livy 3.32.6, 3.33.3–5; Dion. Hal. *Ant. Rom.* 10.56.2.

106 Livy 3.33.3 (Ogilvie's *OCT*). Broughton 1951, 45–6.

In 398, during Rome's long war with Veii, the Romans allegedly sent an embassy to Delphi, to consult the oracle. Although
the Romans had supposedly sent ambassadors to Delphi during
the regal period, this was the first embassy sent by the Republic.
The names of the ambassadors are provided by Plutarch: Cossus
Licinius, Valerius Potitus and Fabius Ambustus.[107] There are
some difficulties with the identity of these men,[108] but the names
Licinius, Valerius and Fabius are clear. The Fabii too produced an
historian, Q. Fabius Pictor, who also happened to lead an expedition to Delphi in 216.[109]

16. Polybius says that the first treaty between Rome and Carthage
    was struck in the first year of the republican period, that is, when
    L. Iunius Brutus and M. Horatius were the consuls (see number 1
    above). Diodorus, on the other hand, says that Rome's first treaty
    with Carthage was struck during the consulship of M. Valerius
    and M. Popilius (348).[110] It may be that the consuls' names are as-
    sociated with this important event merely for dating purposes and
    nothing more, but the existence of these two incompatible tra-
    ditions, the significance of any treaty, but especially the first, be-
    tween Rome and Carthage, not to mention the appearance of yet
    another Valerius, make the striking of this particular treaty worth
    noting.[111]

What stands out in all this is, first of all, the considerable number of
Valerian (see 1, 3, 5, 6?, 8, 9, 10, 11, 12, 15 and 16), Licinian (2, 3, 4, 6 and
15) and Postumian (3?, 6, 9, 13, 14 and 15) 'firsts', although there are several
'firsts' for the Papirii as well (7 and 8). While the Valerian, Licinian and
Papirian 'firsts' have mostly been observed before, the various Postumian

107   Plut. *Cam.* 4.4.
108   See Broughton 1951, 86.
109   Livy 22.57.5, 23.11.1–6; Plut. *Fab.* 18.3; App. *Hann.* 27. Richardson 2012, 107–8.
110   Diod. 16.69.1; Oros. 3.7.1 (the first); also Livy 7.27.2, although Livy does not expli-
      citly say that it was the first.
111   Diodorus' claim that the treaty of 348 was the first is frequently dismissed; see
      Chapter 4 on the problems involved.

'firsts' have not. What is also noticeable is the number of Postumian 'runners-up' (3, 9, 11 and 12); on several occasions, Postumii come a close second, and so often to a Valerius. Postumius Albinus wrote his history in the second century BC, while Valerius Antias wrote his sometime in the first. It is difficult not to suspect that Postumius Albinus may have laid claim to a number of 'firsts' for his ancestors, and that some of those claims may have subsequently been usurped by Valerius Antias. Be that as it may, there are just so many Postumian, Licinian and Valerian 'firsts' that the conclusion, however unfashionable it may be, that Postumius Albinus, Licinius Macer and Valerius Antias must have invented stories or at least tampered with the received tradition seems virtually inescapable.

The obvious objection that, if the Postumii, Licinii and Valerii were influential and prominent in early Rome, then they may well have been the first to do any number of things does not seem to be sufficient to get around this, not least because these 'firsts' are in fact scattered across the tradition of a fairly lengthy period of time. In the case of the Licinii, there is also an obvious theme. The Licinii are so often connected with important developments in the struggle of the orders: one (or even two) of the first tribunes of the plebs was allegedly a Licinius (4), the first plebeian *magister equitum* was allegedly a Licinius (3), the first plebeian consular tribune was allegedly a Licinius as well (6) and it was evidently even claimed that the first plebeian consul was a Licinius (2).[112] Clearly it was perfectly possible for historians to invent or insert claims, and clearly it was also perfectly possible for subsequent historians to invent or insert rival ones.

The case of the Papirii, a *gens* that does not appear to have produced an historian, clearly demonstrates that the appearance of such claims in the literary evidence was not due simply to the intervention of those few individuals who wrote history. While it may be useful to remember that both Cicero and Livy said that funeral speeches and the like were to blame

---

112   Licinius Macer's own political views (he may have been a *popularis* statesman) should be taken into account, as they may have influenced his work; see, for example, Oakley 1997a, 92; Wiseman 2009, 19–24, 59–63, 78–80; Oakley 2013c, 320–2. Cornell 2018, 186–200 raises doubts about the historian's identity; see Wiseman 2018, XV for a reply. For immediate purposes, it is enough to note once again Livy 7.9.5 (p. 8 n. 18).

for various problems in Rome's historical traditions,[113] it is, however, quite obvious that, if widespread cultural practices such as funeral speeches were indeed the direct cause of these particular claims, then the distribution of them would almost certainly be very different. Similarly, Romans were expected to emulate their ancestors, and this expectation could in turn affect the ways in which individual Romans were believed to have behaved.[114] This may very well explain some of the repetition of behaviour associated with these 'firsts', and may have even given some plausibility to several of the claims,[115] but again, if this alone were the cause, then the distribution of the 'firsts' would quite probably be different, and the fact that the Postumii, Licinii and Valerii produced historians would presumably have to be dismissed as nothing more than an extraordinary coincidence.[116] For these reasons, it seems safer to conclude that the intervention of a writer of some description was needed, if not to invent such claims, then at least to incorporate them into the literary tradition.

Although no Papirius appears to have written a work of history, there is nonetheless some evidence for Papirii who wrote. C. Papirius, the *pontifex maximus* allegedly in office following the expulsion of the kings, and so presumably the first *pontifex maximus* of the republican period, was said (by Dionysius) to have copied down various writings on religious rites that had originally been composed by Numa.[117] This work is usually presumed to be the same as the *ius Papirianum*, although that was, according to Pomponius, the work of a Sex. Papirius.[118] Pomponius also knew of a P. Papirius, who compiled the laws of the kings, the *leges regiae*.[119] The *ius Papirianum* was, like the *leges regiae*, almost certainly a later, antiquarian

---

113   See n. 1 above. Note Livy's words, 8.40.4: *vitiatam memoriam funebribus laudibus reor falsisque imaginum titulis, dum familiae ad se quaeque famam rerum gestarum honorumque fallente mendacio trahunt* (see p. 7 n. 16).

114   Cf. Richardson 2012, 17–55.

115   See, for instance, nn. 51, 86, 104 and 109 above.

116   Hence the position of Walter 2003b, 153, and Beck and Walter 2004, 171 plays down the role of the historian too much.

117   Dion. Hal. *Ant. Rom.* 3.36.4.

118   Pompon. *Dig.* 1.2.2.2. According to Pomponius, the *ius Papirianum* also included laws passed by Romulus.

119   Pompon. *Dig.* 1.2.2.36.

reconstruction;[120] however, while it may conceivably have included some mention of C. Papirius, and perhaps even of M'. Papirius, the first *rex sacrorum*, mention of any later Papirius would obviously be anachronistic, if the *ius Papirianum* was indeed presented simply as the work of C. Papirius. In any case, not only is the evidence for these writings late and difficult, the nature and possible influence of them are also difficult to ascertain.[121]

Rüpke has argued that C. Papirius Maso, a *pontifex* whose career he dates to the third century BC, may have been involved in 'publishing the pontifical formulae in written form'.[122] The evidence for Papirius Maso's literary activities is no less difficult. Valerius Maximus merely says that Maso wrote out the formula for surrender (*verba deditionis*),[123] and so it is inevitably risky to suppose that this is evidence for any larger project. Rüpke, however, connects Papirius Maso's work with that of the *pontifex maximus*, Ti. Coruncanius, who was conceivably Maso's colleague. Coruncanius was likewise involved, Rüpke argues, in 'committing those formulae to writing' as well as 'documenting precedents', and he suggests that 'Maso's participation in this project may then have been reflected in the increased presence of his own family members ... in the early period.'[124] This is possible, but

---

120 The *terminus ante quem* for its invention is presumably the career of Granius Flaccus (*Dig.* 50.16.144), who may have lived in the first century BC (a Granius Flaccus dedicated a book to Iulius Caesar: Censorinus *DN* 3.2); Cic. *Fam.* 9.21.2, in his list of patrician Papirii, does not mention C. (or P. or Sex.) Papirius, which is telling; see Gabba 2000, 90–4. Watson 1972, 103–4, however, tries vainly to defend the evidence and dismiss all the inconsistencies in it. On the wider problems associated with such early writings, cf. Wiseman 2008, 1–15; also Chapters 1–3 above.

121 The evidence for the *leges regiae* is collected in Franciosi 2003. The material comes from a wide range of sources, but the origin of it all is another matter entirely. The range and diversity of the material may tell against the existence of an Urtext.

122 Rüpke 2008, 826 n. 4.

123 Val. Max. 6.5.1b.

124 Rüpke 2008, 826 n. 4. Glinister 2017, 71–2 rejects Rüpke's conclusions; she argues for the existence of family records (she cites Cic. *Fam.* 9.21, in which Cicero informs Papirius Paetus about the history of the Papirii!) and dismisses out of hand the evidence for the unreliability of such material. The approach is entirely aprioristic (see the Introduction), and also fails to account for the general absence of evidence for early priests, an absence that strongly tells against the existence of early records (see pp. 140–3). Besides, the first patrician Papirius that Cicero knew

the argument is obviously circular. On the positive side, however, a context such as this may well explain why most of the Papirian 'firsts' involve the holding of priesthoods. A religious context would have further significance too. It would suggest that it was not just Rome's annalists who were 'in a position to impose a fraudulent version of Rome's history on their contemporaries and on succeeding generations', but that Roman writers of other kinds may have been in such a position too.

That conclusion may well be supported by the identity of one of Rome's first Vestal virgins. According to Plutarch, Numa initially appointed just two Vestals, although more were subsequently added, until the total had been raised to six. The first were Gegania and Verenia, and it has been suggested that Verenia may owe her position (and no doubt her existence as well) to the antiquarian Veranius.[125] Among other things, Veranius wrote about pontifical matters, a topic that would easily have allowed for discussion of the appointment of Vestals, and he evidently described some of the Vestals' ritual duties too.[126]

There is no need to suppose that the glorification of ancestors in the manner discussed in this chapter was widely practised by Rome's historians, and the fact that the most conspicuous patterns in the distribution of the 'firsts' involve only a minority of families suggests that it was not. But the evidence is enough to warn against simply denying Rome's historians (and other writers) any opportunity to invent, to modify what other historians had already written and to differ with popular traditions of one kind or another, and to do so, moreover, on occasion precisely in order to glorify their ancestors.

---

of was L. Papirius Mugillanus, the censor of 443 BC; that is, Cicero appears to have been unaware of M'. and C. Papirius.

125   Plut. *Numa* 10.1; Wiseman 1985a, 268–9; Syme 1988, 634 n. 41; Smith 1998, 152. The original appointment of the Vestals was evidently a matter of antiquarian speculation, cf. Dion. Hal. *Ant. Rom.* 2.67.1, 3.67.2; Plut. *Numa* 10.1; Fest. 468L; Paul. Fest. 475L; see also Gell. *NA* 1.12.19 on Amata (on which, cf. Wildfang 2006, 40–1 for various explanations; Gegania and Verenia, as well as Canuleia and Tarpeia, are all missing from Wildfang's catalogue of Vestals on pp. 142–3).

126   Macrob. *Sat.* 3.5.6, 3.20.2; Fest. 152L on the preparation of *muries*. See Wiseman 1985a, 266–9 on Veranius' identity and work. For the appointment of Vestals, see Gell. *NA* 1.12. I am grateful to Peter Wiseman for drawing my attention to the possible source of this 'first'.

CHAPTER 8

L. Iunius Brutus the Patrician and the Political Allegiance of Q. Aelius Tubero

According to Dionysius of Halicarnassus, those writers who have in-vestigated Rome's history most accurately state that L. Iunius Brutus (Rome's liberator and first consul) did not leave any children. They offer, Dionysius says, much evidence in support of this, but one argu-ment in particular is especially compelling: L. Iunius Brutus was, they say, a patrician, while those who claimed descent from him were all ple-beian, and so stood only for those magistracies for which plebeians were eligible by law (the offices of aedile and tribune); but they did not stand for the consulship, as plebeians were not eligible to hold it. Only later did the Iunii reach that office, after it had been opened up to the plebs.[1]

The Iunii were plebeian and had always been so. The story that L. Iunius Brutus was patrician, although potentially attractive to those who have confidence in the value of the early consular *fasti* and who consequently find the presence of plebeian names in them an inconvenience,[2] is simply unhistorical. For a start, L. Iunius Brutus never existed, and the mythical liberator probably only became a Iunius in the fourth century BC.[3] The origin and cause of this story are easily found, however, and they may shed some light not just on Dionysius' sources – and on the political allegiances

---

[1]   Dion. Hal. *Ant. Rom.* 5.18; for Brutus the patrician see also 5.48.2.

[2]   See Broughton 1951, 1 and 4 n. 1; for belief in the existence of patrician Iunii, see also Mommsen 1864, 108; De Sanctis 1980, 412. On plebeian names in the *fasti*, cf. for instance the approach taken by Gjerstad (1973, 83–97), although Gjerstad himself rejects L. Brutus' consulship (77–8); more recently still, Drummond 1989, 175–6; Forsythe 2005, 161–2 (although Forsythe includes other hypotheses in his discussion and defends L. Brutus' consulship on different grounds, 154–5).

[3]   Cf., variously, Alföldi 1965, 77, 82–3, 351–2; Gjerstad 1973, 77–8; Welwei 2000; Wiseman 2014.

of one of them in particular – but also on the nature and value of the literary tradition of early Rome.

A Roman noble was expected to live up to the achievements of his ancestors, and that often meant that he had, if at all possible, to emulate his ancestors' deeds.[4] One of the best illustrations of this is found in the career of M. Iunius Brutus, who conspired, along with numerous others, to murder C. Iulius Caesar. M. Iunius Brutus claimed descent from L. Iunius Brutus, the man who had expelled L. Tarquinius Superbus, Rome's seventh and last king. On his mother's side, M. Brutus was also descended from C. Servilius Ahala. Ahala had famously murdered Sp. Maelius when the latter had tried to establish himself as king.[5] If there was anyone at Rome who could be expected to take swift action against an aspiring monarch, it was M. Brutus. Consequently, when Caesar established his autocracy, Marcus came under pressure to act. Messages were left for him on his tribunal, some of which challenged his claim to be descended from L. Brutus.[6] The natural implication is obviously that, if Marcus was indeed descended from Lucius, he would not have been able to tolerate Caesar's position. True heirs behaved like their ancestors; it was natural that they did, and it was expected that they would.[7] Not surprisingly, these

---

4   For example, Cic. *Off.* 1.78, 1.116, 1.121, *Rab. Post.* 2; Val. Max. 5.8.3; cf. also nn. 6 and
      11 below. For various approaches to this well-known phenomenon, see Flower 1996,
      passim, for example, 22, 221; Treggiari 2003, esp. 155–7 on *imitatio* and *aemulatio*;
      Walter 2003a; Walter 2004; Lentano 2007, *passim*, esp. 113–223; Lentano 2008;
      Richardson 2012, 17–55.

5   M. Brutus advertised his ancestry on his coins, for which see Crawford 1974, 455–6,
      on no. 433, 1 and 2. He also commissioned Atticus to research his ancestry; see Nep.
      Att. 18.3; Cic. *Att.* 13.40.1. See also Cic. *Phil.* 2.26, 10.14, *Brut.* 331, *Orat.* 153; Plut.
      Brut. 1.1–5, *Caes.* 62.1.

6   Plut. *Brut.* 9.5–10.6, *Caes.* 62.4; Suet. *Iul.* 80.3; App. *BCiv.* 2.112–13; Cass. Dio
      44.12.2–3.

7   On the influence and importance of Brutus' ancestry, see variously MacMullen
      1966, 7–10; Flower 1996, 88–9; Gotter 2000, 330–3; Welwei 2000, 53–4; Walter
      2003a, 272–4; Lentano 2007, 127–34; Lentano 2008, 891–5; Richardson 2012,
      21–3, 44–6.

ideas and expectations could, in turn, be used to justify all manner of behaviour.[8]

According to Plutarch, those who did not approve of M. Brutus' role in Caesar's murder denied that Marcus really was descended from L. Brutus. They pointed out that L. Brutus had executed his own sons for conspiring to restore Tarquinius Superbus to his throne, and so had left no children. They also argued, Plutarch says, that M. Brutus was descended from a plebeian.[9] Since the Iunii were plebeian, that argument must logically presuppose that L. Iunius Brutus was patrician, and it is in this context that Dionysius' claim that he was is to be understood. By asserting that L. Iunius was patrician, Marcus' opponents were trying to disparage his claims to be descended from Lucius, and thus, in turn, to deprive Marcus' actions of their legitimacy;[10] it is conceivable too that they were also attempting to undermine some of the associated rhetoric, namely that Iulius Caesar was a king, just as Tarquinius Superbus had been. Cicero, in contrast, who was more than happy with Caesar's fate, made sure that he insisted on the correctness of M. Brutus' claims. How could Marcus *not* have acted as he had, seeing every day as he did the *imago* of L. Iunius Brutus, as well as that of Servilius Ahala?[11]

Dionysius' source appears therefore to have been an opponent and critic of M. Brutus and, it is probably safe to assume, an adherent of Iulius Caesar. The constitutional details that Dionysius includes at this point in

8   Cf., for example, Suet. *Claud.* 24.1, and Ryan 1993; Val. Max. 5.8.3; the idea was parodied by Plaut. *Pers.* 53–61, on which cf. Walter 2003a, 262; Lentano 2007, 179; Richardson 2012, 43–5.

9   Plut. *Brut.* 1.6; Cass. Dio 44.12.1.

10   Cf. Mastrocinque 1988, 95–6; Rawson 1991, 490–1; Welwei 2000, 54.

11   Cic. *Phil.* 2.26: *etenim si auctores ad liberandam patriam desiderarentur illis actoribus, Brutos ego impellerem, quorum uterque L. Bruti imaginem cotidie videret, alter etiam Ahalae?* [Besides, if those who acted to free their fatherland required others to prompt them, would I be needed to incite the Bruti, both of whom saw the *imago* of L. Brutus every day, and one of whom also saw that of Ahala?] For the *imagines* as stimuli, cf. Polyb. 6.53.9–10; Sall. *Iug.* 4.5–6; Gregory 1994, 91; see also the various works cited in nn. 4 and 7 above. For Cicero's view of Caesar's position (viz. that he was a king), see for instance *Att.* 14.11.1, *Fam.* 11.3.4, 11.8.1, 11.27.8, *Phil.* 2.34, 2.108, 2.114.

his narrative regarding the magistracies that the plebs was eligible to hold may be relevant. Dionysius' source was presumably someone who took an interest in legal and constitutional matters, or someone who was at least sufficiently well versed in them to be able to use them in support of his argument;[12] and it may be that his source was perhaps also someone who had reason to be conscious of, or interested in, the disparities that had once existed between patricians and plebeians. Also relevant may be Dionysius' comments about the accuracy of his source.

Traditional *Quellenforschung* – which typically involves attempting to discern the precise sources that an author used – is both an unfashionable and a highly conjectural science, but that does not mean that the approach should be abandoned altogether.[13] Its current lack of popularity is primarily the result of a reaction to the excesses and overconfidence of certain scholars of previous generations. As for its conjectural nature, it is important merely to realise that any argument about the sources that an ancient writer may have used will usually only ever amount to a hypothesis, a hypothesis that must be tested just like any other. Inevitably it is possible, therefore, to do no more than make a suggestion about the identity of Dionysius' source, and then to explore, with all due caution, some of the implications of that suggestion, to see if it is at all plausible.

Very early on in his work Dionysius provides a list of his sources (*Ant. Rom.* 1.7.3). The list appears to be confined only to those who wrote in Latin and it is not comprehensive in any case. Other authors not included in the list, some of whom wrote in Latin, are mentioned elsewhere by Dionysius

12   This may not seem like an argument that would require specialist knowledge, but note how unperturbed people in antiquity generally appear to have been about the presence of plebeian names in the early consular *fasti*; cf. Livy 6.42.9: *L. Sextius de plebe primus consul factus* [L. Sextius the first consul elected from the plebs], 7.1.1–2; and yet Livy has earlier recorded the election to the consulship of numerous men who appear to have been from plebeian families: 1.60.3, 2.17.1, 2.18.1, 2.21.1, 2.33.3, 2.34.1, 2.34.7, 2.40.14, 2.41.1, 2.63.1, 3.10.5, 3.25.1, 3.30.1, 3.31.5, 4.1.1.

13   *Pace* Cornell 1995, 4–5; Cornell 2005, 64: 'there is nothing whatever to be gained by trying to identify the individual writer or writers being followed by Livy or Dionysius at any given point (that is, from *Quellenforschung* as traditionally practiced).' The following discussion, it is hoped, may reveal some of the benefits to be had from '*Quellenforschung* as traditionally practiced'.

(for instance, C. Sempronius Tuditanus, whom Dionysius cites at *Ant. Rom.* 1.11.1). The field can be narrowed down very easily and quite considerably. Most of the authors Dionysius names in his work simply lived too early to have been able to contribute to debates that took place in the first century BC.[14] Dionysius also claims to have conversed with learned contemporaries, and it is not impossible that the source he refers to at *Ant. Rom.* 5.18 was someone to whom he had spoken. But this is unlikely. Dionysius' vocabulary makes it clear that his source wrote rather than spoke. For the same reason, it is also clear that Dionysius had not simply got hold of a political pamphlet of some kind, or some such document: his vocabulary seems to imply that his source was a general work on Roman affairs, rather than something devoted to a specific political issue.[15]

There are several possible sources that Dionysius may have drawn on for his claim that Brutus was a patrician; but, of those several possibilities, there is one in particular that certainly seems to meet all the various criteria outlined above, and that is the work of Q. Aelius Tubero, Dionysius' patron and the man to whom he dedicated his essay on Thucydides. Dionysius describes Tubero as a clever man and a careful compiler of historical data,[16] and this accords extremely well with the complimentary tone he adopts at *Ant. Rom.* 5.18. The comments on which magistracies plebeians could legally hold are perfectly appropriate too, for Aelius Tubero also wrote about

14 A list of the sources that Dionysius cites by name can be found in the indices for Jacoby's Teubner edition (1925). It may be possible to narrow the field down further: those historians of the first century BC who dealt only with recent and contemporary events and who did not write *ab urbe condita* (such as Asinius Pollio, who, as it happens, evidently praised Brutus and Cassius, Tac. *Ann.* 4.34.4) may not have been of much interest to Dionysius; naturally that does not mean that he did not consult their works, but it may be less likely. To what extent does Dionysius' choice of words at *Ant. Rom.* 5.18 (see n. 15 below) preclude historical works of a restricted or focused nature?

15 Dion. Hal. *Ant. Rom.* 5.18.1: ὡς οἱ τὰ Ῥωμαίων σαφέστατα ἐξητακότες γράφουσι [as write those who have investigated the history of the Romans most accurately]. For the circulation of political pamphlets that dealt with Brutus' ancestry, see Cass. Dio 44.12.1.

16 Dion. Hal. *Ant. Rom.* 1.80.1. See Cic. *ap.* Gell. *NA* 1.22.7 and Pompon. *Dig.* 1.2.2.46 on Tubero's knowledge of legal matters.

legal and constitutional matters.[17] Finally, there is the issue of Tubero's views regarding Iulius Caesar and M. Brutus.

Although Tubero and his father, Lucius, both fought alongside Pompey during the Civil War, both were later pardoned by Caesar. In 46 BC Tubero unsuccessfully prosecuted Q. Ligarius – who also fought against Caesar in the Civil War, but who was in the end likewise pardoned, despite Tubero's efforts – and thereafter he retired from public life.[18] It may, then, seem rather unlikely that Tubero would have ever become in any way a supporter of Iulius Caesar, and yet there is good evidence that, despite his former allegiances, that is precisely what must have happened. Furthermore, there exists at least one possible and plausible explanation for this apparent change of heart. The Aelii were plebeian, but at some stage they were evidently granted patrician status. It has been very plausibly argued that it was Iulius Caesar who was responsible for this grant.[19] If it was, then that may well have provided sufficient motive for some expression of support for him, and along with that, the subsequent censure of Brutus. And it is conceivable too that this transition may have made Tubero especially sensitive to, or conscious of, the restrictions that had previously been imposed on the plebeians, and so on his own ancestors.

Tubero wrote about Iulius Caesar. While there is nothing in those fragments of his work that are directly concerned with Caesar that could safely be taken as evidence for Tubero's opinion of him,[20] a fragment of

17   References in nn. 16 and 18. Note Tubero fr. 1 Huschke (= Gell. *NA* 14.7.13) where the style of argumentation is reminiscent of Dion. Hal. *Ant. Rom.* 5.18.

18   Q. Ligarius was an opponent of Caesar (e.g. Plut. *Cic.* 39.5) and he remained one, but Tubero had his own axe to grind (cf. Cic. *Lig.* 9, 11, 23, 24, 29; Caes. *BCiv.* 1.31.3; Pompon. *Dig.* 1.2.2.46); on Ligarius' trial, cf. Walser 1959. For Tubero's career, see Klebs 1893a; Klebs 1893b; Beck and Walter 2004, 346–8; Chassignet 2004, LXXVI–LXXXI; Oakley 2013a, 362–4.

19   Plebeian: cf., for example, Livy 30.39.8. Pomponius, however (*Dig.* 1.2.2.46), says that Q. Tubero was a patrician. As Wiseman 1979b, 138 rightly concludes, the Aelii must have been 'granted patrician status either by Caesar, under the *lex Cassia*, or perhaps by Octavian, under the *lex Saenia* in 30 B.C.' It makes no significant difference to the current argument if it was instead Octavian who made the Aelii patrician, but Caesar is certainly the likelier candidate.

20   *FRHist* 38 F15 (= Suet. *Iul.* 83.1) and F16 (= Suet. *Iul.* 56.7, where the attribution to Tubero depends on an emendation of the text). Neither fragment, at least, betrays any hostility to Caesar.

his account of the story of Romulus and Remus is considerably more re-
vealing. In the days before Rome was founded, the herdsmen of Numitor
and Amulius grazed their flocks on the site where the city would later
stand. On one occasion a dispute arose among the herdsmen; Romulus
and Remus became involved, and shortly thereafter, and in circumstances
variously related, Remus was seized by Numitor's men and taken into cus-
tody. There were, it would appear, essentially two different versions of the
story of Remus' capture. According to one, while Romulus was occupied
with religious matters, Remus was taken by Numitor's men; according to
the other, while the brothers and their followers were performing the rites
of the Lupercalia, and so had separated into two groups and were unarmed,
Remus and his *Luperci* were ambushed.[21] Aelius Tubero evidently told this
second version, but he appears to have made one important modification
to the story: Tubero appears to have added a third group of *Luperci*.[22]

Traditionally there were just two groups of *Luperci*, the *Luperci Fabiani*
and the *Luperci Quinctiales*, and these two groups were connected with
Remus and Romulus respectively.[23] In 45 BC a third group was added. This
group was called the *Luperci Iuliani*, and it was established in honour of
Iulius Caesar.[24] Dionysius (who is the source for Tubero's version of the
story of Remus' abduction) does not say how Tubero accounted for the
third group that had allegedly existed in Romulus' and Remus' day, who
was supposed to have led it, or even what it was called, but it seems safe to
assume that Tubero must have incorporated the *Luperci Iuliani* into his
narrative.[25] There is no other obvious explanation for the existence of a third

---

21 For the first version, see Plut. *Rom.* 7.1–3; Dion. Hal. *Ant. Rom.* 1.79.12–14; for
    the second, Livy 1.5.3 (with minor variation in the details); Dion. Hal. *Ant. Rom.*
    1.80.1–2.
22 *FRHist* 38 F3 (= Dion. Hal. *Ant. Rom.* 1.80.1–3).
23 Ov. *Fast.* 2.375–8; Fest. 308L; Paul. Fest. 78L; *OGR* 22.1; *CIL* 6.1933, 6.33421,
    11.3205.
24 Suet. *Iul.* 76.1; Cass. Dio 44.6.2, 45.30.2.
25 So too Walt 1997, 175 and n. 729; Beck and Walter 2004, 351–2; Chassignet 2004,
    LXXIX–LXXX, 239 n. 3. Note Weinstock 1971, 332–3 on the possible justification
    for the creation of the *Luperci Iuliani*. Oakley 2013b, 470 suggests that the allusion
    to the *Luperci Iuliani* could be due to Dionysius himself; while not impossible, the
    chronology may tell against it (see Dion. Hal. *Ant. Rom.* 1.3.4 and n. 27 below);
    Dionysius' handling of the story does not encourage the idea that he has modified

group of *Luperci*. And there is only one reason why anyone would have wished to do such a thing. By inserting the *Luperci Iuliani* into the traditional story of Romulus and Remus, Tubero must have been attempting to give them a heritage that made them every bit as old and authentic as the *Luperci Fabiani* and the *Luperci Quinctiales*.

Not only, therefore, does this fragment provide good evidence for Tubero's allegiances, it also demonstrates that he was quite prepared to modify his account of Rome's history in order to flatter Caesar. It is perfectly conceivable then that Tubero may have also been the source behind Dionysius' discussion of L. Iunius Brutus' patrician status and the offices for which the plebeian Iunii were eligible; indeed, it is possible that he may have even been responsible for the specific claim that L. Brutus was patrician.[26]

Tubero's version of the story of Romulus and Remus also provides a useful *terminus post quem* for the composition of this part of his history. It may provide something of a *terminus ante quem* too: presumably Tubero

---

Tubero's version of it on account of anything he had witnessed in his own day, and Dionysius usually makes it clear when he is discussing things he has seen for himself (*Ant. Rom.* 1.32.2, 1.37.2, 1.64.5, 1.68.1–2. 2.23.5, 6.13.4–5, 7.72.12, 7.72.18, etc.); any suggestion that he may have been drawing on some other, unnamed source seems an unnecessary complication.

26 Tubero would not have been the first to deny that the Iunii Bruti were descended from L. Brutus; a fragment of Posidonius (*ap.* Plut. *Brut.* 1.7–8) shows that the ancestry of the Iunii Bruti had been questioned previously, but only, it would appear, on the grounds that Brutus had executed his children (and thus, in reply to this argument, Posidonius claimed that Brutus had had a third son, who was an infant, and that the later Iunii were descended from him). Oakley 2013a, 367 n. 27 questions the attribution to Tubero of the story that L. Brutus was patrician; he does so on the grounds that 'anxiety about the relationship of later plebeian families to earlier patrician ones pre-dates Tubero'; that is certainly true (Oakley cites Cic. *Brut.* 62, for which see p. 7 n. 16 above) but, when their claim to be descended from Brutus was already vulnerable, would the Iunii Bruti have risked making it more so with claims that their famous ancestor had been patrician (note, obviously, Dion. Hal. *Ant. Rom.* 5.18.1)? And would they have really stood to gain anything, when Brutus already had the reputation of being the very founder of the Republic (again, note Dion. Hal. *Ant. Rom.* 5.18.1: Brutus was the best of the Romans; Plut. *Publ.* 6.4: Romulus' achievement was inferior)? But, if not the Iunii Bruti themselves, then who else would have invented such a claim and for what purpose? Plut. *Brut.* 1.6 is explicit about the context and so there is no need to propose another.

wrote his account before, or at least not too long after, the *Luperci Iuliani* disappeared, for once they had ceased to exist, as they soon did,[27] there would have been little point in inventing a pedigree for them. If Tubero was writing his account of Romulus and Remus and the foundation of Rome in the late 40s or in the 30s BC, he would, it is reasonable to suppose, have been dealing with the expulsion of the kings and the foundation of the Republic, and so with the career of L. Iunius Brutus, at about this same time, perhaps at the most just a few years later – that is, at any rate, during precisely the period when M. Brutus' ancestry really mattered.

It is of course impossible to prove that the source to which Dionysius refers at *Ant. Rom.* 5.18 was indeed the work of Aelius Tubero. However, the hypothesis that Dionysius was referring to Tubero's history does seem to accord very nicely with what little else can be inferred about the work. Moreover, where politically contentious issues are concerned, matters of chronology become especially important, and here too, a good case can be made for Tubero's suitability.[28]

It hardly needs to be said that considerably more is at stake than simply tracing the possible source of one small passage of Dionysius' history. If the hypothesis put forward here is correct, then the claim that L. Iunius Brutus was a patrician must inevitably constitute yet further evidence of the way in which contemporary politics could affect what and how Roman historians wrote about Rome's early history.

* *

When stories told about the past could be matters of such contemporary relevance and debate even centuries after the purported events, then the

---

27 Cic. *Phil.* 13.31 shows that the Senate deprived the *Luperci Iuliani* of their funding; it is, however, quite conceivable that their position was restored by the triumvirs (see Wiseman 2008, 78). Any revival was presumably short-lived, and their existence may have been brought to an end by Octavian (cf. Suet. *Aug.* 31.4, which is obviously not to be taken literally). I am very grateful to Professor Peter Wiseman for drawing my attention to this possibility and also to *Classical Philology*'s anonymous readers for several other helpful suggestions.

28 Wiseman 1994, 54–5 suggests a similar date (i.e. the triumviral period) for another story – this time, of a Catilinarian-style conspiracy – found in Dionysius (also from his fifth book, *Ant. Rom.* 5.53–7); Wiseman further suggests that Dionysius' source for this story was none other than Aelius Tubero.

very act of producing an account of those events undoubtedly had the potential to be contentious. Under such circumstances, the writing of history could easily have involved much more than a desire simply to record, understand or try to reconstruct the events of the past;[29] indeed, it did not necessarily even need to involve any such desires at all.

The events of the past mattered, and not just in the heated years of late republican Rome. They had always mattered. The difference is that many of the issues, debates and even events of the late republican period are better known (or, indeed, are simply known), on account of the nature and scale of the evidence, and that means that their influence on the way stories about the past were told, assessed, modified and even fabricated is sometimes discernible. But when, in the second century BC, Polybius asserted that historians must write impartially – even blaming their friends or praising their enemies, if circumstances require it – he was not needlessly insisting on a principle to which everyone adhered. He was criticising those historians who had not met his own, quite clearly exceptional, standards.

The specific context of Polybius' comment is his assessment of the handling of the First Punic War by the historians Philinus of Agrigentum and Fabius Pictor.[30] They had evidently written partisan accounts of the war, but it is clear that such partisanship (Philinus' in particular, but clearly that of others too) had also contributed to the creation of different and, in places, mutually incompatible accounts of Rome's prior dealings with Carthage. Since Philinus' and Pictor's works have not survived, however, the full extent of the problems that Polybius encountered is unknown.

Rome's relationship with Carthage was naturally not the only one that had an impact on what the Romans said about their past. When Cato the Elder, for instance, claimed in his history, as he appears to have done, that Rome's constitution was superior to those of other states, including Sparta and Athens, because Rome's was the work of many people and a long period of time, he was hardly offering an impartial interpretation of Rome's early history. And more may have been behind that claim than just interpretation. Even when it came to contemporary events, Cato's work

29   Note Wiseman 2018, XIII–XVI.
30   Polyb. 1.14.

was hardly impartial, containing as it did Cato's own speeches while also omitting the names of other people.[31]

Nor – to return to later times – did Livy criticise Licinius Macer for praising his family or Valerius Antias for exaggerating and distorting the account of events for no good reason. Macer apparently favoured his family to such an extent that parts of his work became patently unreliable, and some of that distortion may still be detectable today. Of course Macer's responsibility cannot be proved, since his work has been lost, but the hypothesis that he was behind some of the stories told about the early Licinii certainly works well to explain the nature of those stories and the patterns in the evidence. And that hypothesis cannot be arbitrarily dismissed on the grounds that Rome's historians simply and faithfully passed on what their predecessors had said, with variation only to be found in matters of style and in the handling of incidental details. That idea is inherently implausible to begin with. The Romans would, once again, need somehow to be unique among humans.

Given the nature of the extant evidence, of course individual details and episodes in the tradition can only rarely be connected with specific authors and their works and, even then, hardly ever easily. But when ancient writers discuss problems in their sources, as they do from time to time,[32] it is clearly not an appropriate response to trivialise or otherwise dismiss their comments, especially on the basis of preconceived ideas about the existence and use of early documents and the general reliability of the literary evidence. What ancient writers have to say about the problems they encountered needs to be taken seriously, no matter how inconvenient it may be. It does not help, either, that the amount of variation in the literary evidence is persistently underestimated. When it is not explained away or just ignored, variation is often missed entirely, sometimes simply on account of flawed methodologies, following which it is supposed, most notably,

---

31 Cic. *De or.* 1.227, *Brut.* 89, *Sen.* 38; Nep. *Cato* 3.4; Livy 45.25.3, *Per.* 49; Val. Max. 8.1.*absol.*2; Plin. *HN* 8.11; Gell. *NA* 6.3.7; Cornell 2013a, 213–16.

32 On the frequency of such comments, note pp. 117 and 146–7, but hopefully much of the discussion in this book has helped to show at least something of the extent of the difficulties, variation and inconsistencies that are found in the literary evidence.

that incompatible versions of events only need to be handled selectively but otherwise given little or no further consideration. Any methodology that involves ignoring the very nature of the evidence is almost inevitably going to lead to erroneous conclusions.

As for what went on before the Romans first began to write down something of what they knew or thought they knew about their past, matters are considerably more difficult. But there is certainly no reason to think that Rome's historians were the first to handle the traditions of the past in ways designed to meet the needs of the present (whatever those needs may have been at the time), or simply in light of the circumstances of the present. What the Romans had thought and said about Romulus, the founder of Rome, about their kings, who at some stage came to be conceived of as founders too, about Brutus the founder of the Republic and about the Republic itself several centuries or so before Livy's day and, even more so, several centuries before Polybius' is only really a matter of conjecture. But there is nonetheless good reason to conclude that there was never any single, fixed and agreed account of these events that was simply repeated from one generation to the next.

There is material in the extant literary evidence that certainly does look to be much older and, in the case of early inscriptions that had somehow made their way into some written account of events, there is good reason to have confidence in their value as contemporary evidence. This early material is important in its own right, but it is further important because some of it is really quite inconsistent with what the Romans themselves said, at least in later times. That ought not to be unexpected. What did Romans in the second and first centuries BC really know about the beginnings of their city and state, that is to say, about events that took place centuries before any account of them had been entrusted to letters? It is, therefore, a problem when those few scraps of contemporary evidence are passed over, as they not infrequently are, in favour of what the Romans in the second and first centuries thought they knew. And it is equally a problem when what is clearly evidence for disagreement and incompatible accounts of events is treated simply as an invitation to handle the evidence selectively, to pick out this or that detail from this or that version in order to piece together something new or, worse, simply to fit the desired reconstruction.

It is better to ask what the evidence for disagreement suggests in the first place. Is the disagreement politically motivated, for instance, or has some author perhaps simply included in his account something that, for one reason or another, does not actually fit? The answers to questions such as these greatly affect how the evidence should be handled and what can be done with it.

There is much that the Romans said about their past that is quite obviously contrived and consequently needs an explanation. It is hardly plausible to imagine, for instance, that the Roman state simply came into existence the very moment Romulus founded it; nor is it plausible to imagine that, following the end of Romulus' reign, the Roman Senate and people immediately began to elect their kings; nor is it plausible to imagine that, after just one king (and only one king) had come to power on hereditary grounds and had (as a result) proved to be a tyrant, the Romans immediately founded their Republic, with all its ideals of shared power and limited tenure of office, and also with the events of each year henceforth duly recorded alongside the names of the appropriate consuls (with only the occasional slip here and there).

How are these stories about Rome's origins and early development to be explained, if they are not historical? And what can be done with those occasional pieces of early evidence that happen to have survived? This book has offered a few attempts to provide some answers to these questions. The answers are necessarily hypothetical, and for that reason they may well invite that easy, unfortunately common but nonetheless wholly inadequate response, whereby the conjectures of others are dismissed as 'mere speculation'. A more appropriate approach is to test these hypotheses against the evidence, to see if they explain it sufficiently well and, if they do not, to look for something better. But to continue to insist that Roman accounts of Rome's early history are based on a 'foundation', 'core' or 'backbone' of evidence and are therefore broadly reliable is not only, at best, to operate on faith, but it is also to risk leaving untested – and also unexplained – the various reconstructions and hypotheses of the Romans themselves.

Bibliography

Adam 2001: Anne-Marie Adam, 'Des «condottieri» en Étrurie et dans le Latium a l'époque archaïque?', *Latomus* 60 (2001), 877–89.

Adcock 1957: Frank E. Adcock, 'Consular Tribunes and their Successors', *Journal of Roman Studies* 47 (1957), 9–14.

Alföldi 1965: Andrew Alföldi, *Early Rome and the Latins* (Ann Arbor: University of Michigan Press, 1965).

Ameling 2011: Walter Ameling, 'The Rise of Carthage to 264 BC', in Dexter Hoyos, ed., *A Companion to the Punic Wars* (Malden, MA: Wiley-Blackwell, 2011), 39–57.

Ampolo 1976–7: Carmine Ampolo, 'Demarato: Osservazioni sulla mobilità sociale arcaica', *Dialoghi di Archeologia* 9–10 (1976–7), 333–45.

Ampolo 1980: Carmine Ampolo, 'Le origini di Roma e la «cité antique»', *Mélanges de l'École française de Rome – Antiquité* 92 (1980), 567–76.

Ampolo 1983a: Carmine Ampolo, 'La storiografia su Roma arcaica e i documenti', in Emilio Gabba, ed., *Tria Corda: Scritti in onore di Arnaldo Momigliano* (Como: Edizioni New Press, 1983), 9–26.

Ampolo 1983b: Carmine Ampolo, 'Sulla formazione della città di Roma', *Opus* 2 (1983), 425–30.

Ampolo 1988: Carmine Ampolo, 'La nascita della città', in *Storia di Roma 1: Roma in Italia* (Turin: Giulio Einaudi Editore, 1988), 153–80.

Ampolo 2013: Carmine Ampolo, 'Il problema delle origini di Roma rivisitato: Concordismo, ipertradizionalismo acritico, contesti. I', *Annali della Scuola Normale Superiore di Pisa. Classe di Lettere e Filosofia* 5, 5/1 (2013), 217–84, 441–7.

Ampolo and Manfredini 1988: Carmine Ampolo and Mario Manfredini, eds, *Plutarco: Le vite di Teseo e di Romolo* (Milan: Arnoldo Mondadori Editore, 1988).

Andreae 2004: Bernard Andreae, 'La Tomba François ricostruita', in Anna Maria Moretti Sgubini, ed., *Eroi etruschi e miti greci: Gli affreschi della Tomba François tornano a Vulci* (Calenzano: Edizioni Cooperativa Archeologia, 2004), 41–57.

Armstrong 2016: Jeremy Armstrong, *War and Society in Early Rome, from Warlords to Generals* (Cambridge: Cambridge University Press, 2016).

Armstrong and Richardson 2017: Jeremy Armstrong and James H. Richardson, 'Authors, Archaeology, and Arguments: Evidence and Models for Early Roman Politics', *Antichthon* 51 (2017), 1–20.

Astin 1978: Alan E. Astin, *Cato the Censor* (Oxford: Clarendon Press, 1978).

Badian 1966: Ernst Badian, 'The Early Historians', in T. A. Dorey, ed., *Latin Historians* (London: Routledge and Kegan Paul, 1966), 1–38.

Badian 1979: Ernst Badian, 'Two Polybian Treaties', in Φιλίας χάριν: *Miscellanea di studi classici in onore di Eugenio Manni* I (Rome: Giorgio Bretschneider, 1979), 159–69.

Badian 1990a: Ernst Badian et al., 'Diskussion. Sektion II: Quellen und Quellenkritik', in Walter Eder, ed., *Staat und Staatlichkeit in der frühen römischen Republik* (Stuttgart: Franz Steiner Verlag, 1990), 208–17.

Badian 1990b: Ernst Badian et al., 'Kommentar. Sektion V: Magistratur und Gesellschaft', in Walter Eder, ed., *Staat und Staatlichkeit in der frühen römischen Republik* (Stuttgart: Franz Steiner Verlag, 1990), 458–75.

Beard 1990: Mary Beard, 'Priesthood in the Roman Republic', in Mary Beard and John A. North, eds, *Pagan Priests* (London: Duckworth, 1990), 19–48.

Beck 2011: Hans Beck, 'The Reasons for the War', in Dexter Hoyos, ed., *A Companion to the Punic Wars* (Malden, MA: Wiley-Blackwell, 2011), 225–41.

Beck and Walter 2001: Hans Beck and Uwe Walter, *Die frühen römischen Historiker I: Von Fabius Pictor bis Cn. Gellius* (Darmstadt: Wissenschaftliche Buchgesellschaft, 2001).

Beck and Walter 2004: Hans Beck and Uwe Walter, *Die frühen römischen Historiker II: Von Coelius Antipater bis Pomponius Atticus* (Darmstadt: Wissenschaftliche Buchgesellschaft, 2004).

Bellen 1991: H. Bellen, 'La monarchia nella coscienza storica dello stato repubblicano: Un problema di continuità della storia Romana', *Athenaeum* 79 (1991), 5–15.

Beloch 1926: Karl Julius Beloch, *Römische Geschichte bis zum Beginn der punischen Kriege* (Berlin: Walter de Gruyter and Co., 1926).

Bernard 2012: Seth G. Bernard, 'Continuing the Debate on Rome's Earliest Circuit Walls', *Papers of the British School at Rome* 80 (2012), 1–44.

Bernardi 1953: Aurelio Bernardi, 'L'interesse di Caligola per la successione del *rex Nemorensis* e l'arcaica regalità nel Lazio', *Athenaeum* 31 (1953), 273–87.

Bernardi 1988: Aurelio Bernardi, 'La Roma dei re fra storia e leggenda', in *Storia di Roma 1: Roma in Italia* (Turin: Giulio Einaudi Editore, 1988), 181–202.

Bianchi 2010: Edoardo Bianchi, *Il* rex sacrorum *a Roma e nell'Italia antica* (Milan: Vita e Pensiero, 2010).

Bianchi 2018: Edoardo Bianchi, 'Il *rex sacrorum* alla luce di alcuni studi recenti', *Mediterraneo Antico* 21 (2018), 627–40.

Bickerman 1944: Elias J. Bickerman, 'An Oath of Hannibal', *Transactions and Proceedings of the American Philological Association* 75 (1944), 87–102.

Bickerman 1952: Elias J. Bickerman, '*Origines gentium*', *Classical Philology* 47 (1952), 65–81.

Billows 1989: Richard Billows, 'Legal Fiction and Political Reform at Rome in the Early Second Century B.C.', *Phoenix* 43 (1989), 112–33.

Billows 1992: Richard Billows, Review of Frank W. Walbank, Alan E. Astin, Martin W. Frederiksen, Robert M. Ogilvie and Andrew Drummond, eds, *The Cambridge Ancient History, Volume VII part 2: The Rise of Rome to 220 B.C.* (2nd edn, Cambridge: Cambridge University Press, 1989), *Phoenix* 46 (1992), 190–5.

Bispham and Cornell 2013: Edward Bispham and Timothy J. Cornell, 'Q. Fabius Pictor', in Timothy J. Cornell, ed., *The Fragments of the Roman Historians, Volume I: Introduction* (Oxford: Oxford University Press, 2013), 160–78.

Blaive 1998: Frédéric Blaive, 'De la *designatio* à l'*inauguratio*: Observations sur le processus de choix du *rex Romanorum*', *Revue internationale des droits de l'antiquité* 45 (1998), 63–87.

Boddington 1959: Ann Boddington, 'The Original Nature of the Consular Tribunate', *Historia* 8 (1959), 356–64.

Bormann 1893: Eugen Bormann, 'Die älteste Gliederung Roms', in *Eranos Vindobonensis* (Vienna: Alfred Hölder, 1893), 345–58.

Bradley 2015: Guy Bradley, 'Investigating Aristocracy in Archaic Rome and Central Italy: Social Mobility, Ideology and Cultural Influences', in Nick Fisher and Hans van Wees, eds, '*Aristocracy' in Antiquity: Redefining Greek and Roman Elites* (Swansea: Classical Press of Wales, 2015), 85–124.

Bravo and Griffin 1988: Benedetto Bravo and Miriam Griffin, 'Un frammento del libro XI di Tito Livio?', *Athenaeum* 66 (1988), 447–521.

Bremmer 1982: Jan Bremmer, 'The *suodales* of Poplios Valesios', *Zeitschrift für Papyrologie und Epigraphik* 47 (1982), 133–47.

Brennan 2000: T. Corey Brennan, *The Praetorship in the Roman Republic* (Oxford: Oxford University Press, 2000).

Bringmann 2007: Klaus Bringmann, *A History of the Roman Republic*, trans. W. J. Smyth (Cambridge: Polity Press, 2007).

Briquel 2000a: Dominique Briquel, 'La lente genèse d'une cité', in *Histoire Romaine I: Des origines à Auguste* (Paris: Fayard, 2000), 47–83.

Briquel 2000b: Dominique Briquel, 'Le sillon du fondateur', in *Histoire Romaine I: Des origines à Auguste* (Paris: Fayard, 2000), 11–45.

Briquel 2016: Dominique Briquel, 'Monuments of the Regal Period and the Beginnings of the Republic: The Ambiguity of *realia*', in Marta García Morcillo, James H. Richardson and Federico Santangelo, eds, *Ruin or Renewal?*

Places and the Transformation of Memory in the City of Rome (Rome: Edizioni Quasar, 2016), 27–47.

Briscoe 2013a: John Briscoe, 'L. Cassius Hemina: Commentary', in Timothy J. Cornell, ed., *The Fragments of the Roman Historians, Volume III: Commentary* (Oxford: Oxford University Press, 2013), 160–84.

Briscoe 2013b: John Briscoe, 'L. Cornelius Sisenna', in Timothy J. Cornell, ed., *The Fragments of the Roman Historians, Volume I: Introduction* (Oxford: Oxford University Press, 2013), 305–19.

Briscoe 2013c: John Briscoe, 'Paulus Clodius', in Timothy J. Cornell, ed., *The Fragments of the Roman Historians, Volume I: Introduction* (Oxford: Oxford University Press, 2013), 264–5.

Broughton 1951: Thomas Robert S. Broughton, *The Magistrates of the Roman Republic, Volume I: 509 B.C.–100 B.C.* (New York: American Philological Association, 1951).

Bucher 1987 [1995]: Gregory S. Bucher, 'The *Annales Maximi* in the Light of Roman Methods of Keeping Records', *American Journal of Ancient History* 12 (1987 [1995]), 2–61.

Calore 2000: Antonello Calore, *"Per Iovem lapidem" alle origini del giuramento: Sulla presenza del 'sacro' nell'esperienza giuridica romana* (Milan: Giuffrè Editore, 2000).

Capogrossi Colognesi 2014: Luigi Capogrossi Colognesi, *Law and Power in the Making of the Roman Commonwealth*, trans. Laura Kopp (Cambridge: Cambridge University Press, 2014).

Carandini 2006: Andrea Carandini, ed., *La leggenda di Roma, Volume I: Dalla nascita dei gemelli alla fondazione della città* (Milan: Arnoldo Mondadori Editore, 2006).

Carandini 2011a: Andrea Carandini, ed., *La leggenda di Roma, Volume III: La costituzione* (Milan: Arnoldo Mondadori Editore, 2011).

Carandini 2011b: Andrea Carandini, *Rome: Day One*, trans. Stephen Sartarelli (Princeton, NJ: Princeton University Press, 2011).

Cary 1919: Max Cary, 'A Forgotten Treaty between Rome and Carthage', *Journal of Roman Studies* 9 (1919), 67–77.

Castagnoli 1958: Ferdinando Castagnoli, 'Roma antica', in Ferdinando Castagnoli, Carlo Cecchelli, Gustavo Giovannoni and Mario Zocca, *Topografia e urbanistica di Roma* (Bologna: Licinio Cappelli Editore, 1958), 3–186.

Chassignet 2004: Martine Chassignet, *L'Annalistique romaine, tome III: L'annalistique récente, l'autobiographie politique (fragments)* (Paris: Les Belles Lettres, 2004).

Classen 1965: C. Joachim Classen, 'Die Königszeit im Spiegel der Literatur der römischen Republik (Ein Beitrag zum Selbstverständnis Römer)', *Historia* 14 (1965), 385–403.

Cloud 1971: J. Duncan Cloud, '*Parricidium*: From the *lex Numae* to the *lex Pompeia de parricidiis*', *Zeitschrift der Savigny-Stiftung für Rechtsgeschichte: Romanistische Abteilung* 88 (1971), 1–66.

Coarelli 1999: Filippo Coarelli, 'Sepulcrum Romuli', in Eva Margareta Steinby, ed., *Lexicon Topographicum Urbis Romae, Volume IV* (Rome: Edizioni Quasar, 1999), 295–6.

Cornell 1978: Timothy J. Cornell, 'The Foundation of Rome in the Ancient Literary Tradition', in Hugo Mck. Blake, Timothy W. Potter and David B. Whitehouse, eds, *Papers in Italian Archaeology I: The Lancaster Seminar* (Oxford: British Archaeological Reports, 1978), 131–40.

Cornell 1982: Timothy J. Cornell, Review of T. Peter Wiseman, *Clio's Cosmetics: Three Studies in Greco-Roman Literature* (Leicester: Leicester University Press, 1979), *Journal of Roman Studies* 72 (1982), 203–6.

Cornell 1983: Timothy J. Cornell, 'The Failure of the Plebs', in Emilio Gabba, ed., *Tria Corda: Scritti in onore di Arnaldo Momigliano* (Como: Edizioni New Press, 1983), 101–20.

Cornell 1986: Timothy J. Cornell, 'The Formation of the Historical Tradition of Early Rome', in Ian S. Moxon, John D. Smart and Anthony J. Woodman, eds, *Past Perspectives: Studies in Greek and Roman Historical Writing* (Cambridge: Cambridge University Press, 1986), 67–86.

Cornell 1988: Timothy J. Cornell, 'La guerra e lo stato in Roma arcaica (VII–V sec.)', in Enrico Campanile, ed., *Alle origini di Roma. Atti del Colloquio tenuto a Pisa il 18 e 19 settembre 1987* (Pisa: Giardini Editori, 1988), 89–97.

Cornell 1991: Timothy J. Cornell, 'The Tyranny of the Evidence: A Discussion of the Possible Uses of Literacy in Etruria and Latium in the Archaic Age', in *Literacy in the Roman World* (Ann Arbor: JRA Supplement 3, 1991), 7–33.

Cornell 1995: Timothy J. Cornell, *The Beginnings of Rome: Italy and Rome from the Bronze Age to the Punic Wars (c. 1000–264 BC)* (London: Routledge, 1995).

Cornell 2001: Timothy J. Cornell, 'Cicero on the Origins of Rome', in Jonathan G. F. Powell and John A. North, eds, *Cicero's Republic* (London: Institute of Classical Studies, 2001), 41–56.

Cornell 2003: Timothy J. Cornell, 'Coriolanus: Myth, History and Performance', in David Braund and Christopher Gill, eds, *Myth, History and Culture in Republican Rome: Studies in Honour of T. P. Wiseman* (Exeter: University of Exeter Press, 2003), 73–97.

Cornell 2004: Timothy J. Cornell, 'Deconstructing the Samnite Wars: An Essay in Historiography', in Howard Jones, ed., *Samnium: Settlement and Cultural*

Change (Providence, RI: Center for Old World Archaeology and Art, 2004), 115–31.

Cornell 2005: Timothy J. Cornell, 'The Value of the Literary Tradition Concerning Archaic Rome', in Kurt A. Raaflaub, ed., *Social Struggles in Archaic Rome: New Perspectives on the Conflict of the Orders* (2nd edn, Malden, MA: Blackwell Publishing, 2005), 47–74.

Cornell 2009: Timothy J. Cornell, 'Political Conflict in Archaic Rome and the Republican Historians', in Giuseppe Zecchini, ed., *'Partiti' e fazioni nell'esperienza politica romana* (Milan: Vita e Pensiero, 2009), 3–30.

Cornell 2012: Timothy J. Cornell, 'Comments', in Gabriele Cifani and Simon Stoddart, eds, *Landscape, Ethnicity and Identity in the Archaic Mediterranean Area* (Oxford: Oxbow Books, 2012), 20–1.

Cornell 2013a: Timothy J. Cornell, 'M. Porcius Cato', in Timothy J. Cornell, ed., *The Fragments of the Roman Historians, Volume I: Introduction* (Oxford: Oxford University Press, 2013), 191–218.

Cornell 2013b: Timothy J. Cornell, 'M. Porcius Cato: Commentary', in Timothy J. Cornell, ed., *The Fragments of the Roman Historians, Volume III: Commentary* (Oxford: Oxford University Press, 2013), 63–159.

Cornell 2014a: Timothy J. Cornell, 'The *Lex Ouinia* and the Emancipation of the Senate', in James H. Richardson and Federico Santangelo, eds, *The Roman Historical Tradition: Regal and Republican Rome* (Oxford: Oxford University Press, 2014), 207–37.

Cornell 2014b: Timothy J. Cornell, 'Livy's Narrative of the Regal Period and Historical and Archaeological Facts', in Bernard Mineo, ed., *A Companion to Livy* (Malden, MA: Wiley-Blackwell, 2014), 245–58.

Cornell 2018: Timothy J. Cornell, 'Which One is the Historian? A Neglected Problem in the Study of Roman Historiography', in Kaj Sandberg and Christopher J. Smith, eds, Omnium Annalium Monumenta: *Historical Writing and Historical Evidence in Republican Rome* (Leiden: Brill, 2018), 182–201.

Crawford 1974: Michael H. Crawford, *Roman Republican Coinage* (Cambridge: Cambridge University Press, 1974).

Cristofani 1990: Mauro Cristofani, ed., *La grande Roma dei Tarquini, catalogo della mostra* (Rome: L'Erma di Bretschneider, 1990).

De Cazanove 1988: Olivier de Cazanove, 'La chronologie des Bacchiades et celle des rois étrusques de Rome', *Mélanges de l'École française de Rome – Antiquité* 100 (1988), 615–48.

De Cazanove 1992: Olivier de Cazanove, 'La détermination chronographique de la durée de la période royale a Rome', in *La Rome des premiers siècles: Légende et histoire* (Florence: Leo S. Olschki Editore, 1992), 69–98.

De Martino 1972: Francesco De Martino, 'Intorno all'origine della repubblica romana e delle magistrature', in Hildegard Temporini, ed., *Aufstieg und Niedergang der römischen Welt* I.1 (Berlin: De Gruyter, 1972), 217–49.

De Martino 1988: Francesco De Martino, 'La costituzione della città-stato', in *Storia di Roma 1: Roma in Italia* (Turin: Giulio Einaudi Editore, 1988), 345–65.

De Sanctis 1960: Gaetano De Sanctis, *Storia dei Romani* II (2nd edn, Florence: La Nuova Italia, 1960).

De Sanctis 1980: Gaetano De Sanctis, *Storia dei Romani* I (new edn, Florence: La Nuova Italia, 1980).

Degrassi 1947: Atilius Degrassi, ed., *Inscriptiones Italiae, XIII Fasti et elogia, fasc. 1 Fasti consulares et triumphales* (Rome: Libreria dello Stato, 1947).

Delfino 2009: Alessandro Delfino, 'L'incendio gallico: Tra mito storiografico e realtà storica', *Mediterraneo Antico* 12 (2009), 339–60.

Dovere 2009: Elio Dovere, '«*Nec diuturno rege esset uno*». Rilievi sull'interregno d'età arcaica', *Latomus* 68 (2009), 319–39.

Drews 1981: Robert Drews, 'The Coming of the City to Central Italy', *American Journal of Ancient History* 6 (1981), 133–65.

Drogula 2015: Fred K. Drogula, *Commanders and Command in the Roman Republic and Early Empire* (Chapel Hill: University of North Carolina Press, 2015).

Drogula 2017: Fred K. Drogula, 'Plebeian Tribunes and the Government of Early Rome', *Antichthon* 51 (2017), 101–23.

Drummond 1989: Andrew Drummond, 'Rome in the Fifth Century II: The Citizen Community', in Frank W. Walbank, Alan E. Astin, Martin W. Frederiksen, Robert M. Ogilvie and Andrew Drummond, eds, *The Cambridge Ancient History, Volume VII part 2: The Rise of Rome to 220 B.C.* (2nd edn, Cambridge: Cambridge University Press, 1989), 172–242.

Dubuisson 1985: Michel Dubuisson, *Le latin de Polybe: Les implications historiques d'un cas de bilinguisme* (Paris: Klincksieck, 1985).

Dyck 2004: Andrew R. Dyck, *A Commentary on Cicero, De Legibus* (Ann Arbor: University of Michigan Press, 2004).

Eckstein 1997: Arthur M. Eckstein, '*Physis* and *Nomos*: Polybius, the Romans, and Cato the Elder', in Paul Cartledge, Peter Garnsey and Erich Gruen, eds, *Hellenistic Constructs: Essays in Culture, History, and Historiography* (Berkeley: University of California Press, 1997), 175–98.

Eckstein 2010: Arthur M. Eckstein, 'Polybius, "The Treaty of Philinus", and Roman Accusations against Carthage', *Classical Quarterly* 60 (2010), 406–26.

Erskine 1991: Andrew Erskine, 'Hellenistic Monarchy and Roman Political Invective', *Classical Quarterly* 41 (1991), 106–20.

Facchetti 2000: Giulio M. Facchetti, *Frammenti di diritto privato etrusco* (Florence: Leo S. Olschki Editore, 2000).

Feeney 2007: Denis Feeney, *Caesar's Calendar: Ancient Time and the Beginnings of History* (Berkeley: University of California Press, 2007).

Finley 1964: Moses I. Finley, 'The Trojan War', *Journal of Hellenic Studies* 84 (1964), 1–9.

Finley 1985: Moses I. Finley, *Ancient History: Evidence and Models* (London: Chatto and Windus, 1985).

Flaig 2003: Egon Flaig, *Ritualisierte Politik: Zeichen, Gesten und Herrschaft im Alten Rom* (Göttingen: Vandenhoeck und Ruprecht, 2003).

Flower 1996: Harriet I. Flower, *Ancestor Masks and Aristocratic Power in Roman Culture* (Oxford: Clarendon Press, 1996).

Flower 2009: Harriet I. Flower, 'Alternatives to Written History in Republican Rome', in Andrew Feldherr, ed., *The Cambridge Companion to the Roman Historians* (Cambridge: Cambridge University Press, 2009), 65–76.

Forsythe 1994: Gary Forsythe, *The Historian L. Calpurnius Piso Frugi and the Roman Annalistic Tradition* (Lanham, MD: University Press of America, 1994).

Forsythe 1999: Gary Forsythe, *Livy and Early Rome: A Study in Historical Method and Judgment* (Stuttgart: Franz Steiner Verlag, 1999).

Forsythe 2005: Gary Forsythe, *A Critical History of Early Rome, from Prehistory to the First Punic War* (Berkeley: University of California Press, 2005).

Franciosi 2003: Gennaro Franciosi, ed., *Leges regiae* (Naples: Jovene Editore, 2003).

Frier 1979: Bruce W. Frier, Libri annales pontificum maximorum: *The Origins of the Annalistic Tradition* (Rome: American Academy in Rome, 1979).

Friezer 1959: E. Friezer, '*Interregnum* and *Patrum Auctoritas*', *Mnemosyne* 12 (1959), 301–29.

Fromentin 2004: Valérie Fromentin, 'Choisir le meilleur: La royauté élective à Rome selon Denys d'Halicarnasse', *Ktèma* 29 (2004), 311–23.

Fronda 2015: Michael P. Fronda, 'Why Roman Republicanism? Its Emergence and Nature in Context', in Dean Hammer, ed., *A Companion to Greek Democracy and the Roman Republic* (Malden, MA: Wiley-Blackwell 2015), 44–64.

Fugmann 1990: Joachim Fugmann, *Königszeit und frühe Republik in der Schrift »De viris illustribus urbis Romae«. Quellenkritisch-historische Untersuchungen I: Königszeit* (Frankfurt: Peter Lang, 1990).

Fugmann 1997: Joachim Fugmann, *Königszeit und frühe Republik in der Schrift »De viris illustribus urbis Romae«. Quellenkritisch-historische Untersuchungen II,1: frühe Republik (6./5. Jh.)* (Frankfurt: Peter Lang, 1997).

Fugmann 2004: Joachim Fugmann, *Königszeit und frühe Republik in der Schrift »De viris illustribus urbis Romae«. Quellenkritisch-historische Untersuchungen II,2: frühe Republik (4./3. Jh.)* (Frankfurt: Peter Lang, 2004).

Fulminante 2014: Francesca Fulminante, *The Urbanisation of Rome and Latium Vetus, from the Bronze Age to the Archaic Era* (Cambridge: Cambridge University Press, 2014).

Gabba 1991: Emilio Gabba, *Dionysius and the History of Archaic Rome* (Berkeley: University of California Press, 1991).

Gabba 2000: Emilio Gabba, *Roma arcaica: Storia e storiografia* (Rome: Edizioni di Storia e Letteratura, 2000).

Galinsky 2014: Karl Galinsky, ed., Memoria Romana*: Memory in Rome and Rome in Memory* (Ann Arbor: University of Michigan Press, 2014).

Gallia 2007: Andrew B. Gallia, 'Reassessing the "Cumaean Chronicle": Greek Chronology and Roman History in Dionysius of Halicarnassus', *Journal of Roman Studies* 97 (2007), 50–67.

Gallia 2012: Andrew B. Gallia, *Remembering the Roman Republic: Culture, Politics, and History under the Principate* (Cambridge: Cambridge University Press, 2012).

Gallup 1905: F. A. Gallup, 'Early Legends and Recent Discoveries', *New York Latin Leaflet* 5.124 (1905), 1–2.

Gantz 1975: Timothy N. Gantz, 'The Tarquin Dynasty', *Historia* 24 (1975), 539–54.

Garbarino 1973: Giovanna Garbarino, *Roma e la filosofia greca dalle origini alla fine del II secolo a.C. Raccolta di testi con introduzione e commento, II – Commento e indici* (Turin: G. B. Paravia and C., 1973).

Gassman 2017: Mattias Gassman, 'The Roman Kings in Orosius' *Historiae Adversum Paganos*', *Classical Quarterly* 67 (2017), 617–30.

Gaughan 2003: Judy E. Gaughan, 'Killing and the King: Numa's Murder Law and the Nature of Monarchic Authority', *Continuity and Change* 18 (2003), 329–43.

Giovannini 1993: Adalberto Giovannini, 'Il passaggio dalle istituzioni monarchiche alle istituzioni repubblicane', in *Bilancio critico su Roma arcaica fra monarchia e repubblica* (Rome: Accademia Nazionale dei Lincei, 1993), 75–96.

Giovannini 1998: Adalberto Giovannini, 'Les livres auguraux', in *La Mémoire perdue: Recherches sur l'administration romaine* (Rome: École française de Rome, 1998), 103–22.

Giua 1967: M. A. Giua, 'La valutazione della monarchia a Roma in età repubblicana', *Studi Classici e Orientali* 16 (1967), 308–29.

Gjerstad 1962: Einar Gjerstad, *Legends and Facts of Early Roman History* (Lund: C. W. K. Gleerup, 1962).

Gjerstad 1967: Einar Gjerstad, 'The Origins of the Roman Republic', in *Les Origines de la République romaine* (Geneva: Fondation Hardt, 1967), 3–30.

Gjerstad 1969: Einar Gjerstad, 'Porsenna and Rome', *Opuscula Romana* 7 (1969), 149–61.

Gjerstad 1973: Einar Gjerstad, *Early Rome V: The Written Sources* (Lund: Berlingska Boktryckeriet, 1973).

Glinister 2006: Fay Glinister, 'Kingship and Tyranny in Archaic Rome', in Sian Lewis, ed., *Ancient Tyranny* (Edinburgh: Edinburgh University Press, 2006), 17–32.

Glinister 2017: Fay Glinister, 'Politics, Power, and the Divine: The *Rex Sacrorum* and the Transition from Monarchy to Republic at Rome', *Antichthon* 51 (2017), 59–76.

Gotter 2000: Ulrich Gotter, 'Marcus Iunius Brutus – oder: Die Nemesis des Namens', in Karl-Joachim Hölkeskamp and Elke Stein-Hölkeskamp, eds, *Von Romulus zu Augustus: Große Gestalten der römischen Republik* (Munich: Verlag C. H. Beck, 2000), 328–39.

Grandazzi 1997: Alexandre Grandazzi, *The Foundation of Rome: Myth and History*, trans. Jane Marie Todd (Ithaca, NY: Cornell University Press, 1997).

Grandazzi 2010: Alexandre Grandazzi, '*Vrbem condere*: De la linguistique à l'histoire? À propos de Varron, *ling.*, V, 143', in Dominique Briquel, Caroline Février and Charles Guittard, eds, Varietates Fortunae: *Religion et mythologie à Rome. Hommage à Jacqueline Champeaux* (Paris: Presses de l'université Paris-Sorbonne, 2010), 159–73.

Green 2007: Carin M. C. Green, *Roman Religion and the Cult of Diana at Aricia* (Cambridge: Cambridge University Press, 2007).

Gregory 1994: Andrew P. Gregory, '"Powerful Images": Responses to Portraits and the Political Uses of Images in Rome', *Journal of Roman Archeology* 7 (1994), 80–99.

Gruen 1984: Erich S. Gruen, *The Hellenistic World and the Coming of Rome* (Berkeley: University of California Press, 1984).

Hahm 2000: David E. Hahm, 'Kings and Constitutions: Hellenistic Theories', in Christopher Rowe and Malcolm Schofield, eds, *The Cambridge History of Greek and Roman Political Thought* (Cambridge: Cambridge University Press, 2000), 457–76.

Hall 2014: Jonathan M. Hall, *Artifact & Artifice: Classical Archaeology and the Ancient Historian* (Chicago: University of Chicago Press, 2014).

Hanell 1946: Krister Hanell, *Das altrömische eponyme Amt* (Lund: C. W. K. Gleerup, 1946).

Harris 1990: William V. Harris, 'Roman Warfare in the Economic and Social Context of the Fourth Century B.C.', in Walter Eder, ed., *Staat und Staatlichkeit in der frühen römischen Republik* (Stuttgart: Franz Steiner Verlag, 1990), 494–510.

Hedrick 2002: Charles W. Hedrick, Jr, 'The Prehistory of Greek Chronography', in Vanessa B. Gorman and Eric W. Robinson, eds, Oikistes: *Studies in Constitutions, Colonies, and Military Power in the Ancient World Offered in Honor of A. J. Graham* (Leiden: Brill, 2002), 13–32.

Heurgon 1964: Jacques Heurgon, 'L. Cincius et la loi du *clavus annalis*', *Athenaeum* 42 (1964), 432–7.

Heurgon 1973: Jacques Heurgon, *The Rise of Rome to 264 B.C.*, trans. James Willis (London: B. T. Batsford, 1973).

Hölkeskamp 1993: Karl-Joachim Hölkeskamp, 'Conquest, Competition and Consensus: Roman Expansion in Italy and the Rise of the *Nobilitas*', *Historia* 42 (1993), 12–39.

Hölkeskamp 1999: Karl-Joachim Hölkeskamp, 'Römische *Gentes* und griechische Genealogien', in Gregor Vogt-Spira and Bettina Rommel, eds, *Rezeption und Identität: Die kulturelle Auseinandersetzung Roms mit Griechenland als europäisches Paradigma* (Stuttgart: Franz Steiner Verlag, 1999), 3–21.

Holloway 1994: R. Ross Holloway, *The Archaeology of Early Rome and Latium* (London: Routledge, 1994).

Holloway 2008: R. Ross Holloway, 'Who Were the *Tribuni Militum Consulari Potestate?*', *L'Antiquité Classique* 77 (2008), 107–25.

Hölscher 1984: Tonio Hölscher, *Staatsdenkmal und Publikum: Vom Untergang der Republik bis zur Festigung des Kaisertums in Rom* (Konstanz: Universitätsverlag Konstanz, 1984).

Hopkins 2017: John Hopkins, 'Tarquins, Romans and Architecture at the Threshold of Republic', in Patricia S. Lulof and Christopher J. Smith, eds, *The Age of Tarquinius Superbus: Central Italy in the Late 6th Century* (Leuven: Peeters, 2017), 135–42.

Hoyos 1985: Dexter Hoyos, 'Treaties True and False: The Error of Philinus of Agrigentum', *Classical Quarterly* 35 (1985), 92–109.

Humm 2014: Michel Humm, 'Numa and Pythagoras: The Life and Death of a Myth', in James H. Richardson and Federico Santangelo, eds, *The Roman Historical Tradition: Regal and Republican Rome* (Oxford: Oxford University Press, 2014), 35–51.

Huschke 1879: Eduardus Huschke, ed., *Iurisprudentiae Anteiustinianae quae supersunt* (4th edn, Leipzig: B. G. Teubner, 1879).

Jacoby 1925: Carolus Jacoby, ed., *Dionysi Halicarnasensis Antiquitatum Romanarum quae supersunt: Supplementum, indices continens* (Leipzig: B. G. Teubner, 1925).

Jahn 1970: Joachim Jahn, *Interregnum und Wahldiktatur* (Kallmünz: Verlag Michael Lassleben, 1970).

Jones 2016: Lucy Jones, 'Memory, Nostalgia and the Roman Home', in Marta García Morcillo, James H. Richardson and Federico Santangelo, eds, *Ruin or Renewal? Places and the Transformation of Memory in the City of Rome* (Rome: Edizioni Quasar, 2016), 183–211.

Kajanto 1965: Iiro Kajanto, *The Latin Cognomina* (Helsinki: Keskuskirjapaino, 1965).

Klebs 1893a: Elimar Klebs, 'L. Aelius Tubero, 150', in *Paulys Realencyclopädie der classischen Altertumswissenschaft* 1 (Stuttgart: J. B. Metzlersche Buchhandlung, 1893), 534–5.

Klebs 1893b: Elimar Klebs, 'Q. Aelius Tubero, 156', in *Paulys Realencyclopädie der classischen Altertumswissenschaft* 1 (Stuttgart: J. B. Metzlersche Buchhandlung, 1893), 537–8.

Klotz 1937: Alfred Klotz, 'Diodors römische Annalen', *Rheinisches Museum für Philologie* 86 (1937), 206–24.

Kraus 1991: Christina S. Kraus, '*Initium turbandi omnia a femina ortum est*: Fabia Minor and the Elections of 367 B.C.', *Phoenix* 45 (1991), 314–25.

Kraus 1994: Christina S. Kraus, ed., *Livy, Ab urbe condita, Book VI* (Cambridge: Cambridge University Press, 1994).

Kunkel 1974: Wolfgang Kunkel, *Kleine Schriften zum römischen Strafverfahren und zur römischen Verfassungsgeschichte* (Weimar: Hermann Böhlaus Nachfolger, 1974).

Kvium 2008: Christian Kvium, 'Identifying Identities – Some Thoughts about *gentes* and *gentiles* in Archaic Rome', in Anders Holm Rasmussen and Susanne William Rasmussen, eds, *Religion and Society: Rituals, Resources and Identity in the Ancient Graeco-Roman World. The BOMOS-Conferences 2002–2005* (Rome: Edizioni Quasar, 2008), 267–85.

La Rosa 1994: Franca La Rosa, 'I "tribuni militum" tra le istituzioni dell'alta repubblica', *Iura* 45 (1994), 15–33.

Lanciani 1901: Rodolfo Lanciani, *New Tales of Old Rome* (London: Macmillan and Company, 1901).

Latte 1936: Kurt Latte, 'The Origin of the Roman Quaestorship', *Transactions and Proceedings of the American Philological Association* 67 (1936), 24–33.

Laurendi 2010: Rossella Laurendi, 'La monarchia etrusca a Roma ed il *nomen* di Servio Tullio: *Epos* e storia. Dati e considerazioni sulla Tavola di Lione e la Tomba François', in *Polis 3. Studi interdisciplinari sul mondo antico* (Rome: L'Erma di Bretschneider, 2010), 123–46.

Lentano 2007: Mario Lentano, *La prova del sangue: Storie di identità e storie di legittimità nella cultura latina* (Bologna: Società editrice il Mulino, 2007).

Lentano 2008: Mario Lentano, 'Bruto o il potere delle immagini', *Latomus* 67 (2008), 881–99.

Linderski 1990: Jerzy Linderski, 'The Auspices and the Struggle of the Orders', in Walter Eder, ed., *Staat und Staatlichkeit in der frühen römischen Republik* (Stuttgart: Franz Steiner Verlag, 1990), 34–48.

Linke 1995: Bernhard Linke, *Von der Verwandtschaft zum Staat: Die Entstehung politischer Organisationsformen in der frührömischen Geschichte* (Stuttgart: Franz Steiner Verlag, 1995).

Linke 2010: Bernhard Linke, 'Kingship in Early Rome', in Giovanni B. Lanfranchi and Robert Rollinger, eds, *Concepts of Kingship in Antiquity* (Padua: S.A.R.G.O.N. Editrice e Libreria, 2010), 181–96.

Lintott 1997: Andrew Lintott, 'The Theory of the Mixed Constitution at Rome', in Jonathan Barnes and Miriam Griffin, eds, *Philosophia Togata II: Plato and Aristotle at Rome* (Oxford: Clarendon Press, 1997), 70–85.

Lintott 1999: Andrew Lintott, *The Constitution of the Roman Republic* (Oxford: Oxford University Press, 1999).

Luce 1977: T. James Luce, *Livy: The Composition of his History* (Princeton, NJ: Princeton University Press, 1977).

McDonnell 1997: Myles McDonnell, Review of Timothy J. Cornell, *The Beginnings of Rome: Italy and Rome from the Bronze Age to the Punic Wars (c. 1000–264 BC)* (London: Routledge, 1995), *Classical Philology* 92 (1997), 202–7.

MacMullen 1966: Ramsay MacMullen, *Enemies of the Roman Order: Treason, Unrest, and Alienation in the Empire* (Cambridge, MA: Harvard University Press, 1966).

Magdelain 1968: André Magdelain, *Recherches sur l'«imperium»: La loi curiate et les auspices d'investiture* (Paris: Presses universitaires de France, 1968).

Magdelain 1990: André Magdelain, *Jus Imperium Auctoritas: Études de droit romain* (Rome: École française de Rome, 1990).

Maltby 1991: Robert Maltby, *A Lexicon of Ancient Latin Etymologies* (Leeds: Francis Cairns, 1991).

Maras 2010: Daniele F. Maras, 'Ancora su Mastarna, *sodalis fidelissimus*', in Giuseppe M. Della Fina, ed., *La grande Roma dei Tarquini* (Rome: Edizioni Quasar, 2010), 187–200.

Mastrocinque 1988: Attilio Mastrocinque, *Lucio Giunio Bruto: Ricerche di storia, religione e diritto sulle origini della repubblica romana* (Trento: Edizioni La Reclame, 1988).

Mazzarino 1945: Santo Mazzarino, *Dalla monarchia allo stato repubblicano: Ricerche di storia romana arcaica* (Catania: G. Agnini Editore, 1945).

Mineo 2014: Bernard Mineo, ed., *A Companion to Livy* (Malden, MA: Wiley-Blackwell, 2014).

Mitchell 2005: Richard E. Mitchell, 'The Definition of *patres* and *plebs*: An End to the Struggle of the Orders', in Kurt A. Raaflaub, ed., *Social Struggles in Archaic Rome: New Perspectives on the Conflict of the Orders* (2nd edn, Malden, MA: Blackwell Publishing, 2005), 128–67.

Möller 2001: Astrid Möller, 'The Beginnings of Chronography: Hellanicus' *Hiereiai*', in Nino Luraghi, ed., *The Historian's Craft in the Age of Herodotus* (Oxford: Oxford University Press, 2001), 241–62.

Möller 2004: Astrid Möller, 'Greek Chronographic Traditions about the First Olympic Games', in Ralph M. Rosen, ed., *Time and Temporality in the Ancient World* (Philadelphia: University of Pennsylvania Museum of Archaeology and Anthropology, 2004), 169–84.

Momigliano 1963: Arnaldo Momigliano, 'An Interim Report on the Origins of Rome', *Journal of Roman Studies* 53 (1963), 95–121.

Momigliano 1969: Arnaldo Momigliano, 'The Origins of the Roman Republic', in Charles S. Singleton, ed., *Interpretation: Theory and Practice* (Baltimore, MD: Johns Hopkins Press, 1969), 1–34.

Momigliano 1975: Arnaldo Momigliano, *Alien Wisdom: The Limits of Hellenization* (Cambridge: Cambridge University Press, 1975).

Momigliano 1989a: Arnaldo Momigliano, 'The Origins of Rome', in Frank W. Walbank, Alan E. Astin, Martin W. Frederiksen, Robert M. Ogilvie and Andrew Drummond, eds, *The Cambridge Ancient History, Volume VII part 2: The Rise of Rome to 220 B.C.* (2nd edn, Cambridge: Cambridge University Press, 1989), 52–112.

Momigliano 1989b: Arnaldo Momigliano, *Roma arcaica* (Florence: Sansoni Editore, 1989).

Momigliano 1990: Arnaldo Momigliano, *The Classical Foundations of Modern Historiography* (Berkeley: University of California Press, 1990).

Momigliano 2005: Arnaldo Momigliano, 'The Rise of the *plebs* in the Archaic Age of Rome', in Kurt A. Raaflaub, ed., *Social Struggles in Archaic Rome: New Perspectives on the Conflict of the Orders* (2nd edn, Malden, MA: Blackwell Publishing, 2005), 168–84.

Mommsen 1859: Theodor Mommsen, *Die römische Chronologie bis auf Caesar* (2nd edn, Berlin: Weidmannsche Buchhandlung, 1859).

Mommsen 1864: Theodor Mommsen, *Römische Forschungen* I (Berlin: Weidmannsche Buchhandlung, 1864).

Mommsen 1879: Theodor Mommsen, *Römische Forschungen* II (Berlin: Weidmannsche Buchhandlung, 1879).

Mommsen 1887a: Theodor Mommsen, *Römisches Staatsrecht* II.1 (3rd edn, Leipzig: Verlag von S. Hirzel, 1887).

Mommsen 1887b: Theodor Mommsen, *Römisches Staatsrecht* III.1 (3rd edn, Leipzig: Verlag von S. Hirzel, 1887).

Monaco 1995: Lucia Monaco, 'La "gens postumia" nella prima repubblica. Origini e politiche', in Gennaro Franciosi, ed., *Ricerche sulla organizzazione gentilizia romana* III (Naples: Jovene Editore, 1995), 267–98.

Moore 2017: Daniel W. Moore, 'Learning from Experience: Polybius and the Progress of Rome', *Classical Quarterly* 67 (2017), 132–48.

Moormann 2001: Eric M. Moormann, 'Carandini's Royal Houses at the Foot of the Palatine: Fact or Fiction?', *Bulletin Antieke Beschaving* 76 (2001), 209–12.

Moretti Sgubini 2004: Anna Maria Moretti Sgubini, *Eroi etruschi e miti greci: Gli affreschi della Tomba François tornano a Vulci* (Calenzano: Edizioni Cooperativa Archeologia, 2004).

Mouritsen 2015: Henrik Mouritsen, 'The Incongruence of Power: The Roman Constitution in Theory and Practice', in Dean Hammer, ed., *A Companion to Greek Democracy and the Roman Republic* (Malden, MA: Wiley-Blackwell, 2015), 146–63.

Mouritsen 2017: Henrik Mouritsen, *Politics in the Roman Republic* (Cambridge: Cambridge University Press, 2017).

Münzer 1920: Friedrich Münzer, *Römische Adelsparteien und Adelsfamilien* (Stuttgart: J. B. Metzlersche Verlagsbuchhandlung, 1920).

Münzer 1953a: Friedrich Münzer, 'Postumius, 52a', in *Paulys Realencyclopädie der classischen Altertumswissenschaft* 22 (Stuttgart: J. B. Metzlersche Buchhandlung, 1953), 932–3.

Münzer 1953b: Friedrich Münzer, 'Postumius, 52b', in *Paulys Realencyclopädie der classischen Altertumswissenschaft* 22 (Stuttgart: J. B. Metzlersche Buchhandlung, 1953), 933–4.

Musti 1970: Domenico Musti, *Tendenze nella storiografia romana e greca su Roma arcaica: Studî su Livio e Dionigi d'Alicarnasso* (Rome: Edizioni dell'Ateneo Roma, 1970).

Musti 1974: Domenico Musti, 'Polibio e la storiografia romana arcaica', in *Polybe* (Geneva: Fondation Hardt, 1974), 105–39.

Nicolet 1974: Claude Nicolet, 'Polybe et les institutions romaines', in *Polybe* (Geneva: Fondation Hardt, 1974), 209–58.

Niebuhr 1851: Barthold Georg Niebuhr, *The History of Rome* I, trans. Julius Charles Hare and Connop Thirlwall (new edn, London: Taylor, Walton, and Maberly, 1851).

Northwood 2013: Simon Northwood, 'A. Postumius Albinus', in Timothy J. Cornell, ed., *The Fragments of the Roman Historians, Volume I: Introduction* (Oxford: Oxford University Press, 2013), 185–90.

Novara 1982: Antoinette Novara, *Les idées romaines sur le progrès d'après les écrivains de la République* I (Paris: Les Belles Lettres, 1982).

Oakley 1997a: Stephen P. Oakley, *A Commentary on Livy, Books VI–X, Volume I: Introduction and Book VI* (Oxford: Clarendon Press, 1997).

Oakley 1997b: Stephen P. Oakley, Review of Timothy J. Cornell, *The Beginnings of Rome: Italy and Rome from the Bronze Age to the Punic Wars (c. 1000–264 BC)* (London: Routledge, 1995), *Classical Review* 47 (1997), 358–61.

Oakley 1998: Stephen P. Oakley, *A Commentary on Livy, Books VI–X, Volume II: Books VII and VIII* (Oxford: Clarendon Press, 1998).

Oakley 2005a: Stephen P. Oakley, *A Commentary on Livy, Books VI–X, Volume III: Book IX* (Oxford: Clarendon Press, 2005).

Oakley 2005b: Stephen P. Oakley, *A Commentary on Livy, Books VI–X, Volume IV: Book X* (Oxford: Clarendon Press, 2005).

Oakley 2013a: Stephen P. Oakley, 'L. and Q. Aelius Tubero', in Timothy J. Cornell, ed., *The Fragments of the Roman Historians, Volume I: Introduction* (Oxford: Oxford University Press, 2013), 361–7.

Oakley 2013b: Stephen P. Oakley, 'L. and Q. Aelius Tubero: Commentary', in Timothy J. Cornell, ed., *The Fragments of the Roman Historians, Volume III: Commentary* (Oxford: Oxford University Press, 2013), 469–75.

Oakley 2013c: Stephen P. Oakley, 'C. Licinius Macer', in Timothy J. Cornell, ed., *The Fragments of the Roman Historians, Volume I: Introduction* (Oxford: Oxford University Press, 2013), 320–31.

Oakley 2013d: Stephen P. Oakley, 'C. Licinius Macer: Commentary', in Timothy J. Cornell, ed., *The Fragments of the Roman Historians, Volume III: Commentary* (Oxford: Oxford University Press, 2013), 418–49.

Ogilvie 1965: Robert M. Ogilvie, *A Commentary on Livy Books 1–5* (Oxford: Clarendon Press, 1965).

Ogilvie 1976: Robert M. Ogilvie, *Early Rome and the Etruscans* (London: Fontana Press, 1976).

Ogilvie and Drummond 1989: Robert M. Ogilvie and Andrew Drummond, 'The Sources for Early Roman History', in Frank W. Walbank, Alan E. Astin, Martin W. Frederiksen, Robert M. Ogilvie and Andrew Drummond, eds, *The Cambridge Ancient History, Volume VII part 2: The Rise of Rome to 220 B.C.* (2nd edn, Cambridge: Cambridge University Press, 1989), 1–29.

Orlin 1997: Eric M. Orlin, *Temples, Religion, and Politics in the Roman Republic* (Leiden: E. J. Brill, 1997).

Pais 1898: Ettore Pais, *Storia di Roma* I.1 (Turin: Carlo Clausen, 1898).

Pais 1899: Ettore Pais, *Storia di Roma* I.2 (Turin: Carlo Clausen, 1899).

Pais 1906: Ettore Pais, *Ancient Legends of Roman History*, trans. Mario E. Cosenza (London: Swan Sonnenschein and Co., 1906).

Pais 1913: Ettore Pais, *Storia critica di Roma durante i primi cinque secoli* I.1 (Rome: Ermanno Loescher and Co., 1913).

Pais 2014: Ettore Pais, 'The Fabii at the River Cremera and the Spartans at Thermopylae', in James H. Richardson and Federico Santangelo, eds, *The Roman Historical Tradition: Regal and Republican Rome* (Oxford: Oxford University Press, 2014), 167–85.

Pallottino 1987: Massimo Pallottino, 'Il fregio dei Vibenna e le sue implicazioni storiche', in Francesco Buranelli, ed., *La tomba François di Vulci* (Rome: Edizioni Quasar, 1987), 225–33.

Penella 2004: Robert J. Penella, 'The *Ambitio* of Livy's Tarquinius Priscus', *Classical Quarterly* 54 (2004), 630–5.

Pinsent 1971: John Pinsent, Review of Marta Sordi, *Roma e i Sanniti nel IV secolo a.C.* (Bologna: Cappelli Editore, 1969), *Journal of Roman Studies* 61 (1971), 271–2.

Pinsent 1975: John Pinsent, *Military Tribunes and Plebeian Consuls: The Fasti from 444 V to 342 V* (Wiesbaden: Franz Steiner Verlag, 1975).

Pittà 2015: Antonino Pittà, *M. Terenzio Varrone, de vita populi Romani: Introduzione e commento* (Pisa: Pisa University Press, 2015).

Platner 1906: Samuel B. Platner, 'Early Legends and Recent Discoveries', *Classical Journal* 1 (1906), 78–83.

Pobjoy 2013: Mark Pobjoy, 'Sempronius Asellio', in Timothy J. Cornell, ed., *The Fragments of the Roman Historians, Volume I: Introduction* (Oxford: Oxford University Press, 2013), 274–7.

Poletti 2013: Stefano Poletti, 'Il Servio Tullio di Livio e le sue "contraddizioni": A proposito dell'elezione ritardata in Liv. I, 46, 1 e di altri stratagemmi liviani', *Studi Classici e Orientali* 59 (2013), 117–51.

Poucet 1967: Jacques Poucet, *Recherches sur la légende sabine des origines de Rome* (Kinshasa: Éditions de l'Université Lovanium, 1967).

Poucet 2000: Jacques Poucet, *Les Rois de Rome: Tradition et histoire* (Louvain-la-Neuve: Académie royale de Belgique, 2000).

Purcell 2003: Nicholas Purcell, 'Becoming Historical: The Roman Case', in David Braund and Christopher Gill, eds, *Myth, History and Culture in Republican Rome: Studies in Honour of T. P. Wiseman* (Exeter: University of Exeter Press, 2003), 12–40.

Raaflaub 2005: Kurt A. Raaflaub, 'From Protection and Defense to Offense and Participation: Stages in the Conflict of the Orders', in Kurt A. Raaflaub, ed., *Social Struggles in Archaic Rome: New Perspectives on the Conflict of the Orders* (2nd edn, Malden, MA: Blackwell Publishing, 2005), 185–222.

Rawson 1985: Elizabeth Rawson, *Intellectual Life in the Late Roman Republic* (London: Duckworth, 1985).

Rawson 1991: Elizabeth Rawson, *Roman Culture and Society: Collected Papers* (Oxford: Clarendon Press, 1991).

Rawson 2014: Elizabeth Rawson, 'Cicero the Historian and Cicero the Antiquarian', in James H. Richardson and Federico Santangelo, eds, *The Roman Historical Tradition: Regal and Republican Rome* (Oxford: Oxford University Press, 2014), 259–83.

Reid 1912: James S. Reid, 'Human Sacrifices at Rome and Other Notes on Roman Religion', *Journal of Roman Studies* 2 (1912), 34–52.

Rich 2005: John Rich, 'Valerius Antias and the Construction of the Roman Past', *Bulletin of the Institute of Classical Studies* 48 (2005), 137–61.

Rich 2011: John Rich, 'The *fetiales* and Roman International Relations', in James H. Richardson and Federico Santangelo, eds, *Priests and State in the Roman World* (Stuttgart: Franz Steiner Verlag, 2011), 187–242.

Rich 2013a: John Rich, '*Annales Maximi*', in Timothy J. Cornell, ed., *The Fragments of the Roman Historians, Volume I: Introduction* (Oxford: Oxford University Press, 2013), 141–59.

Rich 2013b: John Rich, 'Valerius Antias', in Timothy J. Cornell, ed., *The Fragments of the Roman Historians, Volume I: Introduction* (Oxford: Oxford University Press, 2013), 293–304.

Rich 2018: John Rich, 'Fabius Pictor, Ennius and the Origins of Roman Annalistic Historiography', in Kaj Sandberg and Christopher J. Smith, eds, Omnium Annalium Monumenta: *Historical Writing and Historical Evidence in Republican Rome* (Leiden: Brill, 2018), 17–65.

Richard 1990a: Jean-Claude Richard, 'Les Fabii à la Crémère: Grandeur et décadence de l'organisation gentilice', in *Crise et transformation des sociétés archaïques de l'Italie antique au Ve siècle av. J.-C.* (Rome: École Française de Rome, 1990), 245–62.

Richard 1990b: Jean-Claude Richard, 'Réflexions sur le Tribunat consulaire', *Mélanges de l'École française de Rome – Antiquité* 102 (1990), 767–99.

Richard 1992: Jean-Claude Richard, 'Tribuns militaires et triomphe', in *La Rome des premiers siècles: Légende et histoire* (Florence: Leo S. Olschki Editore, 1992), 235–46.

Richardson 2008a: James H. Richardson, 'Ancient Political Thought and the Development of the Consulship', *Latomus* 67 (2008), 627–33.

Richardson 2008b: James H. Richardson, 'The *pater patratus* on a Roman Gold Stater: A Reading of *RRC* Nos. 28/1–2 and 29/1–2', *Hermes* 136 (2008), 415–25.

Richardson 2011: James H. Richardson, 'The Vestal Virgins and the Use of the *Annales Maximi*', in James H. Richardson and Federico Santangelo, eds, *Priests and State in the Roman World* (Stuttgart: Franz Steiner Verlag, 2011), 91–106.

Richardson 2012: James H. Richardson, *The Fabii and the Gauls: Studies in Historical Thought and Historiography in Republican Rome* (Stuttgart: Franz Steiner Verlag, 2012).

Richardson 2013: James H. Richardson, 'The Dioscuri and the Liberty of the Republic', *Latomus* 72 (2013), 901–18.

Richardson 2015: James H. Richardson, 'Andreas Alföldi and the Adventure(s) of the Vibenna Brothers', in James H. Richardson and Federico Santangelo, eds,

Andreas Alföldi in the Twenty-First Century (Stuttgart: Franz Steiner Verlag, 2015), 111–30.

Richardson 2017: James H. Richardson, 'The Development of the Treaty-Making Rituals of the Romans', *Hermes* 145 (2017), 250–74.

Richardson 2018: James H. Richardson, 'Valerius Antias and the Archives', *Materiali e discussioni per l'analisi dei testi classici* 80 (2018), 57–80.

Richardson 2019: James H. Richardson, 'Some Thoughts on *suffragium* and the Practice of Voting in Archaic Rome', *Hermes* 147 (2019), 283–97.

Ridley 1979: Ronald T. Ridley, 'The Origin of the Roman Dictatorship: An Overlooked Opinion', *Rheinisches Museum für Philologie* 122 (1979), 303–9.

Ridley 1980: Ronald T. Ridley, 'Fastenkritik: A Stocktaking', *Athenaeum* 58 (1980), 264–98.

Ridley 1983: Ronald T. Ridley, '*Falsi triumphi, plures consulatus*', *Latomus* 42 (1983), 372–82.

Ridley 1986: Ronald T. Ridley, 'The "Consular Tribunate": The Testimony of Livy', *Klio* 68 (1986), 444–65.

Ridley 1990: Ronald T. Ridley et al., 'Diskussion. Sektion VI: Außenbeziehungen und innere Entwicklung', in Walter Eder, ed., *Staat und Staatlichkeit in der frühen römischen Republik* (Stuttgart: Franz Steiner Verlag, 1990), 546–59.

Ridley 2014: Ronald T. Ridley, 'The Enigma of Servius Tullius', in James H. Richardson and Federico Santangelo, eds, *The Roman Historical Tradition: Regal and Republican Rome* (Oxford: Oxford University Press, 2014), 83–128.

Ridley 2015: Ronald T. Ridley, 'The Puzzles of Porsenna', *Studi Etruschi* 78 (2015), 77–95.

Ridley 2017: Ronald T. Ridley, 'Lars Porsenna and the Early Roman Republic', *Antichthon* 51 (2017), 33–58.

Riposati 1939: Benedetto Riposati, *M. Terenti Varronis,* De vita populi Romani*: Fonti – Esegesi, Edizione critica dei frammenti* (Milan: Vita e Pensiero, 1939).

Rix 2006: Helmut Rix, '*Ramnes, Tities, Luceres*: Noms étrusques ou latins?', *Mélanges de l'École française de Rome – Antiquité* 118 (2006), 167–75.

Roberts 1918: Lucy G. Roberts, 'The Gallic Fire and Roman Archives', *Memoirs of the American Academy in Rome* 2 (1918), 55–65.

Roller 2018: Matthew B. Roller, *Models from the Past in Roman Culture: A World of Exempla* (Cambridge: Cambridge University Press, 2018).

Rüpke 1992: Jörg Rüpke, 'You Shall Not Kill. Hierarchies of Norms in Ancient Rome', *Numen* 39 (1992), 58–79.

Rüpke 1993: Jörg Rüpke, 'Livius, Priesternamen und die *annales maximi*', *Klio* 75 (1993), 155–79.

Rüpke 1995: Jörg Rüpke, 'Fasti: Quellen oder Produkte römischer Geschichtsschreibung?', *Klio* 77 (1995), 184–202.

Rüpke 2007: Jörg Rüpke, *Religion of the Romans*, trans. Richard Gordon (Cambridge: Polity Press, 2007).

Rüpke 2008: Jörg Rüpke, *Fasti Sacerdotum: A Prosopography of Pagan, Jewish, and Christian Religious Officials in the City of Rome, 300 BC to AD 499*, trans. David M. B. Richardson (Oxford: Oxford University Press, 2008).

Ruschenbusch 1963: Eberhard Ruschenbusch, 'Die Zwölftafeln und die römische Gesandtschaft nach Athen', *Historia* 12 (1963), 250–3.

Ryan 1993: Francis X. Ryan, 'Some Observations on the Censorship of Claudius and Vitellius, A.D. 47–48', *The American Journal of Philology* 114 (1993), 611–18.

Scapini 2011: Marianna Scapini, *Temi greci e citazioni da Erodoto nelle storie di Roma arcaica* (Nordhausen: Verlag Traugott Bautz, 2011).

Scardigli 2011: Barbara Scardigli, 'Early Relations between Rome and Carthage', in Dexter Hoyos, ed., *A Companion to the Punic Wars* (Malden, MA: Wiley-Blackwell, 2011), 28–38.

Scullard 1980: Howard H. Scullard, *A History of the Roman World, 753 to 146 BC* (4th edn, London: Methuen and Co., 1980).

Sealey 1959: Raphael Sealey, 'Consular Tribunes Once More', *Latomus* 18 (1959), 521–30.

Serrati 2006: John Serrati, 'Neptune's Altars: The Treaties between Rome and Carthage (509–226 B.C.)', *Classical Quarterly* 56 (2006), 113–34.

Siewert 1978: Peter Siewert, 'Die angebliche Übernahme solonischer Gesetze in die Zwölftafeln: Ursprung und Ausgestaltung einer Legende', *Chiron* 8 (1978), 331–44.

Sisani 2004: Simone Sisani, 'Il Foro Romano', in Filippo Coarelli, ed., *Gli scavi di Roma, 1878–1921* (Rome: Edizioni Quasar, 2004), 59–68.

Skutsch 1985: Otto Skutsch, *The* Annals *of Quintus Ennius* (Oxford: Clarendon Press, 1985).

Small 1991: Jocelyn Penny Small, 'The Tarquins and Servius Tullius at Banquet', *Mélanges de l'École française de Rome – Antiquité* 103 (1991), 247–64.

Smith 1998: Christopher J. Smith, 'Onasander on How to be a General', in Michel Austin, Jill Harries and Christopher J. Smith, eds, *Modus Operandi: Essays in Honour of Geoffrey Rickman* (London: Institute of Classical Studies, 1998), 151–66.

Smith 2006a: Christopher J. Smith, '*Adfectatio regni* in the Roman Republic', in Sian Lewis, ed., *Ancient Tyranny* (Edinburgh: Edinburgh University Press, 2006), 49–64.

Smith 2006b: Christopher J. Smith, *The Roman Clan: The Gens from Ancient Ideology to Modern Anthropology* (Cambridge: Cambridge University Press, 2006).

Smith 2011a: Christopher J. Smith, 'The Magistrates of the Early Roman Republic', in Hans Beck, Antonio Duplá, Martin Jehne and Francisco Pina Polo, eds, *Consuls and Res Publica: Holding High in the Roman Republic* (Cambridge: Cambridge University Press, 2011), 19–40.

Smith 2011b: Christopher J. Smith, 'Thinking about Kings', *Bulletin of the Institute of Classical Studies* 54 (2011), 21–42.

Smith 2012: Christopher J. Smith, 'The Origins of the Tribunate of the Plebs', *Antichthon* 46 (2012), 101–25.

Sohlberg 1991: David Sohlberg, 'Militärtribunen und verwandte Probleme der frühen römischen Republik', *Historia* 40 (1991), 257–74.

Sordi 1972: Marta Sordi, 'La leggenda dei Dioscuri nella battaglia della Sagra e di Lago Regillo', *Contributi dell'Istituto di storia antica* 1 (1972), 47–70.

Staveley 1953: E. Stuart Staveley, 'The Significance of the Consular Tribunate', *Journal of Roman Studies* 43 (1953), 30–6.

Staveley 1956: E. Stuart Staveley, 'The Constitution of the Roman Republic 1940–1954', *Historia* 5 (1956), 74–122.

Stewart 1998: Roberta Stewart, *Public Office in Early Rome: Ritual Procedure and Political Practice* (Ann Arbor: University of Michigan Press, 1998).

Stibbe 1980: Conrad M. Stibbe et al., *Lapis Satricanus: Archaeological, Epigraphical, Linguistic and Historical Aspects of the New Inscription from Satricum* (The Hague: Nederlands Instituut te Rome, 1980).

Strachan-Davidson 1888: James L. Strachan-Davidson, *Selections from Polybius* (Oxford: Claredon Press, 1888).

Stuart Jones 1928: Henry Stuart Jones, 'The Primitive Institutions of Rome', in Stanley A. Cook, Frank E. Adcock and Martin P. Charlesworth, eds, *The Cambridge Ancient History, Volume VII: The Hellenistic Monarchies and the Rise of Rome* (Cambridge: Cambridge University Press, 1928), 407–35.

Syme 1988: Ronald Syme, *Roman Papers, Volume V*, ed. Anthony R. Birley (Oxford: Clarendon Press, 1988).

Szemler 1972: George J. Szemler, *The Priests of the Roman Republic: A Study of Interactions Between Priesthoods and Magistracies* (Brussels: Latomus, Revue d'Études Latines, 1972).

Taifacos 1979: Ioannis G. Taifacos, 'Cicerone e Polibio: Sulle fonti del *De re publica*', *Sileno* 5–6 (1979), 11–17.

Taylor 1951: Lily Ross Taylor, Review of Krister Hanell, *Das altrömische eponyme Amt* (Lund: C. W. K. Gleerup, 1946), *The American Journal of Philology* 72 (1951), 69–72.

Taylor 2013: Lily Ross Taylor, *The Voting Districts of the Roman Republic: The Thirty-five Urban and Rural Tribes* (reprinted with updated material by Jerzy Linderski, Ann Arbor: University of Michigan Press, 2013).

Terrenato 2011: Nicola Terrenato, 'The Versatile Clans: Archaic Rome and the Nature of Early City-States in Central Italy', in Nicola Terrenato and Donald C. Haggis, eds, *State Formation in Italy and Greece: Questioning the Neoevolutionist Paradigm* (Oxford: Oxbow Books, 2011), 231–44.

Testa 2012: Alessandro Testa, 'Verità del mito e verità della storia: Una critica storico-religiosa a recenti ipotesi sui *primordia* di Roma', *Mediterranea* 9 (2012), 195–231.

Torelli 2011: Mario Torelli, '*Bellum in privatam curam* (Liv. II, 49, 1). Eserciti gentilizi, *sodalitates* e isonomia aristocratica in Etruria e Lazio arcaici', in Concetta Masseria and Donato Loscalzo, eds, *Miti di guerra, riti di pace. La guerra e la pace: Un confronto interdisciplinare* (Bari: Edipuglia, 2011), 225–34.

Treggiari 2003: Susan Treggiari, 'Ancestral Virtues and Vices: Cicero on Nature, Nurture and Presentation', in David Braund and Christopher Gill, eds, *Myth, History and Culture in Republican Rome: Studies in Honour of T. P. Wiseman* (Exeter: University of Exeter Press, 2003), 139–64.

Ungern-Sternberg 2005: Jürgen von Ungern-Sternberg, 'The Formation of the "Annalistic Tradition": The Example of the Decemvirate', in Kurt A. Raaflaub, ed., *Social Struggles in Archaic Rome: New Perspectives on the Conflict of the Orders* (2nd edn, Malden, MA: Blackwell Publishing, 2005), 75–97.

Ungern-Sternberg 2011: Jürgen von Ungern-Sternberg, 'The Tradition on Early Rome and Oral History', in John Marincola, ed., *Greek and Roman Historiography* (Oxford: Oxford University Press, 2011), 119–49.

Urso 2005: Gianpaolo Urso, *Cassio Dione e i magistrati: Le origini della repubblica nei frammenti della Storia romana* (Milan: Vita e Pensiero, 2005).

Vaahtera 1993: Jyri E. Vaahtera, 'The Origin of Latin *suffrāgium*', *Glotta* 71 (1993), 66–80.

Vaahtera 2000: Jyri E. Vaahtera, 'Roman Religion and the Polybian *politeia*', in Christer Bruun, ed., *The Roman Middle Republic: Politics, Religion, and Historiography, c. 400–133 B.C.* (Rome: Institutum Romanum Finlandiae, 2000), 251–64.

Valditara 2008: Giuseppe Valditara, *Lo stato nell'antica Roma* (Soveria Mannelli: Rubbettino Editore, 2008).

Vasaly 2015: Ann Vasaly, *Livy's Political Philosophy: Power and Personality in Early Rome* (Cambridge: Cambridge University Press, 2015).

Versnel 1970: Henk S. Versnel, *Triumphus: An Inquiry into the Origin, Development and Meaning of the Roman Triumph* (Leiden: E. J. Brill, 1970).

Versnel 1980: Henk S. Versnel, 'Historical Implications', in Conrad M. Stibbe et al., *Lapis Satricanus: Archaeological, Epigraphical, Linguistic and Historical Aspects of the New Inscription from Satricum* (The Hague: Nederlands Instituut te Rome, 1980), 97–150.

Versnel 1997: Henk S. Versnel, 'IUN]IEI: A New Conjecture in the Satricum Inscription', *Mededelingen van het Nederlands Instituut te Rome* 56 (1997), 177–97.

Vervaet 2014: Frederik J. Vervaet, *The High Command in the Roman Republic: The Principle of the* summum imperium auspiciumque *from 509 to 19 BCE* (Stuttgart: Franz Steiner Verlag, 2014).

Veyne 1986: Paul Veyne, 'Postumius Magnus légat en 146 (IG², II,3780)', *Historia* 35 (1986), 112–13.

Von Fritz 1950: Kurt von Fritz, 'The Reorganisation of the Roman Government in 366 B.C. and the So-Called Licinio-Sextian Laws', *Historia* 1 (1950), 3–44.

Walbank 1957: Frank W. Walbank, *A Historical Commentary on Polybius, Volume I* (Oxford: Clarendon Press, 1957).

Walbank 1967: Frank W. Walbank, *A Historical Commentary on Polybius, Volume II* (Oxford: Clarendon Press, 1967).

Walbank 1979: Frank W. Walbank, *A Historical Commentary on Polybius, Volume III* (Oxford: Clarendon Press, 1979).

Walser 1959: Gerold Walser, 'Der Prozeß gegen Q. Ligarius im Jahre 46 v.Chr.', *Historia* 8 (1959), 90–6.

Walsh 1961: Patrick G. Walsh, *Livy: His Historical Aims and Methods* (Cambridge: Cambridge University Press, 1961).

Walt 1997: Siri Walt, *Der Historiker C. Licinius Macer: Einleitung, Fragmente, Kommentar* (Stuttgart: B. G. Teubner, 1997).

Walter 2003a: Uwe Walter, 'AHN MACHT SINN. Familientradition und Familienprofil im republikanischen Rom', in Karl-Joachim Hölkeskamp, Jörn Rüsen, Elke Stein-Hölkeskamp and Heinrich Theodor Grütter, eds, *Sinn (in) der Antike: Orientierungssysteme, Leitbilder und Wertkonzepte im Altertum* (Mainz: Philipp von Zabern Verlag, 2003), 255–78.

Walter 2003b: Uwe Walter, 'Opfer ihrer Ungleichzeitigkeit: Die Gesamtgeschichten im ersten Jahrhundert v.Chr. und die fortdauernde Attraktivität des "annalistischen Schemas"', in Ulrich Eigler, Ulrich Gotter, Nino Luraghi and Uwe Walter, eds, *Formen römischer Geschichtsschreibung von den Anfängen bis Livius* (Darmstadt: Wissenschaftliche Buchgesellschaft, 2003), 135–56.

Walter 2004: Uwe Walter, '"Ein Ebenbild des Vaters". Familiale Wiederholungen in der historiographischen Traditionsbildung der römischen Republik', *Hermes* 132 (2004), 406–25.

Watson 1972: Alan Watson, 'Roman Private Law and the *Leges Regiae*', *Journal of Roman Studies* 62 (1972), 100–5.

Watson 1992: Alan Watson, *The State, Law and Religion: Pagan Rome* (Athens: University of Georgia Press, 1992).

Weinstock 1971: Stefan Weinstock, *Divus Julius* (Oxford: Clarendon Press, 1971).

Welwei 2000: Karl-Wilhelm Welwei, 'Lucius Iunius Brutus – ein fiktiver Revolutionsheld', in Karl-Joachim Hölkeskamp and Elke Stein-Hölkeskamp, eds, *Von Romulus zu Augustus: Große Gestalten der römischen Republik* (Munich: Verlag C. H. Beck, 2000), 48–57.

Werner 1963: Robert Werner, *Der Beginn der römischen Republik: Historisch-chronologische Untersuchungen über die Anfangszeit der libera res publica* (Munich: R. Oldenbourg Verlag, 1963).

Werner 1968: Robert Werner, 'Die Auseinandersetzung der frührömischen Republik mit ihren Nachbarn in quellenkritischer Sicht', *Gymnasium* 75 (1968), 45–73.

Wieacker 1988: Franz Wieacker, *Römische Rechtsgeschichte, Erster Abschnitt: Einleitung, Quellenkunde, Frühzeit und Republik* (Munich: C. H. Beck, 1988).

Wikander 1993: Örjan Wikander, 'Senators and Equites V. Ancestral Pride and Genealogical Studies in Late Republican Rome', *Opuscula Romana* 19 (1993), 77–90.

Wildfang 2006: Robin Lorsch Wildfang, *Rome's Vestal Virgins: A Study of Rome's Vestal Priestesses in the Late Republic and Early Empire* (London: Routledge, 2006).

Williamson 1987: Callie Williamson, 'Monuments of Bronze: Roman Legal Documents on Bronze Tablets', *Classical Antiquity* 6 (1987), 160–83.

Wirszubski 1950: Chaïm Wirszubski, *Libertas as a Political Idea at Rome during the Late Republic and Early Principate* (Cambridge: Cambridge University Press, 1950).

Wiseman 1979a: T. Peter Wiseman, 'Cicero, *De Divinatione* 1.55', *Classical Quarterly* 29 (1979), 142–4.

Wiseman 1979b: T. Peter Wiseman, *Clio's Cosmetics: Three Studies in Greco-Roman Literature* (Leicester: Leicester University Press, 1979).

Wiseman 1985a: T. Peter Wiseman, *Catullus and his World: A Reappraisal* (Cambridge: Cambridge University Press, 1985).

Wiseman 1985b: T. Peter Wiseman, 'Competition and Co-operation', in T. Peter Wiseman, ed., *Roman Political Life, 90 BC – AD 69* (Exeter: Exeter University Press, 1985), 3–19

Wiseman 1987: T. Peter Wiseman, *Roman Studies, Literary and Historical* (Liverpool: Francis Cairns, 1987).

Wiseman 1992: T. Peter Wiseman, *Talking to Virgil: A Miscellany* (Exeter: University of Exeter Press, 1992).

Wiseman 1994: T. Peter Wiseman, *Historiography and Imagination: Eight Essays on Roman Culture* (Exeter: University of Exeter Press, 1994).

Wiseman 1995: T. Peter Wiseman, *Remus: A Roman Myth* (Cambridge: Cambridge University Press, 1995).

Wiseman 1996: T. Peter Wiseman, Review of Timothy J. Cornell, *The Beginnings of Rome: Italy and Rome from the Bronze Age to the Punic Wars (c. 1000–264 BC)* (London: Routledge, 1995), *Journal of Roman Archaeology* 9 (1996), 310–15.

Wiseman 1998: T. Peter Wiseman, *Roman Drama and Roman History* (Exeter: University of Exeter Press, 1998).

Wiseman 2001: T. Peter Wiseman, 'Reading Carandini', *Journal of Roman Studies* 91 (2001), 182–93.

Wiseman 2004: T. Peter Wiseman, *The Myths of Rome* (Exeter: Exeter University Press, 2004).

Wiseman 2004–6: T. Peter Wiseman, 'Andrea Carandini and *Roma Quadrata*', *Accordia Research Papers* 10 (2004–6), 103–25.

Wiseman 2008: T. Peter Wiseman, *Unwritten Rome* (Exeter: Exeter University Press, 2008).

Wiseman 2009: T. Peter Wiseman, *Remembering the Roman People: Essays on Late-Republican Politics and Literature* (Oxford: Oxford University Press, 2009).

Wiseman 2013: T. Peter Wiseman, 'The Palatine, from Evander to Elagabalus', *Journal of Roman Studies* 103 (2013), 234–68.

Wiseman 2014: T. Peter Wiseman, 'The Legend of Lucius Brutus', in James H. Richardson and Federico Santangelo, eds, *The Roman Historical Tradition: Regal and Republican Rome* (Oxford: Oxford University Press, 2014), 129–45.

Wiseman 2016: T. Peter Wiseman, *How Old is Exeter? Divining the Distant Past with W. G. Hoskins* (Exeter: The Mint Press, 2016).

Wiseman 2018: T. Peter Wiseman, 'Writing Rome's Past', Review of Kaj Sandberg and Christopher J. Smith, eds, Omnium Annalium Monumenta: *Historical Writing and Historical Evidence in Republican Rome* (Leiden: Brill, 2018), *Histos* 12 (2018), I–XXIII.

Wissowa 1924: Georg Wissowa, 'Lapis (2)', in *Paulys Realencyclopädie der classischen Altertumswissenschaft* 12 (Stuttgart: J. B. Metzlersche Buchhandlung, 1924), 779–82.

Zetzel 1995: James E. G. Zetzel, ed., *Cicero,* De re publica: *Selections* (Cambridge: Cambridge University Press, 1995).

Zevi 1969–70: Fausto Zevi, 'Considerazioni sull'elogio di Scipione Barbato', *Studi Miscellanei* 15 (1969–70), 65–73.

Zevi 2014: Fausto Zevi, 'Demaratus and the "Corinthian" Kings of Rome', in James H. Richardson and Federico Santangelo, eds, *The Roman Historical Tradition: Regal and Republican Rome* (Oxford: Oxford University Press, 2014), 53–82.

Index

Acilius, C. 113
Aebutius, T. (*cos.* 499) 169, 172
aediles 87, 110, 168–9, 191
Aelius, P. (*q.* 409) 173 n. 49
Aelius Stilo, L. 185 n. 104
Aelius Tubero, L. 196
Aelius Tubero, Q. 185 n. 104, 195–9
Aemilius Mamercinus, L. (*tr. mil. c. p.* I 391) 175
Aemilius Mamercus (*q.* 446, *tr. mil. c. p.* 438) 174
Aeneas 22 n. 1, 25, 28, 53 nn. 22 and 24
Aequi 176 n. 59, 180
Alba Longa 24–5, 28, 53, 137 n. 8
Albinius Paterculus, L. (*trib. pl.* 493) 172
Algidus, battle of 180
Amulius 197
Ancus Marcius 31, 47 n. 1, 50, 56 n. 39, 57–60, 62–6, 69, 73–4, 83 nn. 135 and 137, 84, 137 n. 11
anti-monarchic ideology 12–13, 119–20, 128, 132–4
Aollius 55–6
appeal laws 128
Ascanius 28
Asconius 172, 177
Asinius Pollio, C. 195 n. 14
Athens 21, 97, 185, 200
Atilius Luscus, L. (*tr. mil. c. p.* 444) 174
augurs 66, 122, 178
Aulus Gellius 156
auspices 65–7, 156 n. 82
Avillius 55–6

Boni, G. 3, 47–8

Caelian hill 32
Calpurnii 56
Calpurnius Piso, L. 56, 61
Calpus 56
Campania 184
Canuleius, C. (*trib. pl.* 445) 59, 65
Capitoline hill 44, 92, 167
Carthage 15–18, 23 n. 6, 25, 37–8, 49 n. 9, 87–94, 99, 101–3, 105–18, 186, 200
Cassius, Sp. (*cos.* I 502) 44, 101–2, 172
Cassius Hemina, L. 113, 175 n. 55
censors 171, 177
census 83
centuries 83, 95 n. 35, 123–4, 126, 131
Ceres, Liber and Libera, temple of 182
Cincius Alimentus, L. 22 n. 1, 113
Circus Maximus 179
Claudius, Emperor 31–3, 156
Clausus, Attus (Claudius, Ap.) 31, 34, 36, 43–4, 95, 139
Cloelius, Q. (*cos.* 498) 169
Cloelius Siculus, T. (*tr. mil. c. p.* 444) 174
collegiality 12, 17, 100–1, 143, 203
Cominius, Post. (*cos.* I 501) 101, 169
comitia centuriata 95, 174 n. 51
comitia curiata 42 n. 62, 65–6, 76
comitia tributa 42 n. 62
Comitium 48
conflict of the orders 41–2, 45–6, 96–7, 128, 131–2, 134, 158–9, 168, 171–2, 175–6, 180, 187, 191, 194–6
consuls 12–14, 17, 68, 76, 87–8, 99–102, 105, 113, 116–17, 119–20, 125–34, 136, 138–60, 166–76, 178–9, 184, 186–7, 191, 194 n. 12, 203